DIFFUSION OF GOOD GOVERNMENT

RECENT TITLES FROM THE HELEN KELLOGG INSTITUTE FOR INTERNATIONAL STUDIES

Scott Mainwaring, series editor

The University of Notre Dame Press gratefully thanks the Helen Kellogg Institute for International Studies for its support in the publication of titles in this series.

Frances Hagopian, ed.
Religious Pluralism, Democracy, and the Catholic Church in Latin America (2009)

Marcelo Bergman and Laurence Whitehead, eds.
Criminality, Public Security, and the Challenge to Democracy in Latin America (2009)

Matthew R. Cleary
The Sources of Democratic Responsiveness in Mexico (2010)

Leah Anne Carroll
Violent Democratization: Social Movements, Elites, and Politics in Colombia's Rural War Zones, 1984–2008 (2011)

Timothy J. Power and Matthew M. Taylor, eds.
Corruption and Democracy in Brazil: The Struggle for Accountability (2011)

Ana María Bejarano
Precarious Democracies: Understanding Regime Stability and Change in Colombia and Venezuela (2011)

Carlos Guevara Mann
Political Careers, Corruption, and Impunity: Panama's Assembly, 1984–2009 (2011)

Gabriela Ippolito-O'Donnell
The Right to the City: Popular Contention in Contemporary Buenos Aires (2012)

Barry S. Levitt
Power in the Balance: Presidents, Parties, and Legislatures in Peru and Beyond (2012)

Douglas Chalmers and Scott Mainwaring, eds. (2012)
Problems Confronting Contemporary Democracies: Essays in Honor of Alfred Stepan (2012)

José Murilo de Carvalho
Formation of Souls: Imagery of the Republic in Brazil (2012)

Sérgio Buarque de Holanda
Roots of Brazil (2012)

Peter K. Spink, Peter M. Ward, and Robert H. Wilson
Metropolitan Governance in the Federalist Americas: Strategies for Equitable and Integrated Development (2012)

For a complete list of titles from the Helen Kellogg Institute for International Studies, see http://www.undpress.nd.edu

DIFFUSION OF GOOD GOVERNMENT

Social Sector Reforms in Brazil

NATASHA BORGES SUGIYAMA

University of Notre Dame Press

Notre Dame, Indiana

University of Notre Dame Press
Notre Dame, Indiana 46556
www.undpress.nd.edu

Published in the United States of America

Library of Congress Cataloging-in-Publication Data

Sugiyama, Natasha Borges.
Diffusion of good government : social sector reforms in Brazil / Natasha Borges Sugiyama.
pages cm. — (From the Helen Kellogg Institute for International Studies)
Includes bibliographical references and index.
ISBN 978-0-268-04142-7 (pbk. : alk. paper) — ISBN 0-268-04142-3 (pbk. : alk. paper) — ISBN 978-0-268-15845-3 (web pdf)
1. Brazil—Social conditions—20th century. 2. Brazil—Social conditions—21st century. 3. Brazil—Social policy. I. Title.
HN283.5.S84 2012
306.098109'04—dc23
2012037026

∞ *The paper in this book meets the guidelines for permanence and durability of the Committee on Production Guidelines for Book Longevity of the Council on Library Resources.*

To my parents,

Maria Lúcia Borges Sugiyama and Iutaka Sugiyama,

and my husband, Greg Carter.

CONTENTS

List of Tables
ix

List of Figures
xi

Abbreviations
xiii

Acknowledgments
xvii

CHAPTER ONE
The Politics of Social Sector Reforms, Subnational Governance, and the Prospects for Policy Diffusion
1

CHAPTER TWO
Theoretical Debates on Policy Diffusion: A Motivations Approach
24

CHAPTER THREE
Diffusion Trends in Education and Health Policy Reforms
50

CHAPTER FOUR
Education Reform: A Simple Idea Catches On
77

CHAPTER FIVE
Health Reform: A Complex Idea Spreads
113

CHAPTER SIX
Conclusion: Ideology and Social Networks
151

Appendixes
189

Notes
199

References
221

Index
253

TABLES

Table 1.1 Adoption of Bolsa Escola/Renda Minima and PSF by Local Government and Administration 17

Table 1.2 Local Government Partisan and Ideological Divide 18

Table 3.1 Electoral Competition and Bolsa Escola Adoption (1998) 58

Table 3.2 Electoral Competition and PSF Adoption (1998) 58

Table 3.3 Ideology and Bolsa Escola Adoption (1998) 58

Table 3.4 Ideology and PSF Adoption (1998) 59

Table 3.5 The Gestão Pública Network and Bolsa Escola Adoption (1998) 61

Table 3.6 Region and Bolsa Escola Adoption (1998) 61

Table 3.7 Summary of Dichotomous Variables in Bolsa Escola Dataset (1998) 61

Table 3.8 Summary of Dichotomous Variables in PSF Dataset (1998) 62

Table 3.9 The Determinants of Social Policy Diffusion: Bolsa Escola and PSF 69

Table 4.1 Structure of the Brazilian Education System 84

Table 4.2 Characteristics of the Municipal Bolsa Escola and Renda Mínima Programs 90

Table 4.3 Case Studies: Bolsa Escola/Renda Minima Adoption and Nonadoption 95

Table 5.1 Case Studies: PSF Adoption and Nonadoption 128

Table A.1 Cities Included in Survey of Municipal Managers of Conditional Cash Transfer Programs 189

Table B.1 PSF Coverage of Regions' Population over Time (%) 194

Table B.2 Percentage of Municipalities Adopting PSF by State and Region (1998–2008) 195

Table B.3 Number of Municipalities Adopting PSF by State and Region (1998–2008) 196

Table D.1 Adoption of Federal/National CCT Models in the Americas 198

FIGURES

Figure 2.1 Multiple Directions of Diffusion Effects 27

Figure 3.1 Cumulative Adoption of Bolsa Escola in the Sample 54

Figure 3.2 Cumulative Adoption of Programa Saúde da Família in the Sample 55

Figure 3.3 Annual Predicted Probability of Bolsa Escola Adoption for Modal City 73

Figure 3.4 Annual Predicted Probability of PSF Adoption for Modal City 74

Figure 6.1 Explaining Social Policy Diffusion: A Motivational Approach 153

Figure B.1 National Cumulative Adoption of Programa Saúde da Família 193

ABBREVIATIONS

ABRASCO	Associação Brasileira de Pós-Graduação em Saúde Coletiva
ACS	Agentes Comunitários de Saúde
ACM	Antônio Carlos Magalhães
CCTs	Conditional Cash Transfer Programs
CONASEMS	Conselho Nacional de Secretários Municipais de Saúde
CONSED	Conselho Nacional de Secretários de Educação
CEBES	Centro Brasileiro de Estudos de Saúde
CFEMEA	Centro Feminista de Estudos e Assesoria
FGV-SP	Fundação Getúlio Vargas–São Paulo
FNDE	Fundo Nacional do Desenvolvimento da Educação
FUNDEF	Fundo de Manutenção e Desenvolvimento do Ensino Fundamental e de Valorização do Magistério
INAMPS	Instituto Nacional de Assistência Médica da Previdência Social
ILO	International Labour Organisation
IPEA	Instituto de Pesquisa Econômica Aplicada
MDS	Minisério de Desenvolvimento Social e Combate à Fome
MEC	Ministério da Educação e Cultura
MS	Ministério da Saúde
NGO	Nongovernmental organization
NOB	Norma Operacional Básica
PACS	Programa de Agentes Comunitários de Saúde
PAHO	Pan-American Health Organization
PAS	Plano de Atendimento à Saúde–São Paulo
PAS	Programa de Agentes de Saúde–Ceará
PETI	Programa de Erradicação do Trabalho Infantil

PGRM	Programa de Garantia de Renda Mínima
PIASS	Programa de Interiorização das Ações de Saúde e Saneamento
PMF	Programa Médico de Família
PSF	Programa Saúde da Família
QUALIS	Qualidade Integral à Saúde (São Paulo State)
SAS	Secretaria de Assistência da Saúde, Ministério da Saúde
SUS	Sistema Único de Saúde
UNESCO	United Nations Educational, Cultural, and Scientific Organization
UNICEF	United Nations Children's Fund
UNDIME	União Nacional dos Dirigentes Municipais de Educação
WHO	World Health Organization

Political Parties

Left Parties

PC do B	Partido Comunista do Brasil (Brazilian Comunist Party)
PDT	Partido Democrático Trabalhista (Democratic Labor Party)
PMN	Partido da Mobilização Nacional (Party of National Mobilization)
PPS	Partido Popular Socialista (Popular Socialist Party)
PSB	Partido Socialista Brasileiro (Brazilian Socialist Party)
PT	Partido dos Trabalhadores (Workers' Party)
PV	Partido Verde (Green Party)

Center Parties

PMDB	Partido do Movimento Democrático Brasileiro (Party of the Brazilian Democratic Movement)
PSDB	Partido da Social Democracia Brasileira (Party of Brazilian Social Democracy)
PTB	Partido Trabalhista Brasileiro (Brazilian Labor Party)

Right Parties

DEM	Democratas (Democrats)
PDS	Partido Democrático Social (Democratic Social Party)
PFL	Partido da Frente Liberal (Liberal Front Party)
PL	Partido Liberal (Liberal Party)
PPB	Partido Progressista Brasileiro (Brazilian Progressive Party)
PPR	Partido Progressista Reformador (Reformist Progressive Party)
PRONA	Partido da Reedificação da Ordem Nacional (Party of the Reconstruction of National Order)
PRN	Partido da Reconstrução Nacional (National Reconstruction Party)
PSC	Partido Social Cristão (Social Christian Party)
PSD	Partido Social Democrático (Social Democratic Party)
PSL	Partido Social Liberal (Social Liberal Party)
PTR	Partido Trabalhista Renovador (Renovative Labor Party)

States

AC	Acre
AL	Alagoas
AM	Amazonas
AP	Amapá
BA	Bahia
CE	Ceará
DF	Distrito Federal (Federal District, Brasília)
ES	Espirito Santo
GO	Goiás
MA	Maranhão
MG	Minas Gerais
MS	Mato Grosso do Sul
MT	Mato Grosso
PA	Pará

PB	Paraíba
PE	Pernambuco
PI	Piauí
PR	Paraná
RJ	Rio de Janeiro
RN	Rio Grande do Norte
RO	Rondônia
RR	Roraima
RS	Rio Grande do Sul
SC	Santa Catarina
SE	Sergipe
SP	São Paulo
TO	Tocantins

ACKNOWLEDGMENTS

Though I did not know it at the time, the seed for this project was planted many years before I embarked upon the research for this book. From 1998 to 2000, I worked in grant making at the Ford Foundation where I supported efforts to strengthen civil society and promote good governance practices. My work had little to do with Brazil or with the social sector reforms that I examine here. But I did learn about the Ford Foundation's long-standing initiative to support innovations in governance. While innovations awards for good governance practices always struck me as a laudable exercise, I always wondered whether award-winning programs would have an impact beyond their originating jurisdiction and spread elsewhere. If so, how would that happen? Several years later, I had the opportunity to investigate the diffusion of good governance models within the context of Brazilian politics.

As is the case with any major research endeavor, this book would not have been possible without the collaboration and support of numerous individuals. First and foremost, I am indebted to my informants in Brazil who were willing to share their experiences with me. This group includes not only the individuals who participated in interviews and focus groups, but also the many others who simply shared with me the realities of living on the margins. Informal conversations with beneficiaries of health and education programs, as well as the street-level bureaucrats who work day to day with the poor, brought to light how important it is for governments to get the policies right. While the voices of the poor are not the focus of this analysis, they nevertheless inform my own perspective on the high stakes for social sector reform.

This type of research requires extensive field research and I am grateful to a number of institutions and individuals who made it possible for me to spend an extended period in Brazil. The Fulbright-IIE and Boren Fellowships supported my early field research in Belo Horizonte, Brasília, Salvador, and São Paulo. In Brazil, I benefited from institutional affiliations with the Escola de Administração Pública of the Fundação Getúlio Vargas–São Paulo and the Escola de Administração of the Universidade Federal de Bahia. Numerous individuals went above and beyond to assist me in the field, including Peter K. Spink, Marta Ferreira Santos Farah, Luiz Odorico Monteiro de Andrade, José António Gomes de Pinho, António Sérgio Araújo Fernandes, Ilka Camarotti, David Fleischer, Fabio Santos Perreira, and Anderson Lima. I had the privilege of working with several talented graduate assistants who assisted me with data collection and implementation of a phone survey of municipal administrators; they were Ana Paula Karruz, Natália Koga, Evelyn Chaves, Lília Asuca Sumiya, and Francisco Moraes da Costa Marques. I was lucky to find such as dedicated group of graduate students, many of whom have gone on to careers in government and higher education.

A number of other institutions have supported this project by granting me valuable time to analyze and write this book as well as other related works. Those include the Spencer Foundation, the Department of Government at the University of Texas at Austin (Malcolm Macdonald Fellowship), the Teresa Lozano Long Institute for Latin American Studies at the University of Texas at Austin (Summer Research Fellowship), PEO International–Austin/CR Chapter, the University of Wisconsin–Milwaukee (Graduate School Research Award), and the University of Wisconsin System's Institute for Race and Ethnicity (Faculty Diversity Fellowship). Two research libraries, the Benson Library at the University of Texas at Austin and the New York Public Library, were also invaluable.

Throughout this project, I have benefited from the insights of numerous individuals. At the risk of omitting some important friends and colleagues, I here recognize those who contributed the most to the development of this project. I am most grateful to Wendy Hunter and Kurt Weyland, both of whom shared my fascination with Brazilian politics as well as a deep interest in matters of the politics of social inclusion. Wendy provided enthusiasm for research on social policy and Brazilian politics, which served as a constant source of energy. Kurt encouraged me to explore the public health sector as well as engage broad disciplinary debates. His research on diffusion theory serves as an important influence in my own study. Many other individuals at the University of Texas at Austin provided insights and feedback on my early research. Raúl L. Madrid offered early input on the research design and encouraged me to draw on mixed methods. Andrew Karch introduced me to a broader literature in U. S.-state politics and American studies of diffusion. Tse-min Lin lent invaluable guidance on the event history modeling in the book. Gretchen Ritter offered her keen eye and asked crucial questions that furthered the development of my argument. Finally, Robert H. Wilson's contributions predate this work when he introduced me to his research on decentralization and governance in Brazil. Colleagues at other institutions have also contributed to the development of my thinking over the years, including Brian Wampler, Howard Handelman, and James W. McGuire. Of course, any errors and omissions are my own.

This book has been years in the making, and my early research of social sector reforms has appeared in journal articles. My publications in *Comparative Political Studies* (41:2 [2008]) and *Latin American Research Review* (43:3 [2008]) cover portions of chapters 2 and 3. Thanks go to these journals for extending permission to reprint some of the analysis.

I have been fortunate to work with the University of Notre Dame Press and would be remiss if I were to neglect their contributions. I thank anonymous reviewers, Stephen Little, Harv Humphrey, and Scott P. Mainwaring for their commitment to this project and for shepherding my manuscript through all the stages of production. Thanks also go to Margo Shearman for careful editing.

Finally, this is the kind of enterprise that would be impossible to undertake without the encouragement of my family. My parents introduced me to Brazil and instilled a lifetime of intellectual curiosity. In particular I thank my mother, Maria Lúcia Borges Sugiyama, for her love of Brazil and persistence in teaching her children about its language, culture, and history. My father, Iutaka Sugiyama, taught me early on to ask questions, challenge conventional norms, and take on the eye of a keen ethnographer. My brother, Alexandre Borges Sugiyama, has been a constant supporter of my academic career and has served as a trusted informal adviser. Most of all my deepest love and gratitude go to my husband, Greg Carter.

CHAPTER 1

The Politics of Social Sector Reforms, Subnational Governance, and the Prospects for Policy Diffusion

One of the foremost challenges for democratic governments is to ensure that its outputs—public policies—are responsive to the needs of citizens. The difficulty of enacting good public policy is especially acute for developing nations, where the need for basic social services is high due to pressing demands resulting from high rates of poverty and social and income inequality. At the same time, governments must also overcome historic and long-standing political legacies of clientelist practices, the unequal quid pro quo exchanges between patrons and the poor in the form of patronage and vote buying, which have undermined meaningful democratic participation for the poor and accountability of the political elite. Given these challenges, it is no wonder that observers consider good governance practices rare.

Much of the scholarship in comparative politics has sought to explain why policy reform by national governments, particularly equity-enhancing social sector reform, has been difficult (Corrales 1999; Grindle 2004; Kaufman and Nelson 2004; Weyland 1996). We know for instance that the legacies of privileged interests, in which the middle and upper classes have benefited disproportionately from the corporativist state, have created entrenched policies that are difficult for reformers to dismantle (Hunter and Sugiyama 2009). Further, we have learned that late industrialization and the delayed emergence of strong working-class political parties in Latin America have hindered efforts to promote a broad welfare state that can serve as a counterweight to a strong corporativist state (Mainwaring 1999). Those who most need the results of that type of reform, the poor and vulnerable, are the least capable of overcoming political barriers and organizing to pressure the state (Kaufman and Nelson 2004; 12; Grindle 2002, 92). Further, evidence abounds of politicians who use social programs to leverage particularistic benefits and buy votes, thus undermining the potential for meaningful social transformation through public policy (see, for example, Schady 2000). Despite these barriers to national social sector reform, however, we know that social and equity-enhancing public policy that benefits the poor can happen, particularly at the local level.

Several examples of good governance in developing contexts are worth noting. For instance, Judith Tendler's research in the state of Ceará in Brazil's northeast has shown how good performance can take place across a set of programs when an activist state government (supported by a reform-minded governor) supports highly dedicated public workers (1997). Merilee Grindle's work on municipal governance in Mexico has demonstrated that local policy innovation is made possible through public sector entrepreneurship, which is in turn supported by competitive elections, state capacity, and citizen demand-making (2007). In Asia examples of model human development strategies have emerged from the Indian state of Kerala (Drèze and Sen 1989; Ramachandran 2000; McGuire 2010, 135–36). In municipalities in Kenya, India, the Philippines, and South Africa, among others, citizens have engaged in participatory decision making over resource allocation and policy implementation alongside local officials (Grindle 2007, 2). The important issue for both scholars of comparative politics and development practitioners is how to take models of good governance and support them elsewhere. Rather than focus on those unique settings where innovations take place, the emphasis here is on the mechanisms that facilitate the spread of model policies.

This book examines the politics behind good governance programs and investigates the driving forces behind their diffusion. It does so from the vantage point of Brazilian politics, where innovative social sector reforms have sought to provide the poor with increased access to state resources. Much of this innovation has taken place at the subnational municipal level where autonomous governments have been free either to emulate well-regarded programs or ignore them altogether. Like other populous federal developing nations, Brazil is continental in size and has thousands of municipalities[1] that vary in terms of size, population, political cultures, levels of development, and degrees of social inequality and poverty. Since the late 1980s, the country has undergone tremendous policy transformations as local governments have gained political, fiscal, and administrative autonomy. For poor and vulnerable groups, local politics hold special importance as municipal authorities provide essential basic services necessary for their survival, including sewerage services, public safety, education, and health care. Thus, the stakes are high for getting the policy right, and we need to understand when and why politicians are willing to emulate good models. Simply, what motivates politicians to replicate good governance models?

This introduction provides a broad overview of the book and its theoretical approach in order to explain the diffusion of social sector reforms in Brazil. We will look first at the Brazilian political context in which local governments experimented with social policy since democratization in the late 1980s. Then we will turn to the model social sector programs in education and health that are the focus of this book. A broad overview of the analytic approach and a preview of the argument are next, followed by a discussion of the research design of the study and an outline of the book's organization.

Brazil's Subnational Policy Environment

Brazilian politics offers a fascinating environment in which to examine social policy innovations as well as the motivations for subnational political actors' emulation decisions. Much of this results from the institutional setting laid out in the democratic Constitution (1988), which established a federal system where municipalities serve as an independent third tier of government. In practice, municipalities enjoy considerable political, fiscal, and administrative autonomy in addressing important social policy concerns. For instance, the constitution established new social rights, including the right to education and health,[2] and requires that municipal governments undertake more responsibilities to deliver important social services. Proponents of decentralization also argued that local governance would allow for better civil society participation, as these institutional arrangements would lead to the inclusion of different actors in the policy process.[3] Since the constitution mandates the creation of participatory mechanisms for citizens to engage in policy making through local councils, citizens would have a voice in shaping policies and overseeing policy making. As a consequence of this administrative and policy flexibility, local governments have the potential to innovate, design new programs, experiment, and serve as democratic "laboratories."[4]

Much of Brazil's local political context is situated against a backdrop of geographic, social, and economic complexity. With over 5500 municipalities that lie between the productive southern plains, lush northern Amazon, and arid northeast, diversity within Brazil cannot be overstated. Local and regional differences date back to the development of its earliest agricultural and industrial sectors, natural resource endowments, immigration settlements, and establishment of local oligarchs who would dominate regional politics. Today, in Brazil observers can see local government reflect their area's political culture and draw on varying resources. Historical legacies of exclusion have also resulted in dramatically different levels of development, poverty, and social inequality. Until recently, the country had the unfortunate distinction of being one of the most unequal countries in the world.[5] It is common for Brazilian intellectuals, for instance, to refer to their own society as "Belíndia"—a country whose income distribution is so skewed that it comprises a small upper class equivalent to the size of Belgium and a large population of poor comparable to India's.[6] Consequently, Brazil exhibits dramatic disparities in wealth, where the elite shop in the trendiest couture stores and travel via private helicopters while millions of families struggle to meet their most basic needs. These household differences also carry over in geographic terms; the industrial and agricultural rich south and southeast offer a dramatic contrast to the small towns located in the arid northeast where destitution and poverty are dire and families struggle for their survival.

Socioeconomic conditions have structured local politics in meaningful ways. As Hagopian (1996) notes, traditional politics has been an important feature of political organization that draws on clientelism, regionalism, and personalism, and owes its origins to extreme economic inequalities, where local patrons use their wealth, such as landholdings, to increase their power and standing (16–17). For instance, in the hinterlands of the northeast, traditional politics has taken the form of a highly personalistic variant of clientelism, whereas in Rio de Janeiro, the Brazilian Democratic Movement (MDB) established a machine-based form of clientelism during the military period (Dinz 1982, as cited by Hagopian 1996, 16). As the political elite gained access to state resources, the distribution of public benefits (e.g., jobs, contracts, and social services) for votes has sustained their contemporary electoral support. Influential political clans have ruled over politics in many states and municipalities, creating lasting legacies. For instance, the Sarney family has held sway in the state of Maranhão, and the family of Antônio Carlos Magalhães (ACM)[7] has dominated politics in the state of Bahia since the 1970s (Fleischer 2008), at least until recently.

For both traditional and reform-minded politicians, the pathway to national electoral success requires achieving local electoral success. Municipal office, particularly mayoralship, represents an important venue for politicians to build careers and gather long-term political resources. As Samuels (2003) notes, many nationally recognized politicians do not build their careers throughout decades of service in Congress, but rather draw on their electoral experience in municipal executive office. Scholars of Brazilian politics have attributed this to the electoral system for congressional office that undermines the appeal of a legislative career-building strategy. Specifically, open-list proportional representation for congressional elections—with large, statewide, multimember districts in which voters can cast ballots for individual candidates—creates incentives for politicians to run on their personal appeal rather than on partisan allegiance (Ames and Power 2007; Mainwaring 1999). With relatively weak party institutionalization, where party leaders cannot control the electoral prospects of their members in Congress, politicians have found that local executive office provides them with greater political influence and ability to shape their political personas. Further, with federal and fiscal decentralization, mayors have significant economic resources at their disposal and do not need to rely on ad hoc national or state-level transfers in the form of pork barrel politics to build their flagship programs (Samuels and Mainwaring 2004). Given this political setting—where local politics represents an important opportunity for politicians to boost their future electoral prospects—competitive local elections and heightened significance of local politics become the norm. Moreover, as politicians build their reputations they highlight their municipal achievements: their advances in administrative and policy reforms become an important part of that effort.

Brazilian mayors have used their administrative independence and constitutional responsibilities to advance their political agendas. Importantly, mayors enjoy considerable discretion in putting together their cabinets and shaping public policy during their electoral mandate, selecting the department secretaries of all the agencies in their cabinet and typically hiring individuals who are loyal to their political priorities.[8] While these political appointees serve at the pleasure of the mayor, most cabinet members, such as secretaries of education and health, have expertise in their fields. Secretaries are typically academics, high-ranking civil servants, or former elected officials with substantive experience in these policy domains. While mayors may require city council approval for new initiatives, in practice city councils are weak legislative bodies and rarely block major policy initiatives.[9] Thus, mayors and senior technocrats have tremendous discretion and flexibility in experimenting, innovating, and replicating new public policies.

Throughout much of the late 1980s and 1990s, many states and municipalities embraced their newfound flexibilities and operated as policy "laboratories" by experimenting with new administrative and social policies (Abers 2000; Tendler 1997a; Wampler and Avritzer 2004; Wampler 2004). Innovative programs abounded as cities instituted programs such as participatory governance (e.g., Orçamento Participativo, Participatory Budgeting), income-generating cooperatives, recycling programs, culturally inclusive indigenous school curricula, and family doctor programs, just to name a few (Spink, Bava, and Paulics 2002). Local policy experiments were created both across and within policy arenas, but were particularly notable in key sectors of municipal responsibility, such as education and health. That a number of subnational governments would become the vanguard of social policy in Brazil was particularly remarkable, given that the federal government was home to highly specialized technocrats, and that social reforms at the federal level took place very slowly (Ames 2001; Weyland 1996).

In the mid-1990s several municipal governments began to exercise their municipal authority to develop new social programs that linked poverty assistance with incentives-based conditionality tied to education. The idea was to improve human development, particularly the education of poor children, by creating an incentive for them to matriculate in school and attend classes regularly. Two cities, Brasília (the federal district) and Campinas (in São Paulo state), started their respective programs in 1995. Brasília's policy, known as Bolsa Escola (School Grant), was implemented under Governor Cristovam Buarque, of the Workers' Party (Partido dos Trabalhadores, also known as the PT). It had a clear focus on education and sought to improve the district's lagging school indicators among the poor; particularly low educational attainment, low enrollment rates, high repetition, and high drop-out rates. Campinas's mayor José Roberto Magalhães Teixeira, of the Social Democratic Party (PSDB), would implement the Programa de Garantia de Renda Familiar Mínima (Guaranteed Minimum Family Income Program), which combined educational conditionality with complementary health services and social assistance. Despite some important differences, both programs shared an underlying logic: they provided mothers of low-income children with cash grants on the condition they monitor their children's behavior.

Today known as conditional cash transfer programs (CCTs), both Bolsa Escola and Renda Familiar Mínima reflected a new set of ideas. First, the poor (particularly mothers) were considered capable of managing cash benefits and did not need state authorities to tell them how to use those funds. Second, government assistance should be targeted to the neediest groups (i.e., indigent and poor families). Third, assistance would be conditional and would require behavioral changes on the part of the beneficiaries. Local authorities would leverage compliance with program requirements—usually behavioral changes to promote a "demand" for education—in order for mothers to receive the family grant. Finally, these programs focused on overall human development and the causes of intergenerational poverty. Rather than view Bolsa Escola or Renda Mínima as expenses, policy makers approached them as investments in human development. All in all, the programs represented a very different view of what constituted "education" or "social assistance" responsibilities of local governments. They also innovated by reconceptualizing what are typically narrowly defined and highly segmented sectors to include an integrated policy design that sought to achieve mutual aims of promoting human development.

Bolsa Escola and Renda Mínima programs received early recognition for their innovative policy design. Well-respected think tanks and international organizations published favorable evaluations of the programs in Campinas and Brasília. These cities also won awards for the programs, which generated news coverage about the merits of this strategy. Municipal Bolsa Escola and Renda Mínima models quickly spread across municipalities; within two years approximately eighty-eight cities had adopted the program (Araújo and de Souza 1998). By 2001 more than two hundred cities had municipal Bolsa Escola programs (Villatoro 2004). That same year, and on the eve of presidential elections, the federal government created a national Bolsa Escola program that was similar in design but bypassed municipalities.[10] This book focuses on municipal program diffusion, which requires budgetary and administrative obligations on the part of cities.

A second innovative policy reform to emerge among local governments took hold in the area of preventive health, called Programa Saúde da Família (PSF, Family Health Program). PSF emerged out of several local experiences in basic health care provision. One source of learning was community health work in states such as Parana, Ceará, and Mato Grosso do Sul (Viana and Dal Poz 1998, 18). The Ministry of Health formally encouraged other states to develop similar programs in 1991, by creating the Programa de Agentes Comunitários de Saúde (Community Health Agents Program, PACS). PACS primarily served the poverty-stricken north and northeast and drew on community leaders to serve as health agents and combat alarmingly high rates of infant and maternal mortality. The program responded to some of the structural deficits in the region's health care infrastructure (e.g., lower access to clinics, hospitals, and health care professionals, such as doctors) as well as high poverty rates that contributed to poor health outcomes for the population. Armed with information, community health agents would visit households and provide them with information on pre- and postnatal care, including the benefits of breastfeeding. Another set of insights would emerge from experiences in a wealthier municipality in the southeast, Niterói, in the state of Rio de Janeiro. In 1991 Niterói's municipal health department drew largely from the Cuban primary health model[11] to establish the Programa Médico de Família (Family Doctor Program) (Terra and Malik 1998). General practice physicians worked directly with families alongside nurses and community health agents to provide basic health care.

The Programa de Agentes Comunitários de Saúde (PACS) and Programa Médico de Família shared important insights crucial to the development of the family health program. First, both programs viewed primary care as a central focus. Rather than concentrate resources on building facilities, clinics, or hospitals, which provide more complex medical services, policy makers focused on the benefits of preventive health care to address a range of health care needs, including prevention of communicable diseases, maternal mortality, and infant mortality. Second, these programs provided services to families and did so in their communities. Health workers organized their work according to geographic territories, and maps of health needs within each area helped in their delivery of preventive medical care. Third, both programs drew on the idea that community health requires working directly with a member of the community who resides in the territory served and can function as an intermediary between the community and other health care professionals. Finally, these programs sought to change the culture of medical care by promoting proactive engagement rather than reactive responses driven by demand for services.

Policy makers integrated these insights when designing the PSF program. The Programa Saúde da Família started in 1994 in small rural municipalities in the northeast (Viana and Dal Poz 1998). PSF was conceived at a Ministry of Health meeting in Brasília in December 1993, held at the request of municipal health secretaries and sponsored by the health minister. Participants included municipal health secretaries, technocrats in basic health from the ministry, public health specialists from state departments of health, and officials from international organizations (Viana and Dal Poz 1998, 19). Supported by the Ministry of Health, this small-scale program has the goal of improving prevention and basic health by working directly with families through home visits. To facilitate linkages to communities, health care workers operate within designated territories and in teams composed of a doctor, nurse, nurse's aide, and several community health agents. Like its predecessors, PACS and Médico de Família, PSF represented a significant departure from the existing health care model in Brazil, which tended to prioritize clinician and hospital-based care. Like the conditional cash grant programs, the PSF received wide recognition and visibility among health care technocrats. As the program gained wider visibility and credibility, it spread dramatically, from 55 cities in 1994 to 4944 municipalities by 2003. By April 2011 nearly 95 percent of all municipalities (5279 total) had adopted the PSF program (Ministry of Health 2011).

Analytic Approach and Preview of Argument

Thus this book delves into the politics of policy making to understand the mechanisms that drive policy diffusion by examining actors' motivations for emulating well-regarded programs. The political science discipline has long debated the origins of actors' political behavior, particularly those related to resource allocation decisions. In other words, when and why do politicians distribute goods to constituents? To answer this question in the policy diffusion context, this analysis contrasts three paradigmatic models for individuals' resource allocations choices: political self-interest, ideological commitments, and socialized professional norms. It opens up the "black box" of policy making by asking what *motivates* policy makers on the ground to make emulation decisions.[12] Rather than employ the conventional framework used in diffusion studies, which contrasts internal prerequisites with external pressures for policy emulation, this study will offer a theoretical framework for understanding the mechanisms that drive diffusion, as chapter 2 explains in greater depth.

The Argument in Brief

To uncover the motivations for social sector reform, this analysis draws on two policy arenas—education and health—that have traditionally served to reinforce personalistic politics and clientelism. Specialists in Brazilian politics have noted that social policies, including education (Draibe 2004, 380, 385; interview Weber 2011) and health (Weyland 1996, 100, 165), have served as long-standing sources for political patronage. Politicians who employ clientelistic practices to gain political support often rely on education and health sectors because they provide local officials with considerable resources. Simply, fiscal transfers for education and health constitute a large share of municipal revenues.[13] Since local politicians face fiscal constraints, such as high fixed costs for personnel and maintenance, transfers for primary education and basic health services constitute an important source of revenue to sustain patron-client relations. Traditional politicians who regularly engage in clientelism can use new programs such as municipal conditional cash transfer programs and PSF to sustain these relationships through the use of patronage and the political distribution of program resources.

Other politicians, including reformists, also have strong political incentives to adopt innovative policies such as Bolsa Escola and PSF. Since Brazil has compulsory voting and a large poor population, politicians have strong incentives to recruit votes from marginalized constituents. Vulnerable groups in abject poverty are entirely reliant on basic public services and cannot reasonably exit from the public system. In other words, public education is the only option for poor families with young children, and the free public health system is the only health care available for indigent, poor, and informal workers who lack private health insurance. Given the importance of health and education for families, voters are most likely to notice and reward policy changes that improve their life prospects. Remarkably, politicians can offer improvements in these areas without fear of alienating other voters, including powerful elites; Amaury de Sousa's study showed that elites believe investments in education, health, and poverty reduction are necessary for the country's development (as cited in *Véja* 1996). Further supporting the view that these programs are mainstream ideas, Melo argues that strong competition among Brazil's leading political parties explains the timing and adoption of conditional cash transfer programs by the *federal* government (2008, 166, 169). In sum, education and health care policies, as opposed to other types of policies (e.g., the environment and job training), represent the most likely cases for an electoral incentives finding. As we will see, however, electoral competition does not drive emulation decisions.

Contrary to the conventional wisdom that politicians are driven by their electoral ambitions, I find that a political incentives approach offers a surprisingly weak explanation for the diffusion of innovative social policies. Electoral self-interest cannot explain variations across political jurisdictions and policy makers' decisions to implement programs like Bolsa Escola and Programa Saúde da Família. Electoral incentives also fail to explain adoption decisions over time, such as why some cities appear to adopt reform more quickly than others. Rather, two different but complementary approaches explain diffusion: ideology and socialized professional norms.

First, I find that ideology serves as a foundation for many policy makers in guiding them to action and helping them filter their policy choices. My analysis reveals that politicians who self-identify as being on the left or left of center are consistently more eager to adopt model social sector reforms. High-level technocrats with political appointments, such as secretaries of education and health, who share their mayors' ideological dispositions, are also instrumental. For left-of-center mayors and technocrats, policies such as Bolsa Escola and PSF fulfill their desires to enact policy innovations consistent with their socially progressive commitments. Thus while education and health are vulnerable to fraud, these actors emulate programs because of an overarching belief that these strategies will help to address poverty and improve social inclusion in Brazil.

Another altogether different motivation for adopting policy innovations, socialized norms, also matters in the diffusion of municipal social sector reforms. Actors involved in the policy process, mayors and especially technocrats, are embedded in professional networks that transmit information and set norms for their field. Professional associations that support networks of technocrats, such as associations in public health, play a central role in shaping technocrats' views on trends in their field and their desire to keep up with the latest innovations. As the analysis shows, policy professionals want to demonstrate to their peer networks that they understand and follow new professional norms. The speed and extent of policy diffusion is related to the density of professional associations within each sector. Sectors such as public health, with dense and overlapping associations, are more likely to reinforce norms for "good governance" programs and encourage actors' legitimacy-seeking behavior, thus promoting diffusion.

Each motivation for policy emulation—political incentives, ideological commitments, and socialized norms—is defined and constructed narrowly. This allows for analysis of the ways in which each mechanism works independently as well as together. Thus, in some instances, ideology and networks can work together in mutually reinforcing ways by convincing actors that policies not only reflect the latest norms in their fields, but also remain consistent with their ideological commitments. When this type of synergy takes place, as in the case of health sector reform, policy emulation decisions are more likely to endure.

Research Design

This project uses a mix of methodological approaches to capture the diffusion of social policies in Brazil, drawing on surveys, interviews, and statistical analyses to answer the question of what motivates policy makers to emulate social policies.

An important feature of this study is the comparison of two social policies that are situated in distinct sectors—education and health—and which diffuse at different rates. As Rogers notes, a shortcoming of diffusion research is the propensity to study "successful" instances of diffusion (2003, 110). In other words, scholars tend to have a "pro-innovations bias" in focusing on policies that have spread dramatically across jurisdictions. Another component of a pro-innovations bias is that researchers tend to focus on policies they believe are "good" and should spread. This study aims to alleviate some of this bias by selecting two markedly different programs. Although both Bolsa Escola and PSF won "innovations" awards,[14] as we will see, these policies are not universally perceived as "good" or desirable for all jurisdictions. Since awards for these programs are based on a single city's experience, it is entirely possible that the same program, when adopted elsewhere, can fail to address the emulating city's most pressing problems. Some policy makers endorsed these policies and believed the programs "should" spread, while others disagreed.

There are numerous benefits to conducting a large-n event history analysis, also known as survival analysis. First, increasing the number of observations provides greater leverage for causal inference (King, Keohane, and Verba 1994). Second, an event history model, which involves annual observations for each jurisdiction, addresses the problem of potential interdependence among jurisdictions and thus allows for better analyses of internal and external determinants of diffusion (Berry and Berry 1990, 1992; Collier and Messick 1975). Advanced statistical methods, such as event history modeling, also allow for a probabilistic interpretation of whether cities are likely to adopt innovative social policies.

In order to understand larger trends across Brazil and map the pattern of Brazilian social policy diffusion, I use an event history analysis statistically to test the impact of political incentives, ideology, and social networks on diffusion for Brazil's largest cities. To conduct such an analysis, I created a database on social policies for all 224 cities that had populations over 100,000 in the census year 2000. This original database draws on information related to electoral politics, sociodemographic data, and social network connectivity. It also includes information on the adoption patterns of Bolsa Escola, Renda Mínima, and Programa Saúde da Família. Because of limited data access and in order to assess the spread of Bolsa Escola and Renda Mínima, I administered a phone survey of education and social welfare administrators for the entire survey population. (For a list of cities included in the analysis, see appendix A.)

The task of uncovering *motivations* for social policy emulation decisions in Brazil is complex and thus requires multiple analytic approaches. First-order analysis can start from observable data and implications, such as information on electoral competition, politicians' partisan affiliation, and the presence of professional networks in a given community. With this information we can draw inferences and make conclusions. Also important, however, is how actors themselves interpret these programs and explain their role in the decision-making process. As Taylor notes, in order to assess meaning, we must pay attention to the stories people tell: "A person's understanding of her own life, the story she tells (constructs and reconstructs) about herself, which itself of course becomes part of her life, endows events with meaning, with significance for us. For most of us want to see things we have done and events in our lives as having some meaning" (2006, 33). Consequently, in order to assess whether an actor's motivations for emulating an innovative policy are driven by political self-interest, ideology, or socialized norms, we must ask individuals to tell a story. Their narratives will frame the way they understand the event and the meaning it held for them.

The case studies draw extensively on semistructured interviews with 120 Brazilian policy makers involved in health and education policy making at the local level, elected officials, technocrats, community activists, and leaders in nongovernmental organizations. Most interviewees worked in one of the four cities in this study; however, I also interviewed a select number of policy makers who promote one of these programs nationally or work for the federal government and are responsible for setting the federal policy agenda. During face-to-face interviews, respondents discussed their motivations for adopting or advocating for Bolsa Escola/Renda Mínima and Programa Saúde da Família, and reflected on the policy process in general. In instances where local governments did not have the programs or the programs had been dismantled, we discussed why this was so. I conducted interviews in four municipalities in Brazil—Belo Horizonte (in Minas Gerais state), Brasília (in the federal district), Salvador (in Bahia state), and São Paulo (in São Paulo state)—and sought out actors involved with three municipal administrations, from 1994 to 2003. The qualitative evidence allows for process tracing, an approach whereby I identify the mechanisms that connect my theoretically driven variables with the diffusion outcome (George and McKeown 1985).

Several criteria guided selection of the research sites. First, the four cities in this study adopted Bolsa Escola and PSF at different points in time and in a few instances even experienced policy reversal (see table 1.1). The variation in program adoption over time is important because otherwise there would be a potential for selection bias (Geddes 1990, 2003; King, Keohane, and Verba 1994, 129–37). Second, these municipalities were selected to allow for variation in partisan politics. These local governments had mayors who were affiliated with eight different political parties and represented ideological leanings from across the political spectrum, from staunch rightists to leftists; no single party dominates, and all major political parties are represented (see table 1.2). Third, the case study cities also face different levels of socioeconomic development and are geographically dispersed. Fourth, in the context of health policy, these cities had great flexibility in determining their basic health models. Not only did they enjoy fiscal autonomy because of their potential to generate revenues through their local tax base, but they also had a sophisticated health infrastructure and a large number of health professionals. In other words, these municipalities had the administrative flexibility to tailor health policy, and emulation of PSF was far from automatic or a foregone conclusion. Despite these important differences, these cities share characteristics that make comparison possible: all are large state capitals and face similar institutional tensions in local, state, and national-level policy making. The only exception is Brasília, which has a unique status as the federal district. So, overall, the case studies largely conform to a comparable case methodology (Lijphart 1971, 687–89; 1975) that allows for the control of differences across the cases that might otherwise be thought of as important factors in explaining diffusion.

By using both large-n statistical analyses and small-n case studies, this project bridges two research traditions on diffusion. Scholars who frame their work along the lines of "learning" and "policy transfer" typi-

Table 1.1. Adoption of Bolsa Escola/Renda Mínima and PSF by Local Government and Administration

	Bolsa Escola/Renda Mínima	*Programa Saúde da Família*
Brasília (DF)[a]		
1990–1994	—[b]	No
1994–1998	Yes	Yes
1998–2002	No/Yes[c]	No/Yes[c]
Belo Horizonte (MG)		
1992–1996	No	No
1996–2000	Yes	No
2000–2004	Yes	Yes
Salvador (BA)		
1992–1996	Yes	No
1996–2000	No	No
2000–2004	No	Yes
São Paulo (SP)		
1992–1996	No	No
1996–2000	No	No
2000–2004	Yes	Yes

[a] The Federal District, Brasília, operates under the gubernatorial electoral calendar.
[b] Period precedes the creation of Bolsa Escola/Renda Mínima.
[c] The program was suspended or discontinued and then reintroduced under new names.

cally focus on microprocesses and actors, and employ qualitative methods (see for example Bennett 1991; Rose 1993, 2004). By contrast, those who employ statistical analyses of broader diffusion phenomena typically seek the leverage that a large number of cases can offer for generalizability of causal analysis (see, for example, Box-Steffensmeier and Jones 1997, 2004b). Employing both methods enables comparison between this study's findings and those from existing research.

Further, drawing on both qualitative and quantitative studies, this work also overcomes some of the shortcomings that single-method studies face (see Tarrow 2004). Quantitative approaches alone may provide insights on the correlates of diffusion, such as economic development.

Table 1.2. Local Government Partisan and Ideological Divide

	Executive in Office	*Mayor's Party*[a]	*Ideological Leanings*
Brasília (DF)[b]			
1990–1994	Joaquim Roriz	PTR	Right[c]
1994–1998	Cristovam Buarque	PT	Left
1998–2002	Joaquim Roriz	PMDB	Center
Belo Horizonte (MG)			
1992–1996	Patrus Ananias	PT	Left
1996–2000	Célio de Castro	PSB	Left
2000–2004	Célio de Castro Fernando Damata Pimentel (PT)[d]	PSB	Left
Salvador (BA)			
1992–1996	Lídice da Mata	PSDB	Center
1996–2000	Antônio José Imbassahy	PFL	Right
2000–2004	Antônio José Imbassahy	PFL	Right
São Paulo (SP)			
1992–1996	Paulo Maluf	PDS	Right
1996–2000	Celso Pitta	PPB	Right
2000–2004	Marta Suplicy	PT	Left

[a] Mayor's partisan affiliation at the time he or she ran for office.
[b] The Federal District, Brasília, operates under the gubernatorial electoral calendar.
[c] Mainwaring, Meneguello, and Power (2000, 180) inform this designation. The PTR is not classified in Coppedge 1996.
[d] Fernando Damata Pimentel (PT) assumed office in November 2001, after Célio de Castro suffered a stroke.

However, large-n statistical analysis alone cannot explain why a jurisdiction's level of development matters in terms of politics or suggest the mechanisms that link economic development to a policy outcome. Moreover, statistical methods can also obscure causal heterogeneity in emulation decisions, thus limiting understanding of the complex and varied mechanisms that lead to policy emulation (Mahoney and Goertz 2006). In this way, large-n statistical studies can contribute to an underaccounting of "causal complexity" by making interpretation of the underlying relationship between indicators and concepts difficult

(Meseguer and Gilardi 2009). Qualitative research can help uncover the mechanisms that drive diffusion and clarify whether jurisdictions are likely to undergo similar causal processes.

At the same time, scholars note that qualitative comparison analysis also has analytic shortcomings. Lijphart argues that the comparative method is problematic as the number of cases is too small to permit systematic control by means of partial correlations (1971, 684). Geddes (1990) has noted that small-n comparisons often suffer from the problem of selection bias, and King, Keohane, and Verba (1994) have famously critiqued these approaches for their lack of systematic procedures. Defenders of qualitative research note that case studies allow for close analysis and are particularly well suited for explaining complex causal processes (A. Bennett 2010; George and Bennett 2005). In this vein this study draws on "process-tracing procedures" to explain the decision process that actors undertake to reach decisions. According to George and Bennett, "The process-tracing approach attempts to uncover what stimuli the actors attend to; the decision process that makes use of these stimuli to arrive at decisions; the actual behavior that occurs; the effect of various institutional arrangements on attention, processing, and behavior; and the effect of other variables of interest on attention, processing, and behavior" (2005, 35). Given this study's focus on the motivations for emulation decisions, this approach is best suited to capture the policy-making process, including learning, emulation, and occasionally policy reversal.

Mixed methods that incorporate qualitative and quantitative approaches are increasingly popular strategies for analyzing comparative policy outcomes (see, for example, Madrid 2003 and Lieberman 2003). Drawing on both methodological approaches can compensate for the shortcomings inherent in each.[15] While the statistical model provides insights in the requisites for adopting innovative social policies, qualitative process tracing allows for analysis of the politics of the policy process. Further, this study leverages the benefits of small-n analysis to provide better and more meaningful measures of theoretically motivated variables for the event history models. For instance, measures of socialized network connectivity are made possible through interviews where actors identify associations that hold meaning for their professional development. In this way, this study seeks to combine the benefits of quantitative and qualitative methods to explore the same problem with the aim of gaining a richer understanding of political processes.[16]

Significance

In the last twenty years or so a tremendous proliferation of diffusion research has taken place across the social sciences illustrating the profound interest among scholars in accounting for change over time. Why do some ideas and policies spread across place? This study furthers previous understandings of diffusion with a new conceptual framework that focuses on individuals' motivations in replicating policy models developed in other settings. As disciplines have embraced paradigmatic explanations for the determinants of individual behavior, many scholars have either purposefully or unintentionally embedded their fields' assumptions in their diffusion analyses. Rather than assume actors are motivated by a single interest, this book contrasts differing perspectives. The mixed-methods approach provides the foundation for a test of whether political incentives, ideology, or social networks affect the decision-making process. Thus, by exploring contrasting motivations for political action, this study assesses three theoretical approaches that are often examined in isolation from one another.

The findings presented here differ from conventional expectations about politicians and their singular interest in electoral competition, at least when it comes to social policy domains such as education and health. Indeed most observations about social sector reform have highlighted the weak incentives for politicians to initiate reform (see, for example, Corrales 1999; Kaufman and Nelson 2004). Politicians are not thought of as being "altruistic" or for making choices because it is the "right thing to do." Yet the analysis of local governance in Brazil reveals that politicians are more complex than we give them credit for. They can have ideological commitments and desires to make a difference. Politicians also hire highly skilled technocrats who share their vision and are equally shaped by their profession's norms to keep up with shared standards. Altogether, this is a very different portrait of the politics of policy making. In a Latin American context where national politicians appear to have converged around neoliberal economic models and militants bemoan the loss of a meaningful political left, I find that ideological differences and commitments still matter.

While diffusion research has broadly captured the attention of social scientists, this framework is still new to studies of Brazilian politics. Decentralization in Brazil has ushered in a new policy-making landscape where policy emulation and diffusion are increasingly prevalent. Yet scholars of Brazilian politics have not yet explored these diffusion processes. Most country-specific studies of diffusion remain largely relegated to analyses of advanced industrialized nations with federal structures, especially the fifty states in the United States. However, in Brazil subnational diffusion has taken place across thousands of municipal governments. The magnitude of policy emulation for Brazil, potentially reaching over 5500 municipalities, allows for an analysis with a much larger number of cases from which to draw causal insights. Further, the diffusion of social reforms in Brazil suggests that good governance models can spread despite important regional inequalities. Thus, this study does more than integrate an analysis of political behavior into diffusion research; it extends a new analytic framework to the study of Brazilian politics.

More generally, we know that the stakes are high for getting the policies right for third-wave democracies in the developing world. As Karl (2000) notes, poverty and socioeconomic inequality have pernicious effects on democracy; they undermine democratic aspirations, institutions, and rules, and excessive concentrations of wealth and poverty are a formula for political trouble that contributes to the greatest threat facing democracy in the Americas today (156). Thus, in order to achieve high-quality democracies that have meaningful effects for the entire citizenry, governments must actively correct for the centuries-old historical exclusions that have rendered persons belonging to some groups less than full citizens. Development practitioners—particularly those in new public administration—have tended to focus on such issues as state capacity, efficiency, transparency, and policy design and implementation (see Grindle 1997, 5). Although these aims are important and necessary, my focus here is on responsive democratic governance that is equitable and responsive to the social welfare needs of the citizens.

In the context of politics in a developing nation, we would expect good governance to entail public policies that are equity enhancing and pro-poor, and which seek to extend access to state resources to groups that are marginalized and excluded from existing programs.

Organization of the Book

This brief overview serves as a road map for the rest of this book, and each chapter will address the questions first introduced here. Chapter 2 will provide a more thorough discussion on theories of diffusion and actors' motivations for resource allocation decisions. It offers a framework for examining social policy emulation across municipalities, focusing on actors' motivations in replicating policies designed for other cities.

Chapter 3 provides a bird's-eye view of the diffusion of education and health reform, through an analysis of the spread of Bolsa Escola and Programa Saúde da Família. Drawing on original data, we will observe the diffusion of these programs for the country's largest cities. After contextualizing the trends in Bolsa Escola and PSF adoption, an event history model, a discrete time logistic model, statistically tests the theoretically driven variables related to political incentives, ideology, and social networks. A benefit to the event history analysis is that it can facilitate interpretation of time and the probability of adoption.

Chapter 4 examines the emergence of conditional cash transfer programs for education, such as Bolsa Escola and Renda Mínima, and the politics behind their spread across the country. Locally driven innovations to address educational access and attainment are examined in the context of stalled efforts for reform through much of the late 1980s and 1990s at the national level. The analysis draws primarily on case studies of four illustrative cities to reveal the ways in which ideology and professional norms, rather than electoral incentives, influenced policy makers' adoption decisions.

Chapter 5 discusses the emergence of Programa Saúde da Família, an integrated family health program, within the context of the significant reorganization of health policy in the 1990s. National health policy made greater advances in reform, unlike the education sector, and the federal government promoted decentralization with the municipalization of services. As local governments took on greater administrative responsibilities, many political actors implemented the PSF policy. The case studies provide accounts from key actors in the health policy field and reveal how technocrats' connections to professional associations and the presence of leftist mayors drove replication in this policy domain.

Chapter 6 contrasts the diffusion of education reform and that of health policy. The large-n and process-tracing methods offer strikingly consistent accounts for what drives emulation decisions. Together, they also provide insights into key differences between each of the policy arenas. In addition to addressing contrasts between actors' interpretations of these policies, the chapter also underscores how the breadth and depth of networks and informal associations influence the socialization of professional norms. Finally, the ways are examined in which policy making appears to offer a different logic from mainstream analyses of political decision making, which emphasize politicians' electoral self-interest and culture for "buying" votes by distributing particularistic goods. In short, this study highlights the ways in which ideology and socialized norms work together to promote policy emulation, and underscores the potential for continued social sector reform into the future.

CHAPTER 2

Theoretical Debates on Policy Diffusion

A Motivations Approach

A fundamental question that has recently engaged social scientists' attention involves diffusion events. Simply put, how do ideas and practices spread, and why do actors embrace them? The geographic spread of social phenomena includes all types of innovations. Various social science fields have drawn on diffusion as a lens for analyzing the spread of capitalism, welfare regimes, agricultural methods, and adoption of new technologies, for example. As observers of social interactions, we can imagine countless examples of replication across place and time. This chapter addresses diffusion processes that reside at the core of political science debates, including why ideas and policies spread across political territories and the mysteries behind actors' motivations for emulation. Before proceeding further, let us first clarify a few concepts and terms.

What Is Diffusion?

Diffusion phenomena, which evoke images from the natural sciences, such as the spread of a virus across space, are all around us and have captured the attention of a wide range of scholars. Social science disciplines as diverse as sociology, economics, political science, agriculture, and business have also sought to explain socially created events that occur in their respective domains of inquiry. Some occurrences seem to "make sense" as people learn about innovations and quickly adopt them. One classic example in this vein is the spread of hybrid corn among farmers in Iowa, who rapidly embraced the usage of hybrid seeds in the 1940s.[1] In business administration, research has sought to explain the adoption of ideas that do not necessarily result in an improvement. For instance, the QWERTY keyboard for typewriters and computers has been widely recognized as an inefficient layout for typists but remains an entrenched standard worldwide even though manufacturers could produce a more efficient alternative.[2] In the realm of political science research, diffusion phenomena have similarly captured scholars' attention. After all there are countless examples of diffusion, including the spread of smoking regulations in the United States, pension systems across Europe, free-market reforms, women's ministries around the world, electoral quotas for women, and global democracy, among others (for some recent examples see Brinks and Coppedge 2006; Karch 2007; Krook 2006; Orenstein 2003; Shipan and Volden 2006; Simmons and Elkins 2004; True and Mintrom 2001).

While diffusion research has enjoyed great interest in the social sciences, we need to ask, what is diffusion precisely? Scholars use such diverse metaphors as "contagion," "waves," and "transfer" to describe diffusion events (see, for instance, Burt 1987; Stone 1999; Walt 2000). But are they the same? This definitional question underscores the need to clarify the relationship between actors and emulation decisions. For instance, "contagion" suggests a rapid replication process, perhaps due to the infectious nature of the policy. In other words, it is the character of the idea or policy that matters most. Alternatively, the idea of policy "waves" invokes a natural and even inevitable process of adoption. Lastly, "policy transfer" intimates that emulation is caused by some type of learning among actors. Inherent in each of the terms is an underlying assumption about how diffusion takes place and the role that actors play in adoption decisions. Distinguishing among these concepts is more than an exercise in etymology; it gets at the heart of the interaction between actors and policy making. As the purpose of the analysis is to uncover actors' motivations, the definition of diffusion to be used here does not assume policy makers' underlying rationales for decision making.

Diffusion implies autonomous decision making across time and place, while also accounting for potential interdependence between actors. Political actors may learn about an innovation from a neighboring government or international meeting, and choose to copy that innovation in their own countries. Sometimes the impetus to emulate can come from peer influence (horizontal), or reflect internal demands (bottom-up) or external pressures (vertical). These inducements need not reflect benign forces but can include coercion or other stimuli for cooperation. For a visual illustration of the potential influences driving diffusion effects, see figure 2.1.

This study broadly defines diffusion to include processes that affect the likelihood that a reasonably autonomous jurisdiction will adopt an innovative policy developed by another such unit, at some point in time. Various members of a social system can trigger a unit's emulation mechanisms and increase the probability of adoption, including the originating jurisdiction that promotes the new idea, similar decision-making units, and those who reside outside of the decision-making unit (similar to Levi-Faur 2005, 23–26; Weyland 2007, 24–25). Thus in defining innovation, I draw on Rogers (2003, 12), who notes that it is "an idea, practice, or object" that is new to the unit of adoption. The key is the "newness" for the jurisdiction and actors, and not necessarily whether the policy is objectively new, viewed in positive terms, or award winning.

Policy diffusion thus captures a process of decision making that involves some degree of learning, emulation, or mimicry. If separate jurisdictions were to enact the same policy because they share similar conditions (e.g., economic shocks, levels of development, or institutional similarities) but were otherwise isolated from one another, this would not constitute an instance of diffusion. The key here is that diffusion emphasizes the interactive process that leads to replication (i.e., the spread), not just the outcome (i.e., policy adoption).[3]

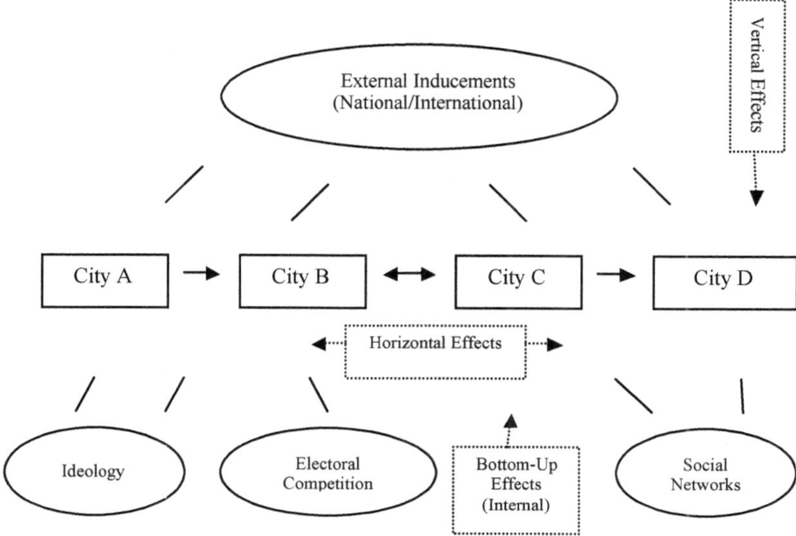

Figure 2.1. Multiple Directions of Diffusion Effects
Source: Modified figure from Levi-Faur 2005, 26.

The conceptualization of diffusion employed in this study is particularly important because the politics of policy making requires that actors advocate for their positions when they choose to adopt an innovation within their jurisdiction. Policy does not lend itself to "automatic" adoption because instituting new programs generally requires the establishment of guidelines, new administrative procedures, and budgetary commitments, all of which require decisive action. Thus, this study emphasizes processes as well as outcomes, including the mechanisms that drive adoption, nonadoption, and reversal. Finally, in classifying diffusion outcomes, I consider that a policy has spread when a jurisdiction enacts a policy that has a similar policy design as the original. Some scholars distinguish between "emulation" and "adoption" as distinct processes. For instance, scholars may use the term *emulation* to emphasize replication in the context of actors' engagement in epistemic communities and desires to keep up with shared norms (e.g., Weyland 2004,

2005). Others, however, use *emulation* or *adoption* to refer to replication that can originate from various other learning processes (e.g., Meseguer 2004; Shipan and Volden 2006; Simmons, Dobbin, and Garrett 2006). Since this work aims to uncover the motivations for policy diffusion and the role of social networks is central to the theoretical framework of this analysis, I make no prior assumptions in selecting terminology to describe diffusion outcomes. For this reason I use *emulation, adoption,* and *replication* interchangeably throughout the book.

Evolution of Diffusion Theory in Political Science

The diffusion research in political science dates back to the late 1960s and 1970s, with seminal studies in American and comparative politics (Collier and Messick 1975; Gray 1973; Walker 1969). Both Collier and Messick (1975) and Walker (1969) persuasively argued that the study of policy trends and policy adoption needed to address the methodological problem of interdependence. Specifically, researchers faced Galton's problem, "that the findings based on the analysis of causal relation within nations (or other units of analysis) may be distorted by the effect of diffusion" (Collier and Messick 1975, 1300). In other words, researchers need to account for the interconnectedness between multiple jurisdictions when examining policy adoption.[4] Policy makers, whether operating at the federal, subnational, or local level, might take into account the decisions of other entities. Thus, to examine the spread of innovations one could not simply examine "prerequisite" conditions, for example levels of economic modernization or human capital, as most policy studies tended to do. Rather, diffusion requires an analysis of external pressures that can affect internal processes, such as spatial proximity to innovative jurisdictions and coercion. By acknowledging that polities are not entirely isolated in their decision-making processes, these early scholars highlighted the need to incorporate analyses of both internal and external pressures for diffusion.

Although these classic studies generated significant attention among scholars for the value of diffusion research, this area of inquiry lay largely dormant until the 1990s. In recent years, both domestic and international events have renewed interest among scholars in policy diffusion research. For instance, political trends toward devolution in the United States led scholars of state politics to examine such diverse issues as the diffusion of education reform (Mintrom 1997; Mintrom and Vergari 1998), welfare reform (Karch 2007), and health maintenance organization regulation (Balla 2001). Other studies have focused on a range of social policy issues, such as the spread of abortion regulation (Mooney and Lee 1995), same-sex marriage bans (Haider-Markel 2001), and antismoking policies (Shipan and Volden 2006). As European integration has taken hold, researchers have explored the propensity for policy transfer and learning across the continent (Bennett 1991; R. Rose 1993, 2004). In the international arena, scholars of comparative politics noted a substantial increase in cross-national replication of state bureaucratic organizations, including science ministries (Finnemore 1993, 1996) and women's ministries (True and Mintrom 2001). More recent analyses of international diffusion waves, such as democratization (Brinks and Coppedge 2006), liberalism (Simmons, Dobbin, and Garrett 2006), economic liberalization (Simmons and Elkins 2004), pension privatization (Madrid 2003), and social sector reform (Weyland 2004, 2005) illustrate that diffusion research continues to have broad appeal and is centrally relevant to the discipline. The fascination with diffusion will only continue as increased channels of communication and globalization facilitate the connectivity between peoples within countries and across the globe.

Also contributing to the resurgence of scholarship on diffusion are advances in methodological techniques that allow for better analysis of the internal and external pressures for policy diffusion. Berry and Berry were among the first diffusion scholars to apply event history analysis,[5] a discrete time logistic regression, to test both internally and externally driven explanations (1990, 1992). Many recent studies of policy diffusion have drawn on this statistical method to examine domestic prerequisites and external pressures for the adoption of innovations (see, for example, Brinks and Coppedge 2006; True and Mintrom 2001). Event history models can also account for different explanations for policy diffusion, including the importance of structural factors, such as coercion through financing from national governments (Karch 2007; Shipan and Volden 2006), as well as actor-orientated explanations that focus on networks of learning and the role of policy entrepreneurs (Balla 2001; Mintrom 1997; Mintrom and Vergari 1998).

Remarkably, this diverse literature not only identifies some of the reasons for policy makers to adopt policy innovations, but also describes the process by which novel ideas spread across time and place. As Rogers (2003) explains, most diffusion events follow a similar S-shaped distribution across time, with five categories of groups that participate in replication: innovators, early adopters, early majority, late majority, and laggards. In the beginning, adoption is rare, with a slow rate of replication as only few units replicate an innovation. Subsequent diffusion typically takes place more rapidly as a larger number of entities in the system follow. Then the slope starts to level off as fewer of the remaining units adopt in each successive period. While this general S-shaped curve applies to most diffusion phenomena, there are important variations. Some innovations diffuse more rapidly than others, resulting in steeper curves, while others diffuse more slowly, producing more gradual slopes (Rogers 2003, 11, 22–23). We have also learned that these temporal features cluster spatially. Innovations tend to spread first to neighbors and then to nearby regions before reaching the rest of the world (Berry 1994; Mooney 2001; Orenstein 2003; Rogers 2003, 90–91). The field as a whole has made significant progress in describing waves of diffusion, including the timing and location of replication. Yet most of the focus has been on single examples of diffusion events. In other words, there is a tendency to examine only one phenomenon at a time and select examples of rapid diffusion. As a result, there is an overall bias in the analyses; scholars privilege cases of innovations that replicate rapidly instead of those that diffuse slowly or not at all. Some of this tendency is understandable as it is difficult to study nonevents (e.g., nondiffusion).[6] But this pro-innovations bias has consequences for understanding broader processes at work. For this reason, I purposefully contrast the diffusion of reforms that also spread to different extents.

This book also extends diffusion research in other ways. While scholarship on policy diffusion is well established among scholars of transnational politics and U.S. state politics, diffusion research has not been readily applied to studies of other federal countries. Both comparative and international politics subfields have examined cross-national and regional diffusion patterns, but have not examined intracountry diffusion. Thus, much of what we know about diffusion processes within a single country comes from studies of the American case. However, other federal countries also share contexts where policies spread across subnational jurisdictions. Brazil, for instance, has a federal system with states and municipal governments with autonomy for policy making and where replication of policy innovations has recently taken hold.[7] Institutional similarities between Brazil and the United States make it possible to draw lessons from the extensive literature on diffusion in the fifty states,[8] as well as draw insights from comparative politics on the cross-national spread of innovations. The existing literature offers a valuable starting point for examining potential factors that explain diffusion in Brazil. Yet at the same time, several shortcomings of conventional approaches to the study of diffusion need to be addressed, including conceptual and methodological limitations.

Since policy issues often have their own unique features (e.g., constituencies and budgetary implications), scholars of policy diffusion necessarily account for these features when testing for the internal prerequisites for diffusion.[9] This line of inquiry has produced a potpourri of factors to explain why jurisdictions would embrace policy innovations (for a comprehensive overview, see Rogers 2003). For instance, scholars identified the presence of policy entrepreneurs (Mintrom 1997), professional associations (Balla 2001), and advocacy coalitions (Haider-Markel 2001) as important variables. Others focused on structural conditions, such as the degree of a jurisdiction's innovativeness, economic resources, or partisanship (Berry and Berry 1992; Klingman 1980; Walker 1969). While these findings yield valuable insights, diffusion studies run the risk of providing analyses that apply only to a small number of policy issues in the United States. For this scholarship to make larger contributions, diffusion research must also engage in broader debates about foundations for individual decision making.

Until recently, one of the most significant gaps in the field was the issue of actors' motivations for policy innovation decisions. As Rogers (2003) notes, the "why" question about adoption is seldom addressed by researchers, in part because of the difficulties in gathering information;

thus, scholars tend to assume motivations are economically driven and overrely on models that are rationalistic. In practice, this often means researchers assume that adoption of innovation is rational,[10] whereas those actors who reject innovations are either nonrational or misguided. In this way, studies tend to incorporate their discipline's dominant paradigms without testing the underlying causes of human behavior. Political scientists who study diffusion often ground their explanations in notions of rationality,[11] and electoral and economic competition (for example, see Berry and Berry 1992; Walker 1969). In contrast, sociologists tend to examine learning in terms of the strength of relational ties and organizational networks (for example, see DiMaggio and Powell 1983; Granovetter 1973, 1983). Underlying assumptions about political behavior and the mechanisms that drive diffusion can be obscured by scholars' embedded assumptions.

Recent works by scholars of American, comparative, and international politics have made improvements along these lines by addressing some of the analytic gaps in accounting for actors' motivations. For instance, Weyland (2005) brings decision making to the forefront of his study on pension reform by investigating whether actors are most influenced by foreign pressures, symbolic and normative imitation, rational learning, or cognitive heuristics when making diffusion decisions.[12] His analysis crosses disciplinary divides by drawing on cognitive psychology to highlight the ways actors use information shortcuts to make decisions. In doing so, Weyland argues that prevailing models in political science that rely on rational choice, "constructivism," "culturalism," and "economic structuralism" have made important contributions but have not offered fully satisfactory explanations (2005, 295). Similarly, Shipan and Volden (2008) and Simmons, Dobbin, and Garrett (2006, 2008) have sought to integrate distinct research traditions by incorporating four diffusion mechanisms in their analyses, including competition, learning, emulation,[13] and coercion. Each of these explanations is typically examined in isolated fashion, and as a result the potential relationship between them is undertheorized. As Shipan and Volden (2008) note in their study of antismoking policies in the United States, there can be normative implications in terms of the quality and timing of the policy outputs; blind mimicry can take place quickly and offer very different results from well thought out, often delayed, decisions attributed to learning. Simmons, Dobbin, and Garrett (2006, 2008) examine the global spread of liberalism and find that while ideational explanations can influence diffusion in some policy venues, such as public sector downsizing, there is greater evidence that competitive pressures explain domestic diffusion decisions in economic domains. In all, these recent additions make important additions to the literature on diffusion by integrating constructivist approaches in their analyses. As these scholars make clear, diffusion research needs to elucidate the mechanisms that drive the spread of new ideas and policies. Without understanding of the microprocesses that lead to policy replication, we cannot fully engage in larger debates about the origins of political decision making.

While these recent contributions make considerable advances in clarifying diffusion processes, important theoretical and methodological gaps still need to be filled. First, assumptions about human decision making have tended to highlight competitive (rational) decision making, (nonrational) mimicry, or socialized learning. Yet another potential explanation—ideology—has not been fully explored. Actors are rarely thought to make choices based on their deeply held beliefs about what they consider to be the right thing to do. But it is possible that individuals are motivated to enact policy when they feel an innovation is consistent with their core beliefs and worldviews. This may be particularly true in the social policy arena, where the politics of redistribution force individuals to confront issues related to poverty and social exclusion. When it comes to social policy innovations, it is possible that ideological commitments may motivate replication decisions.

Second, recent diffusion studies have tended to fall into one of two camps; large-n statistical models providing probabilistic analyses on the determinants of diffusion, or qualitative analyses that draw on constructivist approaches to uncover learning and norms. The introduction of statistical techniques such as event history analysis does have the advantage of capturing both internal prerequisites and external pressures for policy diffusion (Berry and Berry 1992, 1999; Box-Steffensmeier and Jones 2004b). Yet even when statistical analyses offer insights into diffusion, Meseguer and Gilardi note, the reliance on this statistical method can contribute to an underaccounting of "causal complexity" and difficulties interpreting the relationship between indicators and concepts (2009). One solution is to elaborate on event history models by addressing the causal mechanisms for diffusion through qualitative interpretation and process tracing. Resolution of these methodological dilemmas is crucial because the problems associated with causal complexity have important implications for theory building and generalization. For this reason, diffusion research should draw on multiple methods, including both quantitative models and qualitative analysis of the policy process.[14] Doing so not only will uncover potential problems of causal heterogeneity but also will lead to better causal explanation.[15]

Toward a Theory of Social Policy Diffusion

This analysis seeks to uncover the motivating factors that lead actors to adopt programs designed for other cities. We will start by examining the contributions that three broad approaches, which highlight different motivations for political behavior, can make to explaining emulation decisions. Do individuals make decisions based on rational self-interest calculations? Or do they make choices based on their ideological values and beliefs, even when faced with the prospect of electoral costs? Alternatively, do policy makers act because they are socialized into a community that defines and transmits shared norms? These three questions relate to fundamental issues of whether policy makers act in a purely self-regarding way; in a principled way, regardless of self or others; or in an other-regarding, community-oriented way. Framing the motivations that drive political action into three distinct categories—individual political self-interest, abstract ideology, and legitimation before social networks—will clarify how individual behavior drives diffusion.[16]

Conventional rational choice approaches suggest that in an electorally competitive environment, policy makers are driven by self-interest or *political incentives* as they seek to maintain and increase their political power. In this view, purely self-regarding[17] instrumental rationality plays a fundamental role in regulating behavior as individuals seek to realize their goals (Downs 1957; Riker and Ordeshook 1973, 11).[18] Applications of these principles have led to models in which politicians make choices to maximize political support, typically because they desire to win reelection, win a more competitive office in the next election, or simply retain their partisan appointments.

Scholars draw clear linkages between the effects of rational calculus and public policy making. The expectation is that politicians behave strategically and choose policies after having assessed the political costs and benefits of various alternatives; particular policies are simply means for attaining political power (Carmines and Stimson 1993; Downs 1957). In the context of diffusion, Walker (1969) argues that when stiff party competition exists, there is an increased propensity for parties to initiate change and propose new programs in order to distinguish themselves. Lowi also argues that new programs are more likely to be instituted in the beginning of a new administration (1995). Thus, electoral competition and frequent executive turnover contribute to the adoption of new policy, including emulation of external policy models. Berry and Berry (1992) have extended this understanding of electoral cycles and competition in their diffusion studies, embedding assumptions about politicians' rational calculus in the context of elections and politicians' desire to win reelection despite enacting politically unpopular tax policy. They suggest, for instance, that politicians time the enactment of policies based on the electoral cycle; politically unpopular policies might be enacted early in order to give the electorate time to forget the policy come election time (1992, 719). Similarly, politicians might enact popular policies just prior to an election in order to pander to voters. All in all, these scholars assume that politicians make strategic decisions regarding policy enactment and replication with the ultimate goal of winning elections in mind.

Social policies in education and health constitute the most likely cases for a political incentives argument. As in many other Latin American countries, education and health have traditionally served the clientelistic distribution of small-scale benefits designed to gain electoral support. For this reason, scholars of Latin American politics have focused on the politics of clientelism and emphasize politicians' calculus to "buy" the poor's votes. For example, Auyero (2000) and Levitsky

(2003) have documented the clientelistic relationship between Peronists and residents of Buenos Aires; Fox (1994) and Menocal (2001) have discussed the political distribution of the federal Pronasol benefits under Salinas in Mexico; and Schady (2000) uncovered Alberto Fujimori's calculating geographic distribution of Peru's antipoverty programs to maintain political support. Given this context observers commonly claim that social policy making is motivated by politicians who "buy" their electoral support with particularistic benefits rather than by their desire to help the poor.

Another, altogether different explanation for diffusion is that policy makers are driven by their *ideology* and emulate policies irrespective of electoral incentives. Douglass North argues that it is important to consider the role of ideology in accounting for the allocation of resources because not all individual behavior can be explained through neoclassical behavioral assumptions alone (1981, 46–47; 1990, chap. 5).[19] In other words, actors may make seemingly nonsensical and other-regarding choices that deviate from rational choice explanations but which are driven by principled commitments. In the context of electoral politics this could include a politician's support of a public policy even when confronted with the significant political costs of doing so.

Although ideology is one of the most important explanations used in the social sciences, it remains one of the most contested and vilified for its conceptual murkiness.[20] The term has been used inconsistently among social science scholars, broadly falling into two categories: ideology of knowledge (e.g., ideological doctrine), and ideology of politics (e.g., ideological mentality) (Sartori 1969, 398). While operating within this second category, North adds to the confusion by locating "ideology" as any seemingly "irrational" behavior that conflicts with neoclassical economic behavioral expectations. But this conceptualization is also unclear; ideology is not the same thing as irrationality, nor is irrationality a "motivation" for action. Since this study seeks to contrast distinct research traditions with differing views of what drives individuals' motivations in policy making, I locate ideology in terms of decisions driven by abstract maxims regardless of self or others.

In this work, ideology is understood as "a pattern of thoughts and beliefs explaining each person's attitude toward life and their existence in society, and advocating a conduct and action pattern that is responsive to such thoughts and beliefs" (Lowenstein 1953, 52, as cited in Gerring 1997, 958).[21] Key for a study of policy making is that ideology can compel individuals into action by providing both exigency and grounds for political activity. As Mullins argues, a vital component of ideology is its action orientation in policy making; while political ideology provides actors with a "relatively structured and consistent conception of the causal forces operating in the social world, it also incorporates evaluation of what is conceived" (1972, 508). Thus, not only does ideology structure people's worldviews, but it also shapes their interpretation of the consequences of action and inaction.

Social policies are often value laden in politics; they require that politicians prioritize certain groups or make difficult decisions about the distribution of their costs. To uncover the potential effect of ideology for policy emulation, we need to understand the extent to which political actors are driven by their ideological commitments. Actors must first display their own values and then assess the extent to which policies like Bolsa Escola and Programa Saúde da Família (PSF) fit their worldviews. There are observable implications for the role that ideology can play in emulation decisions. Since these policies target the needy, enhance equity, and alleviate poverty, we might expect that those politicians with strong leftist beliefs would be more likely to emulate these programs. As Weyland explains, leftists pursue "the goal of egalitarian transformation through deliberate political action relying on the state as a principal instrument for reshaping the economy and society" (2010, 5). Political actors' own narratives about their ideological beliefs and the meaning[22] they ascribe to social policies, if any, can confirm whether ideology does in fact matter in the diffusion of social reforms.

Sociological approaches, alternatively, suggest that change occurs as a function of social context and relations to others. The premise is that human behavior is embedded in a matrix of organizational and informal relationships that provide fundamental filters through which preferences are formed (Kaufman 1999, 367–68). Networks in particular can play a crucial role in linking individuals with others, structuring meaning, and defining individual perceptions and preferences (Friedkin 1993; Kilduff and Tsai 2003; Passy 2003). Within the diffusion contexts, scholars have examined a diverse set of networks, including those that exist where an organization links structurally equivalent actors and those that take place through interpersonal connections of individual actors (Wejnert 2002, 306). Professional associations represent the first group, where organizations unite people with similar jobs (e.g., doctors, health administrators, teachers, and others) across geographic territory and can define the scope of legitimate action and structure values for "modern" administrative practices. These networks are sometimes discussed in terms of "epistemic communities" that link individuals and help define new paradigms to address existing problems (Haas 1989). The second type of network, those sustained through interpersonal contact, are also thought to be influential in diffusion processes. For instance, alumni/alumnae of the same educational institution may perceive themselves in comparable terms. These interpersonal networks modulate the adoption of innovations because they serve to homogenize adopters' behaviors (Burt 1987; DiMaggio and Powell 1983, as cited in Wejnert 2002). The key for policy making is that these social relationships not only offer information shortcuts that actors use to access policy innovations, but they also establish a set of normalizing professional standards for members of the community to follow (Walker 1969).

Scholars of diffusion have noted that various types of formal and informal social networks can play influential roles in the diffusion process. Formal organizations, such as professional associations, link individuals with structurally equivalent roles who reside in different organizations but nevertheless pressure each other to behave in similar ways (Balla 2001; Friedkin 1988, 69–70, as cited in Kilduff and Tsai 2003, 58). Informal networks can also exist among individuals or across geographical space as "neighborhood effects," where social learning and information exchange travel spatially (Collier and Messick 1975; Granovetter 1973, 1983; Mooney and Lee 1995; Walker 1969).[23] For example, newspapers can have regional circulation, or neighboring city administrators can periodically meet to discuss common problems. Finally, systems theory suggests that individuals participate in networks that include ties to acquaintances (weak ties) as well as close friends (strong ties). Weak ties are thought to be particularly important because they provide people with access to information and resources beyond those available in their inner social circle (Granovetter 1983, 209). Thus, in the context of learning and the spread of information, greater numbers of weak ties are preferable to smaller numbers of strong ties, which tend to be insular and deprive the individual of more information. Individuals with numerous weak ties are more likely to learn about and embrace innovations from elsewhere. In sum, the more actors are connected through informal and professional associations, the more likely they are to share similar values, norms, and discourse.

This sociological framework has been readily adopted by constructivist scholars to explain diffusion events. The core idea is that actors' intersubjective meaning and their desire to gain legitimacy in the eyes of their peers shape policy choices. This focus offers important contrasts to political incentives and ideological approaches. Social networks and the ways they structure preferences need not contribute to "rational" decision making (DiMaggio and Powell 1983). Policy makers may simply desire to "keep up with the Joneses," even when doing what the Joneses do may not be functionally beneficial for them (Weyland 2004). In some instances, emulation can result from a desire to keep up with numerous peers, a "follow the crowd" dynamic, regardless of the appropriateness of doing so. For instance, Finnemore (1993) argues that the worldwide diffusion of science bureaucracies occurred even though many countries lacked a domestic demand for such institutions and had few resources to invest for scientific advances. Alternatively, emulation decisions may emanate from a desire to "follow the leader." When a community of professionals ascribes high reputations to certain actors, this can also spur rapid mimicry, even when the ideas developed by the innovating unit may not readily apply. For instance, Chilean social sector reforms are generally well regarded among Latin American policy experts. As Weyland notes, countries throughout the region replicated the Chilean pension privatization model even when countries such as Bolivia and El Salvador had a larger informal sector and smaller demand for private pension funds (2005, 268). This kind of determination to follow exemplary models, even when they may not be effective, can take place when communities of professionals declare an innovation to be a new norm.[24] A sociological approach thus also differs from a purely self-regarding ideological framework where decision making is based on deeply held beliefs.

Another important distinction between ideological and sociological approaches is that social networks need not comprise individuals who share the same ideological commitments. This is particularly true for professional associations and networks, where membership is based on educational background and functional job duties. Technocrats, known for their expertise in their fields, are hired for their professional knowledge and often experience insulation as career civil servants. In practice, this means technocrats often work for politicians with different partisan affiliations. Given the realities of Brazil's municipal political environment, where health and education professionals work for partisans of varying ideological stripes, professional associations represent an important ideologically neutral space for technocrats to share information and seek peer legitimacy through the adoption of shared professional standards.

As this study brings motivations to the forefront to explain diffusion processes, this framework sets aside questions related to federal financing. In a federal system like that of Brazil, municipal governments and local actors would likely find it useful to tap into federal fiscal resources to increase their budgets. Indeed, research from the United States suggests that fiscal transfers or matching funds can be influential in spurring local governments to participate in new social programs (Derthick 1970; Mossberger 1999; Rose 1973; Welch and Thompson 1980). But financing alone does not constitute a motivation for policy emulation, particularly when the matching grants are limited, as was the case with the education and health reforms examined in this study.[25] For these reasons, the analysis in this study controls for the potential impact of fiscal transfers.

Electoral Incentives, Ideology, and Socialized Norms in Practice

Each of the three approaches to understanding the motivations that drive political behavior—in this case, the decisions to emulate social sector reforms—can be tested empirically. If a political incentives approach explains diffusion, we would expect decision makers to use policies to gain political power by including them in their campaigns for office. We might also see targeted outreach to beneficiaries of social programs or employees of social programs. In contrast, if ideology drives decision making, then politicians would frame adoption of innovations in terms of their ideological commitments and beliefs. They would stand by their choices even if political self-interest pointed in a different direction. Alternatively, actors who are drawn to reforms because of what they have learned through professional networks would express their decisions in terms of the professional norms and trends in their field. In doing so, they would relate their decision making to others, participate in the same networks, and seek to demonstrate how their policies reflect new conventions.

Local-level politics and regional interests have and continue to be an important focus for Brazilian politicians. Historically, differences in geography, settlement, immigration, industry, and levels of economic development have resulted in markedly different regional interests. Since the founding of the First Republic (1889–1930), the country's politics has reflected tensions between divergent local interests and the national government, as elites from states such as Rio Grande do Sul, São Paulo, Rio de Janeiro, and Minas Gerais all vied for political and economic influence. Today, states and municipalities continue to exert political influence through federalism, and as a result state and municipal politics continues to remain relevant, both locally and nationally. More importantly, politicians in Brazil do not view local representation as a lesser post or stepping stone for more influential office with the federal government. Rather, politicians readily move from municipal, state, and national office and back, as opportunities arise. Mayors of state capitals are particularly influential; thus it is not uncommon to see a former senator or governor compete in mayoral elections (Samuels 2003). For instance, prior to winning the mayoral election in São Paulo in 2004, José Serra served as a congressional deputy, senator, planning minister, and health minister, and had run two competitive bids for the presidency against Luiz Inácio Lula da Silva (2002) and Dilma Rousseff (2010). Unlike many Latin American countries where the capital city tends to dominate the national political arena (Myers and Dietz 2002),[26] municipal-level politics in Brazil offers multiple venues for high-stakes electioneering where local contests matter for politicians' careers.

Municipal races for executive office tend to be competitive, and both candidates and incumbents campaign vigorously to win voters' attention. Debates, electoral advertisements, and direct appeals to voters by candidates via neighborhood visits are commonplace features of the campaign season. When incumbents are ineligible for reelection, they nevertheless campaign with vigor beside their handpicked successor. After all, the election of an anointed successor serves as an affirmation for the incumbent that she has done well, and it provides her with further political capital. While many contests are driven by personalism and candidates' charisma, candidates do make reference to their policy positions in campaign advertisements.

Electoral incentives for the emulation of model social policies are particularly strong, and we will examine two policy arenas that have traditionally served to reinforce electoral claims to further politicians' career aims. Politicians of all parties and ideological stripes make direct appeals to the lower classes. Since the two social sector reforms in this study involve targeted programs that benefit indigent and poor groups, all politicians conceivably would find the social policy particularly useful. Both the education policy, Bolsa Escola, and health care reform, Programa Saúde da Família, are award-winning programs that can further the electoral goals of calculating politicians. After all, mayors must distinguish themselves during relatively short mandates and often choose to do so through declarations of policy achievements. As Walker (1969) notes, electoral competition ought to spur the diffusion of innovations as politicians come under pressure to demonstrate their accomplishments. Thus, it is reasonable to suspect that the degree of electoral competition can influence the likelihood that these programs will spread. In highly contested electoral environments, incumbents will feel the need to demonstrate to voters that they are doing something to secure their reelection or further their subsequent electoral ambitions. By contrast, in cities with low levels of electoral competition, incumbents can rest on their laurels and are more likely to retain their electoral advantage regardless of their accomplishments.

Another reason why electoral incentives might spur politicians to engage in social policy innovation draws from the realities of the Brazilian electorate. With the sociodemographic realities of the country, where 46 percent of the population was classified as poor in 2000,[27] candidates cannot afford to ignore the poor and lower classes in majoritarian elections with compulsory voting. For this reason, politicians from all parties and ideological persuasions court the lower classes. Social services, such as health care and education, are particularly important to these voters, who are entirely reliant on public services and cannot reasonably exit from the public system. Given these demographic realities, political parties of all stripes have sought votes from the poor. Research by Amaury de Sousa suggests that politicians can invest resources in social services without readily alienating elite constituencies, as investments in education, health, and poverty reduction are perceived as necessary for the country's development (as cited in *Véja* 1996). Further, Melo (2008) argues that national political competition between the Workers' Party and the Social Democratic Party (PSDB) would result in "one-upmanship" that would largely drive the creation of a national conditional cash transfer program during the Cardoso and Lula administrations. For all these reasons, we might reasonably expect that electoral competition at the local level might spur programmatic policy responses to meet constituents' needs.

While some mayors might adopt innovative social policies in pursuit of electoral rewards from constituents, these programs may also appeal to those who traditionally engage in clientelism and patronage practices. Historically, candidates for local office have sought the support of the poor by offering small goods as vote-buying mechanisms. Vote-buying exchanges can include offers of private goods, such as cash, baskets of food, and clothing, in exchange for votes. But private good need not be limited to candidates' personal resources as politicians often capture government resources and offer them as if they were private goods (Desposato 2007, 102). For example, a politician might offer a "doctor's appointment," "ambulance ride," or school "scholarship" for a child where admission is technically free and open to the public. Patronage, in the form of public sector employment, is another mechanism politicians can use in exchange for votes. Economically vulnerable groups are particularly susceptible to this form of political malfeasance, as "abject poverty forces many people to enter into clientelistic bonds with elites who offer minimal benefits and protection in exchange for obedience and political support" (Weyland 1996, 5–6).

Historically, education and health sectors have been particularly prone to political manipulation by local politicians engaging in traditional politics. For instance, Draibe (2004) notes that the Ministry of Education has been an important center of patronage and clientelism from the military period (1964–84) into the 1990s as education resources became an increasingly valued political prize (380). Although resources came from the federal government, their political distribution mirrored the federal structure, which included regional branch offices as well as state and local secretariats of education. As former state secretary of education Silke Weber of Pernambuco explained, the education sector in the 1990s had entrenched patronage practices and the political distribution of education resources, especially jobs, was common (interview 2011). This tendency also took place in the health sector. As Kurt Weyland documents, proposals to reorganize the health system in the late 1980s faced tremendous resistance as clientelistic politicians feared loss of access to "pork" and control over key positions in the social security apparatus to install political cronies (1996, 165). With these historical patterns in place, how might local politicians react to social policies such as the family health program and Bolsa Escola?

Given the historical legacy of political corruption in distributing education and health resources, we might reasonably expect that local politicians would choose to use these programs to prop up existing clientelist networks.[28] Programs like Bolsa Escola and Renda Mínima are susceptible to quid pro quo politics, such as vote buying, if local administrators employ clientelistic distribution strategies. Municipal conditional cash transfer programs are perhaps the most vulnerable to quid pro quo exchanges, as municipal administrators can select and monitor participants at the individual level. The family health program required selecting priority neighborhoods and hiring new health professionals (e.g., community health agents, nurses' aides, nurses, and doctors), all of which opened the door to personalistic politics. Community health agents were the most numerous new positions and the most vulnerable to manipulation as "leadership" and residency status were often the only requirements for employment. Thus, even though these programs are thought of as "good governance models," their policy designs are still susceptible to political manipulation by politicians who seek to engage in traditional politics.

In sum, there are numerous reasons to believe that electoral incentives are the most likely motivation for politicians to replicate well-known social policies. As local government becomes a high-stakes political arena in which politicians can build their name recognition, mayors must stand out for making advances. The replication of well-known programs becomes an easy way for politicians to claim credit for undertaking innovations. Further, the sociodemographics of high poverty alongside compulsory voting requires that politicians appeal to the needs of poor voters. Some politicians may choose to do so through programmatic achievements, while others might use education and health resources to sustain clientelistic practices. Thus, regardless of politicians' interest in political reform, education and health sectors represent the most likely policy venues in which to find an electoral incentives outcome.

While an electoral motivations explanation for the diffusion of social sector reforms is intuitively appealing, ideology may matter as well when it comes to social policy making in Brazil. Actors with firm ideological commitments and beliefs surrounding the need for social change could respond very strongly to programs such as Bolsa Escola and Programa Saúde da Família. In general, leftists have favored pro-poor policies that seek to overcome the historic marginalization of large segments of the population and guarantee full citizenship. At the same time however, leftists have been wary of many features of neoliberal policy reforms, which tend to emphasize limited state intervention and targeting, rather than broad and universal programs with full social protection. Actors on the right tend to favor neoliberal reforms, the retraction of the state, and probusiness policies.[29] While Power (2000) notes that many politicians refrain from self-identifying as "rightist" because of negative associations with military rule and economic conservativism, in practice the rightist group nevertheless exists and provides a contrasting set of ideological interests and policy prescriptions.[30] The crucial question from the point of view of Bolsa Escola and PSF diffusion is whether politicians and technocrats view these programs in meaningful ideological terms. Although Bolsa Escola and PSF encompass some features of targeted neoliberal social policy, overall these programs represent a new set of strategies that are pro-poor and equity enhancing, and seek to extend citizenship through the extension of social policy. Thus, we might reasonably expect that leftist politicians would replicate these programs if they perceive them to be aligned with personal ideological commitments.

While Brazil is known for highly personalistic politics with relatively low levels of political party institutionalization (Mainwaring 1999), there is increasing evidence that politicians can find meaningful correspondence between their individual-level ideological commitments and the ideological position of main legislative political parties. In other words, the main legislative parties appear on a broad ideological spectrum that ranges from right to left (Coppedge 1996; Mainwaring, Meneguello, and Power 2000, 183; Power and Zucco 2009, 19).[31] For instance, conservative parties, such as PFL (now called DEM) and PL, are more likely to endorse neoliberal economic reform and take more conservative positions on issues related to law and order, abortion, and family morality (Mainwaring, Meneguello, and Power 2000, 165). Leftist parties, such as the Workers' Party and PC do B, have generally embraced more socially progressive and equity-enhancing policies, favoring government involvement in redistributive policies, and until recently resisting neoliberal economic reforms. As Brazil's main political parties offer relatively stable ideological positions, a politician may select a party that corresponds to her commitments. Ideally, we should ask political actors to identify their ideological position and inquire how ideological commitments influence the emulation of innovative social policies. Where such in-depth interviews are not possible, as in the analysis in chapter 3, affiliations with political parties may serve as reasonable proxies for executives' ideological leanings. In other words, we might expect that politicians associated with left-of-center political parties will be more likely to embrace reforms.

Lastly, the social network approach also offers the possibility for understanding emulation decisions within the Brazilian political scenario. Since the *abertura* (political opening)[32] various social movements—for example, women's, students', public health, and labor—have all pushed for democratization and a constitution that would enshrine social rights in addition to basic political rights (Alvarez 1990; Alves 1985; Diamond 1999). As Alvarez, Dagnino, and Escobar (1998) note, the movements from the 1970s and 1980s have undergone a significant transformation, responding not only to the new political scenario under democracy but also to the realities of globalization and the shrinking state under neoliberalism. As a result, the country has seen informal social movements formalize into nongovernmental organizations (NGOs).

Today Brazil has an abundance of civic associations and NGOs,[33] many of which engage in policy debates and participate in "watchdog" activities. Civil society engagement in policy debates has taken place across a diverse sectors, including feminist politics (Alvarez 1999), public health (Weyland 1996, chap. 7), the environment (Scholtz 2005), and trade (Armijo and Kearney 2008), among others. The education sector is well represented among Brazil's civic organizations (Ministry of Justice 2007; Costa and Visconti 2001, 25). For instance, in education and children's welfare, domestic civic and religious organizations such as Abrinq and Pastoral da Criança (Pastorate of the Children) have been active in promoting the well-being and rights of Brazilian children. In the health sector, traditional public health activists who were active in the sanitarian movement (*movimento sanitário*) formed influential organizations such as Associação Brasileira de Pós-Graduação em Saúde Coletiva (ABRASCO) and Centro Brasileiro de Estudos de Saúde (CEBES). Other organizations, such as the Getúlio Vargas Foundation's Public Management and Citizenship Program, have promoted general "good governance" practices by disseminating information on model programs. Given the robust civil society activity throughout Brazil (Encarnación 2003; Oliveira and Haddad 2001), we might expect that these nonpartisan civic associations and NGOs could be instrumental to the promotion of programs such as Bolsa Escola and Programa Saúde da Família.

Informal networks can also structure socializing practices that can further the spread of reforms. Drawing on these insights into the strength of weak ties (Granovetter 1983), we can see how ad hoc individual personal contact among professional acquaintances can thus promote the spread of innovative social policies, for example among professionals trained in the same graduate program or former co-workers, which may reinforce professional norms. Interviews with key actors, such as mayors, other politicians, technocrats, and career civil servants, can establish whether personal ties to other professionals reinforced views on new professional standards or contributed to desires to seek peer legitimacy. Further, policy practitioners may reveal that informal networks often operate spatially with neighborhood effects. For instance, while officials in São Paulo might have more in common with those in other large megacities, they may refer to experiences in proximate cities, such as Santos, or the ABC region.

In practice, social networks matter because they socialize individuals involved in the emulation decisions. Yet we need to clarify which actors are involved in the policy-making practices. Professional networks, particularly those tied to membership organizations, link individuals with expertise, technical training, and applied work in their respective fields. The term *technocrat* is used throughout this work to characterize these individuals. Specifically, technocrats are "people who believe that scientific knowledge is essential for the rational organization of society, and who wish to use their own professional expertise in order to stimulate modernization and development" (Baud 1998, 33). In practice, mid-level technocrats are often career civil servants who benefit from the stability that comes from insulation from political turnover. The Brazilian civil service system also allows career bureaucrats who have passed a competitive exam (*concursados*) to work "on loan" for different jurisdictions, thus enabling a city to hire an expert from elsewhere when needed. In practice, most mayors hire senior technocrats for key advisory posts, such as secretaries of education and health. Secretaries in turn hire their senior directors responsible for major administrative and programmatic initiatives. While these posts are political appointments and high-ranking technocrats serve at the will of mayors, the vast majority of municipal executives hire staff with some technical training and competency. On occasion, politicians may themselves have a technocratic background that drives their interest in a particular policy domain. In this study, for instance, only two city mayors, Célio de Castro of Belo Horizonte, a former physician, and Governor Cristovam Buarque of the Federal District Brasília, a former university rector, had previous professional experience relevant to social sector reform debates.

The impetus to emulate an innovative policy may come from a variety of actors in the policy-making process. Mayors have the most latitude in setting the policy agenda, determining priorities, and setting goals that can further their electoral aspirations or ideological commitments. But it is senior technocrats who are poised to offer specific policy recommendations within these broad parameters. In most instances, secretaries of education and health can initiate discussions with elected officials if they are committed to a particular policy change. The key difference among these actors is motivational. While these high-ranking technocrats do not operate in a political vacuum and need to support mayors' political agendas, their influence is largely driven by their ability to use their expertise to advance effective government (see Whitehead 2000). Technocrats' professional success is thus based on their ability to demonstrate achievements in the design and administration of effective public policy. Politicians come and go, so technocrats' career longevity is driven by their professional expertise and their reputation in their respective fields. In this way, socialized norms through professional channels play a particularly important role for these actors.

In sum, the three potential explanations for why individuals make resource allocation decisions—electoral incentives, ideology, and socialized professional norms—provide a useful analytic lens for understanding the emulation of social policies. Each of these approaches to uncovering individual motivations for social sector reforms is plausible. Nevertheless, there is a general tendency in the diffusion scholarship to employ one's disciplinary paradigmatic assumptions about political behavior, rather than test competing approaches.[34] This chapter draws on recent insights from the broad literature on diffusion as well as core debates within political science to advance an alternative conceptual framework for the study of social policy diffusion. It also presents a rationale for an integrated research design that draws on the strengths of quantitative statistical methods, with careful case study analysis to uncover actors' policy narratives. Next, we will subject to empirical testing the three competing motivational approaches for understanding emulation decisions.

CHAPTER 3

Diffusion Trends in Education and Health Policy Reforms

Throughout much of the 1990s, local governments in Brazil responded to newfound responsibilities afforded through decentralization to develop programs in key social sectors. With greater fiscal, administrative, and political autonomy to design and implement social policies, cities throughout Brazil had the flexibility to alter their social services dramatically. Fiscal transfers from the federal government allowed local governments to fund key needs, such as basic education and health. Political autonomy would also, in theory, mean that democratically elected officials could face some degree of constituent pressure to enact the most pressing reforms. While decentralization processes provided the potential for a potpourri of municipal approaches to address constituents' needs, in practice policy replication and diffusion processes were at the heart of municipal governance through much of the decade. In this context mayors and their staff evaluated innovative models and determined whether to replicate them in their own jurisdiction. Two programs, Bolsa Escola and Programa Saúde da Família, captured the attention of local mayors and policy makers and spread throughout the country. This chapter focuses on emulation and diffusion of these social sector innovations and explores when and why municipalities across Brazil came to adopt them.

Two cities, Brasília in the federal district and Campinas in the state of São Paulo, implemented conditional cash transfer programs for poor mothers in 1995. Brasília and Campinas are not representative of most Brazilian cities as they enjoy relatively high levels of human development. Nevertheless, the Bolsa Escola model quickly caught on, and within two years approximately eighty-eight cities had already adopted the program (Araújo and de Souza 1998). Other cities enacted the program after the federal government introduced a short-lived matching grant to promote the policy's expansion.[1] By 2001 over two hundred municipalities and seven states had adopted Bolsa Escola (Villatoro 2004). A surprising feature of Bolsa Escola diffusion is that some cities were quick to emulate the program. Thus, the adoption of Bolsa Escola by municipal governments is notable because most cities financed the program directly out of their budgets, reflecting a policy commitment to prioritize the program. At the same time, since the program had received so many accolades from national and international experts, it is curious why overall so few governments among Brazil's 5500 municipalities in fact adopted it.

The diffusion pattern for Programa Saúde da Família differed considerably from that of conditional cash transfer programs. At first, PSF operated on a small scale, with only a few small municipalities adopting it. Most of the early adopters were poor, rural, and concentrated in the northeast of the country. By the late 1990s PSF had gained broader credibility and visibility, both within and outside of the Health Ministry, spreading from 55 municipalities in 1994, to 4944 by 2003, to most recently 5238 in 2008. (See appendix B for state-based information on the scope of PSF coverage, by state and population, as well as aggregate data on PSF adoption across the country's municipalities.)

We will start with an overview of municipal Bolsa Escola and Programa Saúde da Família diffusion, and after tracing the diffusion patterns, we will examine some broad tendencies among those cities that chose to adopt each of the two programs. The heart of the chapter integrates the theoretical framework from chapter 2 and tests the motivations for policy emulation—political incentives, ideology, and social networks—in Brazil's largest municipalities, using an event history analysis. After elaborating on the hypotheses and their measures, the study presents the model results and interpretation of the findings.

Tracing the Diffusion of Education and Health Reforms

One of the challenges in a study of this type is simply tracing the diffusion of education and health reform models in Brazil. The autonomy local governments have enjoyed means that their decisions have been largely uncoordinated,[2] and federal authorities were not required to monitor or document the local policy reform choices. Even though Bolsa Escola and PSF are well-known programs that have gained national and international attention, there is very little systematic data available on when and where these programs first spread. The lack of data is due in part to the organic nature of their diffusion; early on these programs traveled without coordinated stimulus or tracking by the national government's ministries. Since municipal Bolsa Escola programs were enacted independently of the Ministry of Education, there was never any systematic effort to track their spread. Although the federal research agency Instituto de Pesquisa Econômica Aplicada (IPEA) conducted a series of evaluations of these policies, the agency rarely examined diffusion and conducted only selected case studies (Lavinas and Barbosa 2000; Lobato and Urani 1998). Furthermore, early research on conditional cash transfer programs often categorized programs differently, depending on the name of the program and whether it focused on education or public assistance. Although the family health program grew out of a meeting held in Brasília with officials from the Ministry of Health, the first to adopt the program did so without significant federal involvement. In the earliest phase (1994–97), only a handful of cities adopted a PSF program. The small project was tracked by a few federal civil servants, and the Ministry of Health and other officials collected aggregated data provided by state authorities rather than by municipal governments.[3] It would take four years for the ministry to collect information systematically on municipal adoption of PSF.

Given the limited information on diffusion available on Bolsa Escola and Renda Mínima, this study draws on original data collection undertaken from 2003 to 2004. To map the pattern of diffusion, I conducted a phone survey of all the 224 cities with populations over 100,000 in the census year 2000. Researchers telephoned municipal civil servants in departments of education and public assistance to inquire whether their cities had a *municipal* education stipend program.[4] If interviewees answered in the affirmative, they were asked what year the program was enacted, how it was administered (i.e., which agency was responsible for the program), and to describe the program more generally (see appendix C for interview questionnaire). Ascertaining a policy's start date is one of the most difficult methodological challenges for diffusion research, because researchers must often ask respondents to reflect back in time to identify the date of adoption; recall data is a characteristic weakness of diffusion research (Rogers 2003, 126). To minimize this problem, interviewers prompted respondents to consider whether there was any legislation or administrative decree that would provide a clear timeline for the program's start. Even though many cities had programs with different names, if respondents described programs that shared a similar design and programmatic goals (e.g., cash transfers with educational conditionality for children), then those cities were classified as having Bolsa Escola. Respondents' answers were also cross-checked with other published records and municipal documents, when available.

The response rate for the phone survey was high, with a total of 93.3 percent of cities participating in the phone interviews. Most respondents were willing to discuss their municipality's programs and services. However, of the total 224 cities in the sample, 15 had officials who either refused to answer questions or were otherwise noncooperative. While it is difficult to explain nonresponses, it is also the case that despite nearly twenty years of democracy in Brazil, many local governments are still reluctant to provide public information.[5] Those nonparticipating cities were dropped as "missing cases."[6] In total, 48 cities (22.9 percent) reported having a program similar to Bolsa Escola by 2003; figure 3.1 shows the overall diffusion pattern of Bolsa Escola programs for the sample in this study.

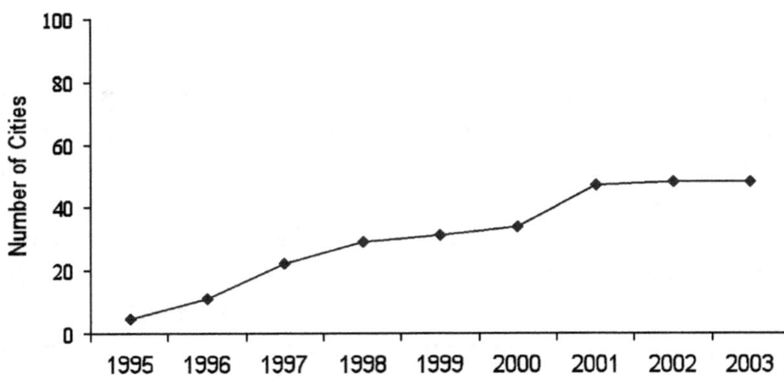

Figure 3.1. Cumulative Adoption of Bolsa Escola in the Sample

A significant portion of the PSF data used in this study draws on information made available by the Ministry of Health, Department of Basic Health Services (Departamento de Atenção Básica). Where possible, data on the early years of the program for the 224 municipalities in this study were cross-checked with secondary sources or deduced based on other statewide information.[7] Otherwise, the decision rule was to code all cities with missing data between 1994 and 1997 as non-adopters. This rule produces data that corresponds with general information about the program's beginnings. Since the program first spread to small rural municipalities in the northeast (Sousa 2002; Viana and Dal Poz 1998), it is reasonable that very few of the cities in the sample would have adopted PSF from 1994 to 1997. The imputed values for PSF also yield an overall trend that is similar to the aggregate national data provided by the Ministry of Health (see appendix B, fig. B.1). By 2003, 89 percent of all the cities in this sample had adopted PSF, and most of those cities that had not adopted the program were in the southern region of the country. Figure 3.2 shows the resulting diffusion trend for PSF in this sample.

Scholars of diffusion note that adoption over time typically follows an S-shaped curve, while a frequency distribution of the number of mean adopters per year approaches a bell-shaped normal distribution

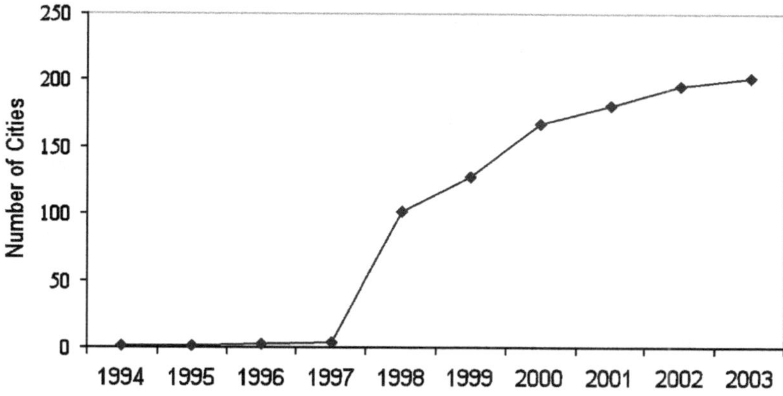

Figure 3.2. Cumulative Adoption of Programa Saúde da Família in the Sample

(Rogers 2003, 273). The S-shaped distribution rises slowly at first, as the first few "innovative" or risk-taking cities adopt the program; the curve's slope increases sharply until approximately half the population has adopted the program, after which the slope decreases (Rogers 2003, 272). Figures 3.1 and 3.2 visually demonstrate the cumulative adoption rates of Bolsa Escola and PSF, and show some important differences between these programs' trajectories. Programa Saúde da Família represents the classic S-shaped distribution. While the Bolsa Escola pattern mirrors some of the overall S-shaped distribution, the program adoption still constituted a relatively rare event by 2003 and had yet to "take off" and spread to half of the sample. In comparing two programs that spread at different rates, we can determine whether these programs nevertheless share similar underlying explanations for their diffusion.

The selection of Brazil's 224 largest cities for the large-n analysis in this study is not intended to be representative of all municipalities, but is instead based on several factors. First, Brazilian municipalities vary significantly in size, from the smallest town, with 795 residents, to the largest megacity, São Paulo, with over 10.4 million people (IBGE).[8] In order to ensure some comparability, this study includes all cities with similar population parameters (i.e., medium to large) in the census year

2000. Second, although these cities represent a small fraction of all cities, they encompass over 51 percent of the total population and are distributed across all of the twenty-six states and the federal district. Thus, although the number of cities is small in comparison to all municipalities, it does allow for an analysis that affects more than half the total population. Third, given the significant barriers in relation to data access and the data-intensive requirements of event history modeling, feasibility precluded the inclusion of all cities. Since data collection included phone surveys of municipal administrators, it was infeasible to collect data for a larger number of cities.

Understanding Policy Diffusion: Tendencies among Municipalities

Having uncovered the patterns of Bolsa Escola and PSF diffusion, we can now ask, what are the main characteristics of those cities that adopted these policies? And, more importantly, how might electoral competition, ideological convictions, and social networks connectivity, among other control factors, influence policy emulation? Let's examine how each of the theoretical variables of interest is measured and provides a snapshot of each factor's relationship to the dependent variables. To accomplish this, I draw on annual observations for the year 1998 to examine simple cross-sectional relationships.[9] The data set for each policy issue has a different sample size; Bolsa Escola (n = 208) and Programa Saúde da Família (n = 223).[10] Thus, the following analysis differentiates between tendencies for Bolsa Escola and PSF.

Political Incentives

To uncover the potential relationship between political interests and policy emulation, I measure each city's degree of electoral competitiveness, drawn from election results for the 224 cities in this study from 1992,[11] 1996, and 2000. Data for this variable came from the federal election bureau (Tribunal Superior Eleitoral), the twenty-seven state election bureaus (Tribunal Regional Eleitoral), the database Voto a Voto from the Fundação Perseu Abramo, and archival records from newspaper articles. The mayoral contests are classified into three categories: highly competitive, competitive, and noncompetitive. Highly competitive races are those in which the winning candidate wins with less than 45 percent of the vote; in competitive elections the winning candidate garners between 45 and 55 percent of the vote; and in a noncompetitive race the winner gains more than 56 percent of all votes.[12] For the event history models, which require annual observations, the competition values for these cities were repeated until the next election cycle.

Within the Bolsa Escola data set, we see that nearly half the cities had highly competitive elections. In fact, about 80 percent of cities had medium to high levels of competition, suggesting that in Brazil's largest cities, meaningful electoral competition is a characteristic of local politics. Interestingly, there are differences in Bolsa Escola adoption decisions based on cities' competitiveness, although the trends are nonlinear. Cities with highly competitive elections were most likely to adopt the policy (17 percent), followed by cities with low levels of competition (15 percent).

Like Bolsa Escola, the cities in the PSF data set also demonstrate a variation in electoral competition. Nearly half the cities have highly competitive elections, and a solid third fall in the medium competition category. However, adoption of PSF, unlike Bolsa Escola, happens most often in cities that have moderate levels of competition; nearly half in this category adopt the health program. Although fewer cities held low competition elections, this subset emulated PSF the least (19 percent).

Ideology

Most Brazilian political parties fall somewhere along a left-right ideological spectrum (Mainwaring 1999; Mainwaring, Meneguello, and Power 2000). Following Mainwaring's typology of partisan ideology (1999, xvii–xix), I group each city's mayor into one of three categories: left, center, and right.[13] Classifications are based on the candidates' partisan affiliation at the time she or he filed with the local elections bureau.[14] A very small fourth category, "nonaligned" captures new parties or small regional parties for which there is little information.

Table 3.1. Electoral Competition and Bolsa Escola Adoption (1998)

	BE Nonadoption		*BE Adoption*		*Total in Sample*	
	Frequency	*%*	*Frequency*	*%*	*Frequency*	*%*
High Competition	83	83	17	17	100	48
Medium Competition	60	89.6	7	10.4	67	32.2
Low Competition	34	85.0	6	15.0	40	19.2
Competition Unknown	1	100	0	0	1	0.5

Table 3.2. Electoral Competition and PSF Adoption (1998)

	PSF Nonadoption		*PSF Adoption*		*Total in Sample*	
	Frequency	*%*	*Frequency*	*%*	*Frequency*	*%*
High Competition	56	53.8	48	46.2	104	46.4
Medium Competition	38	50.7	37	49.3	75	33.5
Low Competition	27	62.8	16	37.2	43	19.2
Competition Unknown	0	0.0	1	100.0	1	0.4

Table 3.3. Ideology and Bolsa Escola Adoption (1998)

	BE Nonadoption		*BE Adoption*		*Total in Sample*	
	Frequency	*%*	*Frequency*	*%*	*Frequency*	*%*
Leftist Mayor	42	82.4	9	17.6	51	24.50
Centrist Mayor	63	79.7	16	20.3	79	38.00
Rightist Mayor	70	93.3	5	6.7	75	36.10
Mayoral Ideology Unknown	3	100	0	0	3	1.40

Table 3.4. Ideology and PSF Adoption (1998)

	PSF Nonadoption		*PSF Adoption*		*Total in Sample*	
	Frequency	*%*	*Frequency*	*%*	*Frequency*	*%*
Leftist Mayor	27	48.2	29	51.8	56	25.0
Centrist Mayor	37	45.1	45	54.9	82	36.6
Rightist Mayor	55	67.1	27	32.9	82	36.6
Mayoral Ideology Unknown	2	66.6	1	33.3	3	1.3

The Bolsa Escola data set for 1998 shows that in aggregate, these cities are governed by executives who represent various ideological perspectives. No single ideological perspective dominates the sample. Most cities' mayors are centrists, followed closely by rightists. Nearly a quarter of these cities have mayors from parties that fall on the left side of the political spectrum. Interestingly, a greater percentage of centrist mayors adopted Bolsa Escola, compared with leftists. Rightists rarely adopted the education cash transfer program.

The data set for PSF, which includes a few more cities, shows a similar distribution in terms of mayoral ideology: there is an equal number of centrists and rightists, while leftists constitute a quarter of the sample. There are notable differences among leftists, centrists, and their right-of-center counterparts when it comes to PSF adoption. Only a third of rightists adopted the family health program, whereas over 50 percent of centrists and leftists adopted it. In other words, centrists and leftists adopt PSF at similar rates.

Social Networks

Social networks for policy making generally reflect the unique specialties of the professionals who work in that policy arena. Thus, to understand the relationship between professional networks and policy diffusion, this study draws on data from two different organizations.

In the case of Bolsa Escola, the Programa Gestão Pública e Cidadania (Public Management and Citizenship Program) was cited by practitioners as an influential source of information and convener for professionals. The program conducts multiple activities, including an annual competition on innovative public policy. Applicants for the award receive information from the Gestão Pública e Cidadania program, and a select number later participate in the organization's meetings and conferences. The program also generates annual data on the cities that apply for an innovation award, dating back to 1996. Interestingly, the number of applications from cities does vary by administration, so the annual data allows for a nuanced analysis of network connectivity.

When it comes to primary health care, health professionals often stated in interviews that the Centro Brasileiro de Estudos de Saúde (CEBES) was an important professional association. This organization, which publishes the well-known journal *Saúde em Debate,* was founded by militants in the *movimento sanitário* (sanitarian movement). Most members are professionals engaged in public health and work for local, state, or federal governments. CEBES staff members provided membership data by municipality. Since membership and subscriptions to the journal have remained constant over the years, data for 2003 was used for all annual observations. Both the network variables were coded dichotomously, "1" for cities where at least one person was linked to the network or where a city applied for an award, and "0" for cities where no one had any formal participation or had not applied for an award.[15]

Given Brazil's continental size, geographic effects can also influence diffusion processes as actors learn through informal social networks. To examine the potential relationship between region and adoption, I classify all cities according to the Brazilian government's geographic categories: north, northeast, southeast, south, and central west.[16]

The Gestão Pública network permeated over a third (32.6 percent) of all municipalities in the study. Cities that were connected to this network adopted the program much more often than did their nonnetworked counterparts; only 5 percent of those cities chose to adopt Bolsa Escola.

Given the selection criteria for cities in this study, it is understandable that the distribution of cases is uneven across the five regions

Table 3.5. The Gestão Pública Network and Bolsa Escola Adoption (1998)

	BE Nonadoption		*BE Adoption*		*Total in Sample*	
Formal Networks	*Frequency*	*%*	*Frequency*	*%*	*Frequency*	*%*
Gestão Pública Network	45	66.2	23	33.8	68	33
No Gestão Pública Network	133	95.0	7	5	140	67

Table 3.6. Region and Bolsa Escola Adoption (1998)

	BE Nonadoption		*BE Adoption*		*Total in Sample*	
Informal Networks	*Frequency*	*%*	*Frequency*	*%*	*Frequency*	*%*
South	34	89.5	4	10.5	38	18.3
Southeast	86	82.7	18	17.3	104	50.0
Central West	10	83.3	2	16.7	12	5.8
Northeast	36	87.8	5	12.2	41	19.7
North	12	92.3	1	7.7	13	6.3

Table 3.7. Summary of Dichotomous Variables in Bolsa Escola Data Set (1998)

	PSF Nonadoption		*PSF Adoption*		*Total in Sample*	
Formal Networks	*Frequency*	*%*	*Frequency*	*%*	*Frequency*	*%*
CEBES Network	78	50.6	76	49.4	154	69.1
No CEBES Network	43	62.3	26	37.7	69	30.9

Table 3.8. Summary of Dichotomous Variables in PSF Data Set (1998)

	PSF Nonadoption		*PSF Adoption*		*Total in Sample*	
Informal Networks	*Frequency*	*%*	*Frequency*	*%*	*Frequency*	*%*
South	26	66.7	13	33.3	39	17.5
Southeast	69	61.1	44	38.9	113	50.7
Central West	7	58.3	5	41.7	12	5.4
Northeast	16	35.6	29	64.4	45	20.2
North	3	21.4	11	78.6	14	6.3

in the country. The differential rate of adoption within each region is most striking. Bolsa Escola adoption is rarest among large cities in the north. In contrast, neighboring regions—the southeast and central west—display higher rates of adoption. Not surprisingly, the cities first to adopt conditional cash transfer programs were located in these regions.

Unlike the professional network associated with Bolsa Escola, which represents a small share of the overall sample, the presence of CEBES is much more pronounced across Brazilian cities; nearly 70 percent of cities have some connection to the health network. While cities with a linkage to CEBES evenly split between PSF adopters and nonadopters, notably the rates of adoption differ between cities with and without a CEBES link. In other words, municipalities without a CEBES connection adopted PSF less often; only 37.7 percent of those cities emulate the family health program.

Since the family health program originated in the northeast, we would expect that municipalities in this region would adopt the policy at greater rates than their counterparts. Almost two-thirds of the municipalities in the northeast do emulate PSF; however, the northern region actually takes the lead, with 78.6 percent adopting the policy. A striking characteristic of PSF adoption by region is the clear geographic pattern that emerges: municipalities in regions farthest from the north have the lowest adoption rates. Thus, the south lags furthest behind the north, with only a third adopting PSF.

Overall, these descriptive statistics provide a snapshot of Bolsa Escola and PSF adoption among Brazil's largest cities. Cross-sectional analysis of the theoretical variables of interest—political incentives, ideology, and social networks—reveals some broad tendencies. However, logistic regression analysis is necessary to test the relative impact of each variable on policy adoption. Next, we will examine in detail the model, which tests three competing explanations for diffusion, while also accounting for the timing of adoption decisions.

An Event History Analysis

This study of policy diffusion tackles several interrelated questions. First, what motivates policy makers to emulate programs like Bolsa Escola and Programa Saúde da Família? Second, why did some cities quickly emulate the program while others lagged? An important feature of policy diffusion is timing. We will next examine both sets of questions by drawing on event history analysis to test the three competing approaches that uncover actors' motivations for policy adoption.[17]

Event history analysis is a standard statistical method used by diffusion scholars to parse both internal and external determinants of policy adoption decisions.[18] The model, similar to a discrete time logistic model that includes time controls, allows for probabilistic interpretation of "risk" or "hazards" of an event occurring. In this study, each logistic model will capture the likelihood that a city will adopt Bolsa Escola/Renda Mínima and PSF, in any given year; Model 1 captures Bolsa Escola and Renda Mínima, while Model 2 analyzes the adoption of PSF. The resulting analysis will reveal the extent to which the independent variables—political incentives, ideology, and social networks—increase the probability for diffusion. To portray the time dimension of Bolsa Escola diffusion, this model includes annual observations for the period 1995–2003, a range that runs from the year Bolsa Escola/Renda Mínima programs were first introduced to the last year for which data is available. Similarly, the family health program started in 1994; thus the data set for Model 2 includes the period from 1994 to 2003.

Model Specification & Hypotheses

The logit equation for each model produces a log-odds of an event occurring. The model specifications follow below:

3.1a Model 1: $Z_b = \ln (P_i/1 - P_i) = \alpha_1 + ß_1(\text{highly competitive})_i + ß_2(\text{competitive})_i + ß_3(\text{leftist mayors})_i + ß_4(\text{centrist mayors})_i + ß_5(\text{Gestão Pública network})_i + ß_6(\text{Lagged neighborhood effect})_i + ß_7(\text{south})_i + ß_8(\text{southeast})_i + ß_9(\text{central west})_i + ß_{10}(\text{northeast})_i + ß_{11}(\text{medium pop. city})_i + ß_{12}(\text{large pop. city})_i + ß_{13}(\text{human development}) + ß_{14}(t^2)_{i+} \ldots ß_{20}(t^9)$.

3.2a Model 2: $Z_p = \ln (P_i/1 - P_i) = \alpha_1 + ß_1(\text{highly competitive})_i + ß_2(\text{competitive})_i + ß_3(\text{leftist mayors})_i + ß_4(\text{centrist mayors})_i + ß_5(\text{CEBES network})_i + ß_6(\text{Lagged neighborhood effect})_i + ß_7(\text{south})_i + ß_8(\text{southeast})_i + ß_9(\text{central west})_i + ß_{10}(\text{northeast})_i + ß_{11}(\text{medium pop. city})_i + ß_{12}(\text{large pop. city})_i + ß_{13}(\text{human development}) + ß_{14}(t^2)_{i+} \ldots ß_{21}(t^{10})$.

Dependent Variables

To measure the effects of political incentives, ideology, and socialized norms on social policy diffusion, I collected data on the adoption of Bolsa Escola/Renda Mínima and Programa Saúde da Família for Brazil's largest cities. In both cases, the data set requirements included determining which cities had these programs and in what year they were replicated. The dependent variables are coded dichotomously ("0" for cities without the program in a given year, and "1" for cities that had adopted the program). Once the event occurs (i.e., the program emulation takes place), observations for that city are dropped from the data set.

Independent Variables

The two models test proxies for the three competing explanations of the diffusion of social programs in Brazil's largest municipalities.

Political Incentives

The first school of thought to explain the underlying motivations for political behavior posits that individuals regularly respond to political self-interest. Walker argues, for instance, that the more electorally competitive the jurisdiction, the more likely policy replication will occur as actors compete for votes (1969). With this logic, we would expect that cities with competitive mayoral races would be more likely to adopt Bolsa Escola and PSF than those facing less contested races.

> Hypothesis 1: The stiffer the jurisdiction's electoral competition, the more likely policy emulation will occur.

Ideology

The second theoretical approach these models will test is whether policy makers' ideological convictions influence the likelihood of program emulation. As Mullins argues, ideology can influence political actors in actionable ways, as it filters their information, shapes their worldview, and guides their evaluation of particular policies (1972). In this vein, politicians with dissimilar ideological convictions would respond differently to particular policies. Both Bolsa Escola and PSF have equity-enhancing goals and aim to extend social services to marginalized and poor population groups. Thus, we would expect that left-leaning progressive actors would be more willing than others, either on the right or at the center, to adopt these programs.

> Hypothesis 2: When cities have left-of-center mayors, they will be more likely to replicate Bolsa Escola and PSF.

Social Networks

A third alternative explanation is that political actors are motivated to emulate programs for diffusion when they are socialized to do so through their professional associations (Balla 2001). Connections between individual policy makers and social networks could spur program diffusion for a number of reasons, including professional socialization, peer pressures, legitimacy considerations, or information exchange. The exact motivational relationship between individuals and their professional associations can be difficult to discern without qualitative evidence; however, statistically we would expect to see that those individuals with connections to networks would be more likely to emulate Bolsa Escola or PSF. Since these policies relate to specific arenas (e.g., health, education/poverty alleviation) we would expect that professionals in each sector would turn to distinct associations.

> Hypothesis 3a: When actors in these cities have linkages to the Gestão Pública e Cidadania network, the likelihood that Bolsa Escola will be adopted increases.

> Hypothesis 3b: When actors in these cities have linkages to the CEBES network, the likelihood that PSF will be adopted increases.

Several diffusion scholars have noted that, in addition to formal membership in professional associations, informal socialization through "neighborhood effects" can also drive diffusion (Mooney 2001; Walker 1969). They posit, for instance, that learning can travel spatially across geographic territories, either because there are opportunities for professionals to meet regionally, or because the circulation of information tends to be regionally based (Mooney 2001; Walker 1969). In this logic, governments that are geographically proximate will be more likely to replicate a neighbor's innovative program.

> Hypothesis 4: The greater the proportion of neighboring cities with Bolsa Escola/PSF, the greater the likelihood that a city will emulate its neighbors.

The measure used for "neighborhood effect" in this study was the proportion of municipalities (in the sample) that had adopted either Bolsa Escola or PSF in their respective state. Since we would expect some time delay between a jurisdiction's decision and its influence on its neighbors, this variable is lagged by a year.

Another measure of regional influence on diffusion is region; thus, municipalities are classified into five areas: north, northeast, southeast, south, and central west. Regional characteristics might matter because the policies in this study were also born in different parts of the country; PSF is most associated with the northeast while Bolsa Escola and Renda Mínima were developed in the southeast and central west.

Control Variables

Scholars also argue that political actors, aside from the immediate goal of winning elections, will respond to fiscal incentives when they are made available, typically through the federal government (Derthick 1970; Mossberger 1999; Rose 1973; Welch and Thompson 1980). Federal financing, through matching grants or incentive grants, provides politicians with resources to demonstrate their accomplishments to their constituents. In the case of Bolsa Escola, the only financing made available to municipalities was limited to those cities with per capita income below their state's average. Few if any of the cities in this data set fell into this category, and the program lasted no more than a year. For this reason, this variable is not included in Model 1.

Although the Ministry of Health has promoted PSF through financing, including line-item transfers, it is very difficult to operationalize the magnitude of the funding because of irregular data collection and availability.[19] For this reason, Model 2 will test the impact of federal transfers with the indirect proxy "year," which allows us to determine whether the years in which the federal government initiated changes in financing correspond to increased likelihoods that PSF would be replicated.

City size is another characteristic that might matter for municipal administration and policy advocacy. Although Brazilian cities face similar levels of financing from the federal government, other factors typically associated with city size might matter. Residents from smaller cities might welcome a health program that relies on home visits from neighbors, whereas residents in large urban cities might shun these intrusions on their privacy. Larger cities also tend to have more universities and nonprofit organizations, enabling civil society engagement in policy debates. For the purpose of this analysis, cities are grouped into three categories: small, medium, and large.[20]

Another factor that could potentially influence policy diffusion is the political response to "internal needs" such as levels of poverty, educational attainment, and access to medical care. The United Nations Development Program in Brazil compiled an aggregate municipal-level index of basic needs, called the Municipal Human Development Index (Índice de Desenvolvimento Humano Municipal, or IDH-M). The index draws on Brazilian census data from 1991 and 2000 to capture over 124 geographic indicators, including population, education, housing, life expectancy, income, and social inequality, among others (Martins and Libânio 2005, 3). Politicians from cities with higher levels of human development might believe these poverty-alleviating and equity-enhancing strategies are unnecessary and therefore decline to adopt them. Thus, the model controls for IDH-M through imputed municipal observations for the years of the study.[21]

Model Results

Remarkably, despite differences between Bolsa Escola and PSF, such as policy area and the extent and rate of their replication, both policies share similar determinants for diffusion. Models 1 and 2 offer remarkably consistent results for understanding the relationship between political incentives, ideology, and social networks on social policy diffusion (see table 3.9).

A surprising result of the event history models is the null finding that electoral competition does *not* spur policy emulation, for either social policy issue. The theoretical findings on the relationship between political competition and the incentives they create for policy renewal and experimentation, based primarily on the United States (for example, Walker 1969; Lowi 1963), do not apply for the largest Brazilian cities included in this sample. In other words, when we control for all other factors, cities with more electoral competition did not adopt either Bolsa Escola or PSF at higher rates than those with less competitive elections.

How does ideology fare in explaining policy diffusion? When compared with cities governed by the right, those governed by leftist mayors are significantly different and in the expected direction; these cities are more likely to adopt both Bolsa Escola and PSF, even when controlling

Table 3.9. The Determinants of Social Policy Diffusion: Bolsa Escola and PSF

	Coefficients (with standard error in parentheses)	
	Model 1 *Bolsa Escola*	*Model 2* *PSF*
Political Competition		
High Competition	−.054 (.413)	−.148 (.249)
Medium Competition	−.017 (.416)	.138 (.254)
Ideology		
Leftist Mayors	1.036 (.462)*	.524 (.257)*
Centrist Mayors	.715 (.466)	.197 (.238)
Social Networks		
Gestão Pública Network	1.271 (.352)**	
CEBES Network		.558 (.220)*
Lagged Neighborhood Effect	−.794 (2.615)	1.465 (.812)
South	.271 (1.141)	−2.166 (.601)**
Southeast	1.295 (1.087)	−1.821 (.565)**
Central West	.455 (1.285)	−1.019 (.691)
Northeast	1.408 (1.091)	−1.171 (.596)*
Controls		
Medium City	.274 (.462)	−.123 (.224)
Large City	1.219 (.440)**	.141 (.263)
Municipal Human Development	8.243 (4.476)*	−4.348 (2.640)
Time		
T2	.032 (.736)	[a]
T3	.818 (.684)	.258 (1.452)
T4	.282 (.741)	.988 (1.270)
T5	−.744 (.889)	5.822 (1.069)**
T6	−.920 (.903)	4.380 (1.061)**
T7	.450 (.757)	5.364 (1.069)**
T8	−2.006 (1.257)	4.378 (1.120)**
T9	[a]	4.901 (1.134)**
T10		4.535 (1.185)**
Constant	−6.174 (1.214)	−1.690 (2.110)
N	1478	1234
Log Likelihood	−174.771	−348.8546
Prob > chi2	0.000	0.000
Pseudo R2	.1745	.3639

* p<.05. ** p<.01.

In Model 1, T2 is 1996; for Model 2, T2 is 1995.

[a] The statistical program Stata dropped the variable because the model perfectly predicted nonadoption.

for other factors. Interestingly, the impact of ideology is most pronounced for partisans on the left, as centrists are not statistically different from their rightist counterparts.

The last set of theoretically driven variables tested in these models corresponds to a sociological approach for explaining diffusion. Although neither model reveals that a lagged neighborhood effect matters for policy diffusion, the other social network variables clearly demonstrate that when cities are linked to influential professional networks, those cities are more likely to adopt Bolsa Escola and PSF. In other words, cities with a member of CEBES are more likely to adopt PSF and cities with a connection to the Gestão Pública e Cidadania network are more likely to emulate Bolsa Escola.

As expected, time, the indirect measure that captures the influence of federal spending, confirms that PSF adoption would increase with the introduction of greater funding in 1998. The likelihood of PSF adoption increases significantly from 1998 to 2003 (T5–T10). Clearly the availability of resources that can defray the costs of program adoption facilitates diffusion. But it is noteworthy that despite this control factor, policy emulation still depends in large part on the ideological perspective of municipal mayors and on the ties professionals have to social networks. Finally, the model shows that internal needs, as measured by levels of human development, are significant for only one of the two policy domains, education. Higher levels of municipal human development have a positive and statistically significant effect on the probability of adoption. Interestingly, IDH-M has no effect on the adoption of preventive public health models.

Interpretation

The logistic models of Bolsa Escola and PSF can tell us about more than just the relationship between the outcome (policy adoption) and its contributing factors. Recall that logit equations 3.1a and 3.2a produce a "log-odds" of an event occurring. Since we normally think in terms of probabilities of events occurring, these equations can be transformed mathematically to yield bounded probabilities, which are more interpretable (see equations 3.1b and 3.2b below).

3.1b Probability of a city adopting Bolsa Escola/Renda Mínima = $1/(1+(\exp(-1^*Z_b)))$, where Z_b is the log-odds of Bolsa Escola/Renda Mínima.

3.2b Probability of a city adopting PSF = $1/(1+(\exp(-1^*Z_p)))$, where Z_p is the log-odds of PSF.

These equations allow for an analysis of the relative impact that the variables of interest have on the probability of Bolsa Escola diffusion. For instance, the modal city in the data set had the following characteristics: it had competitive elections and a centrist mayor, was *not* a part of the Gestão Pública network, had a lagged neighborhood effect score of 0, had a medium-sized population, was located in the southeast, and adopted the program in 1997. Given this scenario, Model 1 predicts that in 1997 the probability the modal city will adopt Bolsa Escola is 3 percent.[22] Although this probability is low and indicates the program is rarely emulated, it is consistent with what we know about its overall adoption rate. When varying certain key characteristics of cities, however, the overall probability of Bolsa Escola adoption increases significantly. For example, when the modal city is governed by a leftist rather than centrist mayor, the probability of adoption increases by one-third to 4 percent. An even greater effect occurs when the modal city both has a leftist mayor and participates in the Gestão Pública network, increasing the predicted probability of Bolsa Escola adoption to 12 percent. Importantly, the predicted probabilities reveal the relative weight of electoral competition, ideology, and networks on the likelihood of adoption. Both ideology and networks matter, yet the professional network has the greatest effect. Further, we see that together, leftists and professional networks operate in a similar direction, thus reinforcing each another.

Drawing on the equations above, we can also uncover the relative probability of Bolsa Escola adoption given time and other demographic characteristics of the sample cities. Overall the model predicts the lowest probability of Bolsa Escola adoption, 0 percent, for a city that in 2002 has highly competitive elections, no connection to the Gestão Pública network, a small population, low levels of human development, and is governed by a mayor from the right and located in the north. By contrast the city with the greatest likelihood of emulating the program, with a predicted probability of 63 percent, would in 2001 have low levels of electoral competition, a leftist mayor, links to the Gestão Pública network, and would rank high in human development and be a large city located in the southeast. While time is not statistically significant in the model, the differing size of the coefficients suggests that adoption is more likely to take place in certain years. In other words, the probability of policy diffusion of the modal city differs according to the year under consideration (see fig. 3.3). Bolsa Escola programs were slightly more likely to be enacted in 1997 and 2001, which corresponds to executives' first year in office. This also corresponds to Lowi's argument that new policies are more likely to be enacted at the beginning of a new administration (1963). Also noteworthy is that mayors choose to adopt municipal Bolsa Escola programs in 2001, even after the federal government instituted its own national program. If mayors had enacted Bolsa Escola at the end of their administrations and prior to the next elections, the timing would suggest that electoral incentives were at play. Instead, the adoption of the education program just after mayoral inauguration suggests that officials took advantage of their electoral mandate and policy windows to carry out important policy priorities.

In the case of Programa Saúde da Família, Model 2 predicts much higher probabilities that cities will adopt the program, when compared with Bolsa Escola diffusion. The modal city in this sample has low competition, a centrist mayor, a lagged "neighborhood effect" score of 0, a medium-sized population, is located in the southeast, and adopted the program in 1998. Given these characteristics, the likelihood that this average city will adopt PSF (in 1997) is 40 percent.[23] However, if this same city were to lose its linkage to the CEBES network, the overall probability would drop to 28 percent. Interestingly, the effect of ideology is especially strong. Holding all other factors constant, if the average city elects a leftist mayor, then the predicted probability that PSF will be implemented increases to 48 percent. Overall the model shows that when different characteristics are in play, the probability of PSF adoption can vary considerably depending on the theoretical variables of interest. In 1998 alone, the probability of adoption is as high as

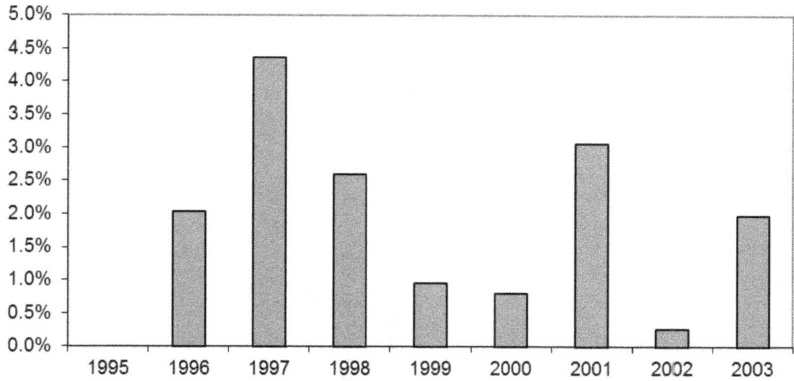

Figure 3.3. Annual Predicted Probability of Bolsa Escola Adoption for Modal City

73 percent for a large city in the northeast with medium competition, a leftist mayor, and CEBES network presence. When that same city has a rightist mayor and loses its CEBES network connectivity, the probability of PSF adoption falls precipitously to 47 percent. While variables such as region or city size can significantly affect the probability of PSF adoption, clearly the motivational variables—ideology and social networks—dramatically influence the likelihood that the health program will diffuse.

There are several reasons to suspect that "time" would impact the probability of PSF adoption. As we see in figure 3.2, on the cumulative adoption of PSF in the sample, there is a dramatic increase in PSF adoption in 1998. The results in Model 2 also indicate that the years 1998–2003 are statistically significant and positively associated with PSF adoption. This finding reflects the history of policy development and mirrors other diffusion research that shows federal financing has strong effects in spurring diffusion decisions (Derthick 1970; Mossberger 1999; Rose 1973; Welch and Thompson 1980). For the modal city in this sample, the yearly effects are remarkable (see fig. 3.4). The probability of adoption jumps dramatically after 1997, from .5 to 40 percent. Also noteworthy, the annual effects are nonlinear and noncyclical. Unlike the timing of Bolsa Escola adoption, where decision making

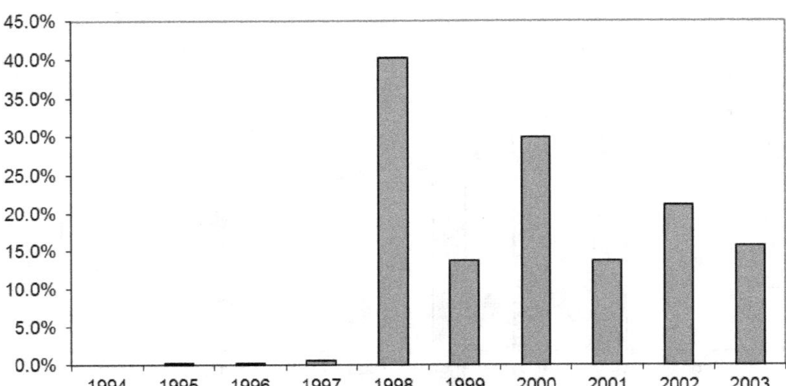

Figure 3.4. Annual Predicted Probability of PSF Adoption for Modal City

appeared to coincide with the electoral calendar, PSF adoption appears unrelated to election cycles. The findings from Model 2 thus reinforce the importance of mayoral ideological commitment and city-level connectivity to CEBES networks, independently from federal funding. Moreover, the effects of ideology and social networks on emulation decisions work independently of electoral competition.

Conclusions

The event history analyses allow us to test three theoretically driven explanations for the diffusion of social policies for a large number of municipalities in Brazil. Surprisingly, the proxies for political competition provide little support for the argument that electoral competition and vote-seeking behavior on the part of politicians spur policy replication. This contradicts conventional assumptions in political science that highly contested elections will spur actors to emulate policies. A particularly noteworthy finding in this regard is that the degree of electoral competition did not matter; politicians in low, medium, and highly competitive environments behaved the same way. By contrast, the proxies for ideology and formal social network connectivity do explain the likelihood that Bolsa Escola and Programa Saúde da Família will diffuse. That both leftist ideology and formal social networks connectivity positively influence the emulation of two programs that spread at different rates is quite remarkable, particularly since scholars of education and health reform often comment that these sectors are more different than similar (Corrales 1999; Grindle 2004). Chapter 6 will further explore the puzzle behind these similar findings and will address the opportunities and limitations for generalization about diffusion across policy arenas.

As King, Keohane, and Verba argue, one of the benefits of quantitative analysis based on a large number of observations is the greater leverage gained to test theories and draw causal inferences (1994). Certainly the event history models in this chapter reinforce the basic argument that ideology and social networks spur diffusion in Brazil's largest cities. However, it is also important to acknowledge the limitations of this method. At the most basic level, the models used in this chapter involve basic assumptions that can influence our analysis. First, the models require a dichotomous categorization of policy adoption—cities either do or do not have a given policy. Yet in practice policy makers may modify or adapt policies for local environments. The "adaptability" of a program may or may not relate to its overall diffusion pattern. Second, these models require dropping observations for cities once they have adopted a program. This analysis certainly allows for understanding what leads up to the decision to emulate a policy, but assumes that policy reversal either does not happen or is irrelevant. Yet in Brazil social policies are often changed, adopted, and reversed when new elected officials take office. Given some of these methodological limitations, it is important to draw on qualitative data to elaborate on the statistical findings and clarify the causal mechanisms that drive diffusion.

This chapter offers valuable insights into the relationship between the variables of interest and policy diffusion, yet the analysis also raises a number of questions that will be addressed in subsequent chapters. First, to what extent do the proxies used to measure political incentives, ideology, and social networks accurately reflect the real-world political dynamics of policy emulation? For instance, political incentives could play out in a number of nonelectoral ways, including the use of clientelism or patronage. Are the findings here simply a reflection of measurement error or limited data? Second, why are leftist mayors so much more likely to adopt Bolsa Escola and Programa Saúde da Família? While both programs have equity-enhancing goals and seek to improve access to education and health care, they also appeal to a broader range of policy makers who like the targeting and "contract" features of these programs. In addition, both programs can represent socially conservative objectives that reinforce traditional gender roles. Thus, there is a need to clarify how these programs are interpreted and how ideology affects decision-making and program emulation. Lastly, the statistical analysis alone cannot reveal the way in which a formal "social network presence" matters. What is it about network connectivity that compels emulation? How do networks shape professional norms? The following chapters, which rely on case study evidence from four Brazilian cities, will shed light on these questions.

CHAPTER 4

Education Reform

A Simple Idea Catches On

Education reform has been a long-standing and pressing need for the Brazilian state. Despite investments made during authoritarian and democratic regimes, Brazil has underperformed on basic indicators such as literacy and measures of language and math learning when compared with other newly industrializing countries (Birdsall, Bruns, and Sabot 1996; Plank, Sobrinho, and Xavier 1996; OECD 2004). While technical improvements in education, including teacher training and curriculum development, may assist educators in making important strides, there is widespread agreement that Brazil's barriers to reform have been largely structural and political (Corrales 1999; Draibe 2004; Grindle 2004). As in many other Latin American countries, education has traditionally served politicians' electoral ambitions through the clientelistic distribution of small-scale goods. For decades local and national-level politicians have enjoyed the electoral spoils that grant them access to education resources and allow for their distribution through political channels. For this reason, equity-enhancing reform proposals that challenge the status quo and undermine politicians' access to patronage resources have been especially hard to enact. This chapter details these challenges to the development of innovative strategies for addressing educational attainment for Brazil's poorest children. How did a relatively simple idea—to provide an education grant for poor families to increase children's educational performance—emerge among local governments in Brazil, and why did this policy approach spread?

Conditional cash transfer programs are not a cure-all for Brazil's educational woes. Yet many mayors across the country were drawn to programs like Bolsa Escola for its potential to address long-standing educational challenges. In what ways did the program appeal to these policy makers? And what motivated municipal authorities to emulate the program for their own cities? To answer these questions, this chapter first contextualizes Brazil's national educational deficits and delayed reforms. The second section addresses how decentralization enabled local innovation and experimentation, including the development of a conditional cash transfer program like Bolsa Escola. The third section draws on case study evidence to uncover the mechanisms that drove emulation decisions. Interviews with policy makers from four research sites reveal why they chose to emulate Bolsa Escola. Although Bolsa Escola lends itself to electioneering behavior, we will see that actors choose to emulate the policy because of their deeply held ideological convictions and desire to keep up with their profession's norms.

National Context for Education Reform

The *abertura* period that began in the late 1970s created an opportunity to address how best to improve Brazilian society and democracy. For Brazilians to exercise their democratic rights effectively and participate in the nation's politics, they must not only benefit from meaningful electoral competition but also have the capacity to evaluate candidates. Education, including basic literacy, is the cornerstone for the development of meaningful citizenship. It is also widely considered key to improving citizens' chances for escaping poverty (de Ferranti et al. 2004). Each additional year of education markedly improves individuals' prospects for upgrading basic life skills and improving earning potential in the job market (Wodon et al. 2001). The need to address both social inclusion and education was certainly pressing during the late 1970s. Census data from 1979 indicated that over a third of the population (38.8 percent) was poor (IPEA data). Moreover, 15.9 percent of the total population fell under the category of extreme poverty and was classified as indigent (IPEA data). At the same time, Brazil's elites enjoyed tremendous wealth, and the country saw extraordinarily high income inequality; the Gini Coefficient during this year was .593 (IPEA data). In 1980, 25.9 percent of the population fifteen years and older was illiterate (INEP n.d., 6). Undoubtedly reform of the education sector was and continues to be necessary.

Studies of educational performance and the quality of overall learning indicate that Brazil is among the worst in the region and woefully underperforms given the fiscal resources dedicated to the sector (OECD 2004, 126; World Bank 2004, 112). The causes of Brazil's dismal educational performance are structural (Hunter and Sugiyama 2009). First, the system favors spending in secondary and higher education, rather than prioritizing primary education. Since most children do not progress to secondary or higher education, the vast majority of them are underserved by the system. The socioeconomic segregation of education services also means the public system favors the needs of middle- and upper-class families, which tend to send their children to prestigious public universities. The structurally unequal spending in education contributes to Brazil's growing inequality and is an important factor in persistent intergenerational poverty. Further, the country's educational deficits raise serious doubts whether Brazil can construct meaningful citizenship for all. Can Brazil consolidate democracy with a population having such low levels of educational attainment?

Education policy has continued to reflect the legacies of policies favoring middle- and upper-income groups. Families with high incomes can bypass low-quality public primary and secondary schools, in favor of private schools that better prepare their children for meritocratic university exams. While upper-income families incur the cost of private education at the primary and secondary levels, they disproportionately benefit from education spending that includes free federal public university enrollment. Low-income families must rely on inadequate public education throughout, and thus their children encounter serious barriers to high education. Nearly 60 percent of university students in Brazil belong to the top income quintile, while higher education accounts for over 20 percent of total education spending. To put this figure into perspective, Brazil's expenditure for university students is nearly four times the average of countries in the Organization for Economic Co-operation and Development (OECD 2004, 7).

Recent figures on Brazil's contemporary education deficits have also troubled policy makers. In ten years, the country had not made significant advances in literacy and school completion. In the early 1990s the combined repetition and dropout rates for primary and secondary education were about 50 percent (Draibe 2004, 383). Data from 1994 also revealed that only 83 percent of children between ages seven and fourteen had access to primary education; figures for secondary school access were even more dismal, with less than 20 percent of students having access (Draibe 2004, 383). Brazil's low-quality education continues to rank it among the worst in the region. It also places Brazil in a worsening position vis-à-vis its international economic competitors. As Birdsall, Bruns, and Sabot note, in the 1960s the quality of Brazil's education system of basic education matched that of other countries with similar incomes. Yet by 1990 Brazil had fallen behind, with lower average quality, particularly compared with high-performing East Asian economies (1996, 7–8). By the mid-1990s it was clear that Brazil's development strategies and subsequent educational deficits would have profound social and economic consequences for the nation. The decline of the education sector had economic consequences, but its causes were independent of the state's overall investment in education. As the World Bank has noted, Brazil's absolute funding to all three levels of education (primary, secondary, and tertiary) has increased by approximately 30 percent since the late 1980s (2004, 110). Thus, reforming education for equity and improved performance requires structural reforms and reprioritizing primary schooling.

Even though the need for education reform was clearly understood by both Brazilian and international development experts, the period from the mid-1980s to the mid-1990s was marked by limited progress. On the one hand, the Constituent Assembly established important administrative, fiscal, and rights frameworks for education reform. Among them was the goal of decentralizing education and delegating preschool and primary education to municipal governments, and establishing the idea that state governments should focus primarily on secondary education. The Constitution also required that states and municipalities spend 25 percent of tax revenue on education; 60 percent of that sum must go to primary education (representing a minimum percentage of 18 percent of tax revenue) (Ministry of Education and Culture, 2004, 6). Most importantly, the Constitution established education as a fundamental social right. On the other hand, much of the Constituent Assembly's work was general and undeveloped. Future legislative sessions and ministers of education would have to tackle contentious topics such as curricular reform, teacher training, student access, and new funding formulas to ensure an equitable system.

Brazil's delays in reforming the education sector at the national level are far from surprising. Education reform is difficult to undertake, and there are numerous political hurdles, including the concentration of costs on a few actors, low incidences of policy entrepreneurship, political disengagement of potential beneficiaries, and the fact that cost-bearing groups often enjoy political advantages (Corrales 1999, vii). Institutional tendencies and political pressures for patronage have made education reform particularly difficult for many federal politicians to undertake. Brazilian presidents often need to dole out cabinet-level appointments in a quasi-parliamentary manner in order to sustain coalitions with other political parties. They typically negotiate ministerial positions with allied party leaders who then agree to legislative unity in return for control over parts of the bureaucracy. This practice has contributed to deprioritization of certain ministries, among them the Ministry of Education and Culture (MEC).

President José Sarney's administration exemplifies the political difficulties of reforming education at the outset of Brazil's new democratic regime. His administration launched an initiative to improve the quality of basic education by making funds available to state and local governments for new projects. This program, called Educação para Todos, sought to provide funds for local governments via a competitive evaluation based on the quality of submitted proposals. But this program was captured by the patronage-oriented leadership within the ministry who seized on the ministry's low administrative capacity. Sarney's allies from the PFL controlled the ministry and used the program to dole out funds for political purposes. As Plank (1990) details, when candidates from the PMDB won twenty-five out of twenty-six governorships in 1986, MEC transfers to state governments fell sharply, while transfers to municipalities allied with Sarney increased by nearly 600 percent. Governors who supported Sarney for a five-year presidential term received ample federal education funds compared with those governors who wanted to limit his term to four years (Plank 1990, 547–48, as cited in Hunter and Sugiyama 2009). Needless to say, MEC became a vehicle for furthering political goals, and any meritocratic features of programs like Educação para Todos were incompatible.

The strong tradition of clientelistic practices within the MEC continued, and from 1985 to 1995 the rightists (PFL and PL affiliates) would continue to dominate ministerial positions for political patronage (Draibe 2004, 380). Even if these education ministers had been committed to initiating substantial reform, the ministry lacked the stability to do so effectively. Given that reform is difficult to undertake, presidents would have had to insulate their ministers from political reprisals in order to facilitate change. Brazilian presidents, however, rarely appointed strong, independent ministers to MEC. As Corrales (1999) notes, one indicator of ministerial political vulnerability is the turnover rate. During José Sarney's presidency (1985–90), five ministers held their posts on average a year, and during Fernando Collor's presidency (1990–92), the average duration of an education minister was ten months. The revolving door at MEC precluded any real opportunity for significant change.

Another factor that likely contributed to stalled reforms was the "low demand" from the system's beneficiaries. Unlike the health sector, the education sector has not traditionally benefited from well-organized civil society advocacy. As Draibe (2004, 385) notes, parents, who are normally advocates for their children's educational interests, have not formed or actively participated in fora such as parent-teacher associations, citywide education councils, or school councils to demand greater educational access and improved quality. Thus the beneficiaries of reform were largely absent from policy-making venues. The absence of civil society organizing is in large part a product of traditionally low participation in this sector; further, large segments of the middle class exited the primary education system in the 1970s, opting instead for private schools that offered better quality education.

A significant turning point for education reform came when President Fernando Henrique Cardoso (PSDB) took office in January 1995. Unlike his predecessors, Cardoso retained tight control over the "social ministries," including the education ministry, and he appointed a fellow PSDB partisan and member of his inner circle, Paulo Renato Souza, to head it. Minister Souza had an unprecedented tenure at the MEC, lasting throughout Cardoso's two-term presidency, and benefited from some of the political protection observers note is necessary to enact unpopular reforms. The president's willingness to insulate the MEC is notable because "demand" for reform on the part of civil society had been and continues to be low.

The mid-1990s brought important reforms that greatly changed education in Brazil. The General Law of Education (1996) and other specific laws and acts finally detailed the responsibilities for education in the federal system (see table 4.1). Thus, decentralization, which had only been outlined in vague terms in the Constitution, gained greater specificity. Changes included the decentralization of the ministry's own programs in primary and secondary education, specification of criteria for transferring resources to states and municipalities (based on a value per student), and the passage of FUNDEF (Draibe 2004, 390). Overall, the most significant changes would take place in primary education, including municipalization,[1] curricular modernization, investment in teacher training, and decentralization of resources.

The FUNDEF[2] (Fundo de Manutenção e Desenvolvimento do Ensino Fundamental e de Valorização do Magistério, or Fund for the Development and Maintenance of Primary Education and Valuing of Teachers) represented the most significant equalizing measure undertaken by the MEC during this period. First, it altered the distribution of spending in education to prioritize primary education. Each state would have its own FUNDEF-fund, composed of 15 percent of all state and municipal tax collection and constitutionally required transfers, which would need to be used exclusively for primary education.[3] The funds

Table 4.1. Structure of the Brazilian Education System

General Title	*Specific Title*	*International Classification*	*Duration/ Grades*	*Cohort/ Ideal Age*	*Authority*
	Early Childhood Education	Nursery Education	4 years	0–3	Municipalities and Federal District
		Preschool Education			
		Preschool	3 years	4–6	
Basic Education	Primary Education (compulsory)	Primary Education	1st grade	7	Municipalities, States, and Federal District
			2nd grade	8	
			3rd grade	9	
			4th grade	10	
	Secondary Education	Lower Secondary	5th grade	11	States and Federal District
			6th grade	12	
			7th grade	13	
			8th grade	14	
Higher Education	Undergraduate		Variable	18–24	Federal Government
	Postgraduate		Variable	Variable	

Source: Ministry of Education and Culture 2004.

would then be allocated to each school equally on a per capita basis. Second, although the per capita spending could differ across states, the amendment ensured greater equity across the country by establishing a minimum threshold for spending per pupil.[4] Poor states that were unable to meet the minimum spending requirement would receive federal funds.

The combination of a federal ministry of education that was intent on devolving programs to subnational governments, together with increased resources for primary and secondary schools, went a long way toward fulfilling the administration's goal of decentralizing education. The MEC's new funding formulas encouraged more municipalities to take responsibility for primary education from state governments, since they would have greater fiscal autonomy. Even low-income cities could do so, because of FUNDEF's equalizing effect. Moreover, MEC policy makers sought to create a program that would encourage municipalities to go after and bring in students because the transfers were based on pupil enrollment rates, thus ensuring that all children were enrolled in school. For the Cardoso administration, FUNDEF thus represented the fulfillment of a campaign commitment to primary education (interview P. Souza 2004).

Although the eight-year period in which Minister Souza oversaw the MEC did bring significant changes to the structure of education provision in Brazil, instituting a Bolsa Escola or similar grant program was not among his top priorities. In Souza's view, the FUNDEF was the mechanism that created a "supply" for education; whereas policies like Programa de Garantia de Renda Mínima (PGRM) or Bolsa Escola created a "demand" for education, which could only take effect after a solid supply was available (interview P. Souza 2004). During the Cardoso administration, the MEC administered two "demand-side" programs: the PGRM, and Bolsa Escola Federal, which replaced it, both of which drew from examples of innovation from local governments. These federal initiatives had "starts and stops" and reflected bottom-up learning based on municipal experimentation, rather than a "top-down" initiative developed by the national government.

Local Experimentation and Innovation

Although national efforts to reform the education sector largely stalled from the mid-1980s to the mid-1990s, states and municipalities have been able to make considerable advances by experimenting with new policies. Certainly, once decentralization and later FUNDEF were in place, municipalities had even greater resources at their disposal for experimenting with new innovative education models. Brazilian mayors used their discretion to hire political appointees who could advance their policy priorities and drew heavily on experts to fill important cabinet posts, such as secretary of education. Most secretaries are experts in the field and come from careers in academia or the civil service, or were former elected officials with substantive experience in this area. For this reason, experimentation in education is largely driven by mayoral priorities and technocratic resourcefulness.

The Gestão Pública e Cidadania program, which sponsors an annual innovation competition for "good governance" practices, offers a useful vantage point from which to examine larger trends in local governance and education reform. City administrators have submitted information on projects, including programs for children with special needs; reform of education administration and information systems; innovative teaching methods; out-of-school activities to reinforce learning; programs focusing on the environment and local development; inclusion of local culture in the curriculum; and various outreach reading programs and libraries, including adult literacy efforts (Spink 2006). In general, many of these programs stayed within the standard domain of education by addressing either learning or curriculum development, while others expanded notions of teaching and education by emphasizing social inclusion or parental outreach.

The local governmental arena presented policy entrepreneurs with fertile ground in which to plant seeds for new ideas and programs. Interestingly, the policy entrepreneurs who led the way to enacting innovative "education" programs were not strictly affiliated with the field of education. Rather, the idea for bundling education with poverty alleviation goals was developed by intellectuals, technocrats, and politicians who wanted to address the pernicious effects of low education outcomes on poverty and inequality, and the cyclical effect of poverty on educational attainment for children. Two leading figures who served as "policy entrepreneurs" and later became advocates for policy replication were Cristovam Buarque and Eduardo Suplicy. Making sense of the origins of Bolsa Escola or Renda Mínima can be tricky. In many cases, ideas do not originate from a single individual, and policies often undergo considerable adaptation before their implementation. In addition, the perception of policy "success" leads many individuals to seek credit for the innovation.[5] The task here is not to give political credit to one individual or another, but rather to present a sense of the murky landscape in which early experimentation occurred and of how these programs originated.

Since the 1970s, Brazilian economists have debated the merits and feasibility of a guaranteed minimum income program (Programa de Renda Mínima).[6] Although these early intellectuals made important theoretical contributions to the debate on poverty, inequality, and democracy, it was not until the 1990s that such a program would make considerable advances in the political arena. Eduardo Suplicy, a career politician and economist by training,[7] has been the most vocal advocate for a national program as a mechanism for social redistribution of wealth and poverty alleviation. Elected to the Senate in 1990, representing the state of São Paulo and affiliated with the Workers' Party, he proposed legislation that would guarantee all individuals[8] over age twenty-five, earning less than two monthly minimum wage salaries, a cash supplement.[9] Suplicy's proposal was heavily debated, with many technocrats and economists questioning the potential economic effects such a program might have on inflation and on the economy in general. Others argued the program was utopian and that Brazil was not ready or even administratively capable of implementing it. Still others wondered whether cash grants were the proper vehicle for poverty alleviation, preferring other programs and approaches. Despite these criticisms the bill gained enough traction to pass in the Senate unanimously on December 16, 1991, only to stall in the House as Presidents Collor, Franco, and Cardoso declined to support it. Suplicy continued to champion the legislation nevertheless,[10] and advocated for governors and mayors to adopt variations of his legislation at the local level.[11]

In the public sphere, economist José Márcio Camargo joined the debate on the merits of Suplicy's proposal when he published an influential opinion piece in the respected newspaper *Folha de São Paulo* (1993). He argued on behalf of a framework for a social policy that would alleviate poverty in the short term and resolve the multigenerational aspect of poverty in the long term, largely supporting Suplicy's efforts. However, Camargo suggested several notable modifications to the existing bill, including giving priority to families with school-age children and making transfers contingent on families' regularly sending their children to school. These modifications would later become the backbone for future Renda Mínima programs.

Given the lack of enthusiasm at the national level for a guaranteed minimum income policy, local governments were a natural venue for advancement of the policy. In 1995 two cities simultaneously adopted minimum income programs: Campinas and Ribeirão Preto, both in the state of São Paulo. The Campinas program, implemented by José Roberto Magalhães Teixeira (PSDB), is the better known of the two, having received awards and undergone several evaluations (Fonseca 2001).[12] Although the program shared the name most closely affiliated with Suplicy, it differed considerably from the national legislation. First, Campinas's Programa de Garantia de Renda Familiar Mínima (PGRFM) policy was not geared to individuals but rather prioritized families as a whole.[13] Further, the program served only families in extreme poverty and with children between infancy and age fourteen.[14] Second, unlike the national bill, the local initiative required beneficiaries to ensure their children's regular school attendance, among other requirements.[15] Notably, although the Campinas program had a strong educational component, it was viewed more broadly as including social assistance.

Though contemporaneous with the Renda Mínima program, Bolsa Escola originated among participants of the Center for Contemporary Brazilian Studies at the Universidade de Brasília (UnB). The interdisciplinary center, spearheaded by then rector Cristovam Buarque, provided a venue for faculty, students, and intellectuals to meet and develop policy which could respond to Brazil's most pressing problems. Center participants quickly identified the problem of basic education as an urgent issue, and noted the strong correlation between poverty and high dropout rates (Aguiar and Araújo 2002, 38). Based on this observation, participants concluded that that poverty and low educational attainment were interrelated and positively reinforcing, and that Bolsa Escola could tackle both. Even though education is compulsory and free in Brazil, parents must still provide a minimum level of resources for their children to attend school (e.g., clothes, shoes, and school supplies). Furthermore, parents face an opportunity cost when sending their children to school (i.e., they must forgo potential labor and income their children can generate through informal work). Second, Buarque argued that just as government has helped students through scholarships to attend institutions of higher learning (to attain master's and doctoral degrees), it would be appropriate for children to receive scholarships for primary education. Thus, the group proposed a school grant (scholarship) for families in poverty, but on the condition that the children regularly attend school; families whose children failed to attend school would lose a monthly payment.

When Cristovam Buarque took office in the federal district of Brasília in 1995, he quickly implemented Bolsa Escola.[16] The program started small, first prioritizing families in the neighborhood Paranoá, which had the lowest socioeconomic indicators in the city. City administrators later expanded it to include more families; by 1998, 25,680 families and 50,673 children were enrolled in the program (Aguiar and Araújo 2002, 43). Eligible families included those whose income fell below half a minimum salary per capita; the monthly benefit was fixed at one minimum salary (R$130).[17] The program raised roughly 10,000 families above the poverty line (Lavinas and Barbosa 2000b, 449). The city also implemented a complementary program, Poupança-Escola (School Savings), as an additional incentive to encourage students to stay in school until completing the lower secondary school, and for those families with older children who stayed in school. In all, the Bolsa Escola program cost the district approximately 1 percent of its annual revenue.

Some policy specialists argue that municipal Renda Mínima and Bolsa Escola policies are substantially different because of their distinct origins, nuances in policy design, and names (Paulics 2004; interview Lavinas 2004; interview Rocha 2003). Table 4.2 provides an overview of the similarities of and differences between two representative municipal programs: Campinas (SP) and Brasília (DF). While it is certainly true that each program displayed unique features, I argue that these programs are essentially similar. First, each program incorporates two objectives within a single program: to improve educational performance and to alleviate poverty. Interestingly, although each program has important education goals, neither was conceived by education specialists, but rather was framed within the larger context of economic and social development. Second, the programs have strict eligibility requirements based on family income and make benefits conditional based on parents' behavior (e.g., regular school attendance). Third, each policy provides cash grants, and parents can determine how best to spend those resources. Fourth, both Renda Mínima and Bolsa Escola represent a flexible policy that can incorporate additional components.

Table 4.2. Characteristics of the Municipal Bolsa Escola and Renda Mínima Programs

	Renda Mínima (Campinas, SP)	*Bolsa Escola (Brasília, Federal District)*
Income Eligibility Threshold	Families in extreme poverty, incomes per capita below R$35, and with children from 0 to 14 years of age	Income per capita below ½ minimum salary (R$130), and with children ages 7 to 14 and matriculated in school
Residency Requirements	Two years from date of the legislation	Five-year residency in Brasília
Conditionality	Regular school attendance Regular health check-ups Monthly meetings	Regular school attendance (90% attendance rate)
Beneficiary	Head of household	Mothers of children
Benefit Amount	The difference between actual family income (per capita) and the minimum income (R$35 per capita)	1 minimum salary (flat)
Administered by	Department of Family, Child, Adolescent, and Social Services	Department of Education

For instance, Campinas's Renda Mínima had health care requirements, and Brasília added parent literacy programs; an important elements of the program was that it appealed to technocrats who wanted to have a more integrated approach to social services. Lastly, and perhaps most importantly, the policy entrepreneurs who have been most vocal in advocating for replication of their respective program have acknowledged that in practice Bolsa Escola and Renda Mínima are essentially similar (interview Buarque 2004; interview Suplicy 2003). For all these reasons, this project examines the diffusion of Renda Mínima and Bolsa Escola as part of the same phenomenon.

Both Bolsa Escola and Renda Mínima policies received early recognition for their "innovativeness" and won numerous awards. For instance, in 1996, the first year of the Innovations Award Program administered by the Public Management and Citizenship Program of the Fundação Getúlio Vargas, city administrators from Brasília and Campinas submitted applications for their respective programs; both received awards that year.[18] The program in Brasília would also win the Children and Peace Prize from UNICEF in 1996, which would spur international and domestic coverage of the program (Aguiar and Araújo 2002, 43). Bolsa Escola in particular became a favorite policy of both Brazilian and international development policy specialists who supported assessments of the program. For instance, the UNESCO office in Brazil produced an evaluation and was an early promoter of the program (Jacobo Waiselfisz, Abramovay, and Andrade 1998). In funding the evaluation, UNESCO introduced the program to policy professionals in the national and international arena. A few other domestic and international organizations followed suit and produced policy papers on Bolsa Escola (Bava et al. 1999; Lavinas, Barbosa, and Tourinho 2001; Lobato and Urani 1998; Vawda n.d.). Although UNESCO[19] and the World Bank never directly supported the policies through financial contributions in Brazil, the program was consistent with their organizations' values and priorities. This is particularly true in the case of the World Bank, which had been advocating for more efficient use of social spending and for targeting to prioritize the poorest groups rather than creating universal coverage.

In addition to technocratic outlets, the mainstream news media took considerable interest in Bolsa Escola and Renda Mínima programs. As early as July 1996 the national weekly news magazine *Vejá* published an article on the Bolsa Escola program in Brasília (Corréa 1996). Other features would follow, including an extensive piece that highlighted Bolsa Escola as one of three notable education programs that removed children from the streets (Policarpo and Brasil 1996). The weekly news magazine *Istoé* also ran articles and opinion pieces on Bolsa Escola. As cities began receiving awards for Bolsa Escola and Renda Mínima programs, journalists often covered municipal achievements in local newspapers. For instance, major news outlets, such as the

Correio Braziliense, Jornal de Brasíla, and *Estado de São Paulo,* ran stories on this public policy.[20] Early international news coverage in *The Economist, Business Week,* and the *Christian Science Monitor* would also increase visibility of the poverty alleviation strategy.[21]

Aside from the wide recognition that Bolsa Escola received in the technocratic community, part of the program's broad appeal was due to its very policy design. Although some of the staff in Brasília who designed particular elements of the program had a feminist perspective on social policy[22]—for instance, having known about microcredit programs for women in Bangladesh such as the Grameen Bank—the program still appealed to mainstream Brazilians holding more conservative views on women's roles. In targeting women, policy makers designed a program that was largely consistent with traditional gender norms and notions of maternity. As Marisa Pacheco, the coordinator of Bolsa Escola, explained, the decision to target the payments to mothers was well received and noncontroversial: "We thought it was important to recognize the culture here in Brazil. Women take a more active role in the family and with their kids. We believe mothers are more likely to keep track of their children's attendance at school, make sure they dress well, eat well, et cetera. And I had a strong belief that women would manage the resources of the Bolsa Escola well" (interview Pacheco 2004). In this way, Bolsa Escola reinforced notions that women would be more responsible because of their maternal roles. Men were perceived as less trustworthy whereas women were thought to be self-sacrificing and would put their children first. Discussions about "women's roles" and "women's work" were an explicit part of technocrats' policy design. Governor Buarque was quick to embrace the gendered features of the program but with a different set of rationales, according to Pacheco: "One justification I used for focusing on women was that we needed to value the work women do as mothers and that the state had an obligation to support this work. Buarque liked this idea and even pushed it a little further, saying that we were generating work for women. Basically, spinning it as a payment for women for work they already do" (interview Pacheco 2004). The implications of the program's construction of gender norms generated very little discussion, in Brasília and later when it would be replicated elsewhere. As Aguiar noted, the policy is attractive in part because it does not attempt to restructure social relations in a radical way (interview 2003). Conservative segments in Brazilian society appreciated the way the program reflected views about women's self-sacrificing nature, while progressive feminists remained largely silent.

Policy entrepreneurs such as Cristovam Buarque and Eduardo Suplicy were vocal advocates for the expansion of Bolsa Escola and Renda Mínima programs. A principal target was the federal government, and both men approached President Cardoso and his senior policy staff to get a national program off the ground (interview Buarque 2004; interview Suplicy 2003; interview P. Souza 2004). Despite their efforts, the Cardoso administration was primarily committed to other social policy approaches, such as changing education financing through FUNDEF. In a concession and despite different priorities, in 1997 the federal government introduced a national program: Programa de Renda Mínima Vinculada à Educação (Lei 9.553, December 10, 1997). The policy supported municipal efforts for Bolsa Escola and Renda Mínima by providing a matching grant to those communities that instituted their own program; the federal program would cover 50 percent of beneficiaries' payments. However, the program was limited in scope and focused on the poorest cities. Only those cities with per capita incomes below their states' average were eligible to participate.

Implementation of the federal Programa de Renda Mínima Vinculada à Educação was short lived. Renda Mínima and Bolsa Escola enthusiasts believed the program was doomed from the start and that the attempt to promote its expansion was half-hearted. Federal technocrats assumed that offering funding would be sufficient incentive for local governments to participate in the program. But eligible cities were often smaller and poorer and had a limited capacity to establish their own program. In practice, only a few state governments, such as the state of Bahia, urged their municipalities to adopt Bolsa Escola. Thus, the vast majority of eligible cities never participated. Overall, the old-fashioned design required formalized cooperative agreements between municipalities and the federal government (interview Pesaro 2004). In 2001 the federal government made a second attempt to support conditional cash transfers through the program Bolsa Escola Federal. In this iteration, federal authorities bypassed municipal governments altogether by directly paying poor mothers a school grant.

Predictably, enacting the federal program in cities that had their own municipal Bolsa Escola and Renda Mínima programs proved to be especially challenging. Federal administrators and politicians criticized these local governments for failing to enact their program in a timely manner and accused politicians from opposition parties of political posturing and deliberate delays.[23] Local officials complained of being railroaded by the federal government (interview Leitão 2004). Since they had their own experience, these local officials argued that they should be granted greater flexibility and given the option of integrating the municipal and federal programs. Technocrats were especially concerned about the registration process and wanted to ensure that the programs would extend coverage to new families rather than provide overlapping benefits. In the end, cities that had already established municipal programs continued to operate their own programs and simply added Bolsa Escola Federal, essentially operating two separate programs. In other words, municipalities across Brazil continued to design, administer, and finance their own Bolsa Escola programs despite the complications caused by the entry of a federal program bearing the same name.

Explaining the Diffusion of Municipal Bolsa Escola in Four Major Cities

Given the early enthusiasm for Bolsa Escola and Renda Mínima programs, with awards and enthusiastic reviews from international development agencies, it is not surprising that other cities would choose to replicate these programs. Some cities across the country were very quick to adopt similar programs, doing so within a year of Brasília and Campinas's enactment. For instance, Salvador emulated the program before major research organizations had widely distributed policy evaluations.[24] That cities replicated the programs so quickly and before assessments of these policies established their effectiveness is remarkable, particularly since most of the earliest publications on these programs were based on case studies (i.e., usually based on one or two cities), and it was unclear

Table 4.3. Case Studies: Bolsa Escola/Renda Mínima Adoption and Nonadoption

	Executive in Office and Party ID[a]	*Bolsa Escola/ Renda Mínima*
Brasília (DF)[b]		
1990–1994	Joaquim Roriz (PTR)	n/a[c]
1994–1998	Cristovam Buarque (PT)	*Innovated*[d]
1998–2002	Joaquim Roriz (PMDB)	No/Yes[e]
Belo Horizonte (MG)		
1992–1996	Patrus Ananias (PT)	No
1996–2000	Célio de Castro (PSB)	Yes
2000–2004	Célio de Castro (PSB)	
	Fernando Damata Pimentel (PT)[f]	Yes
Salvador (BA)		
1992–1996	Lídice da Mata (PSDB)	Yes
1996–2000	Antônio José Imbassahy (PFL)	No
2000–2004	Antônio José Imbassahy (PFL)	No
São Paulo (SP)		
1992–1996	Paulo Maluf (PDS)	No
1996–2000	Celso Pitta (PPB)	No
2000–2004	Marta Suplicy (PT)	Yes

[a] Mayor's partisan affiliation at the time he or she ran for office.
[b] Brasília, the Federal District, operates under the gubernatorial electoral calendar.
[c] This period precedes the development of Bolsa Escola; thus it does not constitute a case of diffusion.
[d] As the originating city for Bolsa Escola, its adoption in 1995 does not constitute a case of diffusion.
[e] The program was suspended or discontinued and then reintroduced under new names.
[f] Fernando Damata Pimentel (PT) assumed office in November 2001, after Célio de Castro suffered a stroke.

whether cities with different sociodemographic characteristics, educational difficulties, or financial resources could benefit from adopting a similar program. So, what explains why certain cities were so eager to replicate these programs? Why were some cities quick to do so? Why did others take a slower pace to adoption? And why did other cities choose not to replicate the programs at all?

To answer these questions, let's turn to some case studies. Table 4.3 presents a synopsis of the replication decisions across the ten cases that were eligible to emulate model programs.

Several broad patterns across the cases are worth noting at the outset. First, adoption of Bolsa Escola occurs at different points in time; each city adopts the policy during different administrative cycles. After Brasília's innovation Salvador was the first city to replicate it, followed by Belo Horizonte, and then São Paulo. Second, all of the administrations to adopt Bolsa Escola were left of center, yet not all cities governed by a leftist adopted the program. For instance, Belo Horizonte (1992–96) had a Workers' Party mayor who did not adopt the policy. This suggests that left-leaning majors are necessary but not sufficient for emulation of this program. Third, a striking feature of Bolsa Escola replication is that it did not necessarily "stick." There are several instances of policy reversal—Brasília and Salvador—where programs were suspended following the start of a new administration. Thus, the case studies provide an opportunity to examine both the determinants of policy diffusion and the reasons for policy reversal.

Political Incentives

An electoral incentives approach offers an intuitively appealing explanation for the spread of Bolsa Escola in Brazil. Policy advocates for Bolsa Escola and Renda Mínima suggest that these programs spread because they are politically attractive (interviews Buarque 2004; Suplicy 2003). In what ways does the nature of the policy itself allow for a political incentives explanation of its adoption? Does electoral competition drive local politicians' day-to-day decision making? Do mayors decide to adopt these programs to win elections? If so, does the electoral calendar determine the timing of policy emulation?

There are several reasons to think Bolsa Escola is the type of policy that calculating politicians are eager to adopt in order to sustain their electoral popularity. First, in Brazil, a country with compulsory voting, poor citizens have the opportunity to sway elections in meaningful ways. Any policy that appeals to poor constituents thus has the potential for an electoral payoff. An example will contextualize the potential impact of the poor's vote: In Salvador in 1991 approximately 35 percent of the population had monthly per capita incomes below 75 reais[25] (Martins and Libânio 2005). While figures for the other case study cities are less dramatic—Belo Horizonte 19 percent, Brasília 17 percent, and São Paulo 8 percent (Martins and Libânio 2005)—this population is still substantial enough to sway elections in competitive races. Second, because the poor are particularly reliant on basic public services, such as primary education, Bolsa Escola would be a highly visible program among beneficiaries. Thus, voters would easily know whom to credit for the program.[26] It is only natural to assume that families receiving the cash grant and rising out of extreme poverty would choose to reward the politicians who backed the policy.

Even though Bolsa Escola targeted a specific group of beneficiaries and distinguished between the "haves" and "have nots," the policy did not exacerbate class cleavages and was widely appealing across income groups. Several factors contributed to its wide acceptance. First, on the surface the program continued the long-standing practice by local governments of offering social assistance to poor and vulnerable populations. Municipalities have traditionally provided a range of benefits to poor families, such as school uniforms, school supplies, and food baskets, albeit on an ad hoc and irregular basis. Others liked the way the program could empower the poor to manage household resources and take responsibility for their children's education. Among others still, there was speculation that increasing cash resources to local economies could have positive economic effects. Although Bolsa Escola's policy design differed from previous public assistance efforts, it fit in with historic municipal efforts to alleviate poverty and assist the poor. Thus, regardless of ideological disposition, whether conservative or socially progressive, politicians in Brazil have reached out to the poor for votes by offering tangible benefits.

Finally, extensive news coverage of municipal cash transfer programs in major national and international news outlets led to familiarity with the model. As detailed above, major media outlets in Brazil covered these award-winning programs from the very beginning. The extensive coverage of Bolsa Escola and Renda Mínima models provided policy makers and politicians with cognitive shortcuts that facilitated decision making. In other words, rather than investigate and create all new education models, actors can draw on the information readily available. By replicating well-known programs, such as Bolsa Escola, politicians can make their mark and claim credit for the implementation of a new "innovation" in their jurisdictions.

The idea that social policy decisions are fueled by electoral competition is certainly a conventional view. Melo argues that politicians, such as Fernando Henrique Cardoso, José Serra, and Lula, either adopted or expanded federal conditional cash transfer programs in order to appeal to voters (2008).[27] In other words, the intense partisan competition between Brazil's most competitive political parties shaped the direction of national social policy making and the eventual scaling up of Bolsa Escola (2008, 166). While Melo's focus is on the national political scene, might it be that subnational electoral competition could also fuel social policy imitation and replication among subnational governments? After all, electoral competition is an important feature of local politics for Salvador, São Paulo, Belo Horizonte, and Brasília, and we would expect that candidates for executive office and current mayors would use their policy position to attract and retain voters. Certainly, the pressure to win elections and distinguish oneself from a competitor is crucially important in the Brazilian municipal arena. Though personalism is still an important feature of Brazilian politics, candidates do refer to their policy positions or specify programs they would enact once in office. Campaigning on the provision of these social programs can offer a clear opportunity to gain votes and clarify the field when voters are faced with numerous candidates. So, did electoral competition fuel the diffusion of this model across Brazil's municipalities?

Despite the program's name recognition and potential for electoral gains, there is little evidence that politicians embraced the policy for political gain. Few candidates actively campaigned on their intention to implement the program. Those who implemented the program were leftist candidates, including Cristovam Buarque in Brasília, Marta Suplicy in São Paulo, and Célio de Castro in Belo Horizonte. The left-of-center candidate Lídice da Mata from Salvador was unfamiliar with the program when she campaigned for office, but her ads centered on maternal themes and promises to improve education. Bolsa Escola was certainly compatible with her political message, and she did implement a version of the conditional cash transfer program once she learned about the innovation. Candidates from the center and right rarely invoked conditional cash transfer programs as campaign promises, despite the potential to gain support for the program. For instance, da Mata's successor, Antônio Imbassahy (PFL), did not make campaign promises to maintain the new program. The only campaign in which a right-wing candidate promised to maintain a municipal CCT occurred during the 1998 election in Brasília, where Governor Buarque sought reelection and faced off against former governor and candidate Joaquim Roriz. Roriz not only promised he would maintain Bolsa Escola but vowed he would make the program even better; instead of enforcing the conditionality of the program, he suggested he would simply make the payments without enforcing "co-responsibility" (interview Buarque 2009). Arguably, Roriz's version of Bolsa Escola would have rendered the program completely different and likened it to handouts that are common with vote-buying schemes. But his promise demonstrated that on the surface it can be difficult for politicians to campaign on dismantling a popular program.

Political appointees, such as trusted political advisers and cabinet members (e.g., secretaries of education and public assistance), constitute another set of actors who can play an important role in linking policy choices with electoral strategies. While it is conceivable that high-ranking political appointees might have advocated for these programs with the goal of providing their mayors and candidates with electoral benefits, in practice this never occurred. Interestingly, when the time came to implement the policy, some Bolsa Escola administrators went ahead with caution. As a coordinator of the program in Belo Horizonte explained, "When executives carry out effective programs and the population views it favorably, it can result in votes. But I think it was difficult at the time to determine what the electoral payoffs would be" (interview Leitão 2004). Several administrative uncertainties gave technocrats pause. First, Bolsa Escola could increase school attendance, but by incorporating previously marginalized and failing students into the system other performance indicators would likely decline. Second, Bolsa Escola was actually disliked by teachers who were skeptical about the program and its benefits.[28] As Marisa Pacheco noted, the Bolsa Escola is not a single solution to education: "Once you bring children into the classroom, other problems arise, including limited classroom space, the need to develop strategies to help students catch up, and the need for improved teacher instruction" (interview Pacheco 2004). But the program also challenged traditional corporatist politics; teachers' unions preferred that education policies enhance teacher pay and classroom supplies (interview Aguiar 2003). Despite these challenges, the Buarque administration proceeded in instituting the pioneering Bolsa Escola program. Mayors Célio de Castro in Belo Horizonte and Lídice da Mata in Salvador quickly emulated Bolsa Escola as well. Marta Suplicy was the only mayor to adopt the program after hiring a cadre of technocrats already familiar with similar municipal policies.[29]

Finally, it is important to note that these candidates and mayors advanced their policy positions independent of partisan mandates. Nor did they embrace these social reforms as part of a party's strategy to win elections. In fact, many mayors adopted these programs without their party's support. As Buarque explained, the policy itself was in line with the views of a subset of members of the Workers' Party who favored a progressive vision of social policy, though in the early and mid-1990s the party itself was reluctant to endorse the policy officially (2004). In Buarque's assessment, around that time the Workers' Party was made up of three distinct streams: (1) those connected via unions; (2) those interested in economic issues; and (3) those interested in social priorities. Workers' Party affiliates who had commitments to social issues were more interested in Bolsa Escola. Since the PT has a São Paulo bias, and Bolsa Escola had an early start in Brasília, it took a while for Bolsa Escola to gain the attention of the mainstream in the party (interview 2004). Another explanation for the PT's slow endorsement of the program may be that policy entrepreneurs, Cristovam Buarque and Eduardo Suplicy, were also competing over the social policy framework the party directorate would embrace. Suplicy also reported his consistent attempts to persuade his own party to endorse a minimum income program (interview 2003). Similarly, throughout the 1990s PSDB leadership looked to the Cardoso administration and senior advisers to establish their party's social sector priorities. While the city of Campinas in São Paulo had established a minimum income program in 1995 under the leadership of a PSDB partisan, the party did not fully endorse it as part of an overall electoral strategy.

In these cases where Bolsa Escola emulation took place, there was a surprising absence of electoral engineering between the program and political campaigning. In theory, the education stipend could have been attractive to a broad set of politicians. After all, politicians have often used education resources to reach out to the poor. A cash benefit program could have been a natural extension of "politics as usual," including patronage politics, clientelism, and pre-election payoffs. Politicians could have directed their staff to target resources to particular schools or neighborhoods, for example. They could also have managed waitlists by offering priority access to clients based on patronage or "personal referrals"; in Portuguese this is called *indicacão.* Since the demand for these programs was high and resources were limited, electoral horse trading could conceivably have taken place. Lastly, when campaigning for re-election, these mayors could have used a directory of beneficiaries for "get out the vote" purposes. Remarkably, in all cases I found no evidence that the politicians who enacted conditional cash transfer programs did so with their campaigns in mind. Moreover, while candidates from the center and right could have adopted these programs, in practice only left-of-center mayors choose to do so. This suggests that politicians' decisions to emulate Bolsa Escola may have been driven by other factors. Since these programs cost municipalities their own resources and federal incentives were nonexistent,[30] something else drove Mayors da Mata, de Castro, and Suplicy to emulate the education program.

Ideology

Traditional ideological divides between the left and the right had a particularly strong impact on the adoption of Bolsa Escola and Renda Mínima programs. Politicians to the left of center, from the Workers' Party (PT), Brazilian Socialist Party (PSB), and the Party of Brazilian Social Democracy (PSDB), tended to emphasize social programs in their campaigns and policy making. Elected officials revealed a dramatically consistent framing of ideological objectives and values when prioritizing issues and selecting public policies. Nearly every politician and technocrat from the Workers' Party, for instance, justified his or her policy choices with ideas about "social rights," governmental responsibilities, and the need to invert spending to prioritize the poorest and most vulnerable sectors of the population.

For many actors ideologically to the left of center, Bolsa Escola and Renda Mínima represented a profound transformation in the relationship between the state and citizens. In their analysis, public assistance programs had historically reflected traditional clientelistic approaches to social assistance. These programs were often administered by the wives of mayors who took them on as part of their charitable first-lady obligations, regardless of whether they had professional credentials in the field. Thus, critics on the left argued that municipal-run programs that offered handouts, such as electronic appliances or baby clothes, were more often than not vehicles for vote buying. Moreover, such programs also failed to address the causes of poverty. In contrast, advocates of Bolsa Escola and Renda Mínima argued that their programs would give children a chance to get out of poverty, while also empowering mothers to decide how to spend the grant. Bolsa Escola program coordinators displayed remarkable convergence of ideological discourse around these general themes. They also expressed a desire to address social exclusion and a belief that education was an important component of citizenship. When politicians discussed why they had chosen to adopt a school grant program, they all cited problems like social inequality and the need to address the "social deficit."

Cities governed by executives from the right-of-center parties took a very different approach and mostly ignored Bolsa Escola and Renda Mínima proposals. In general, right-of-center mayors emphasized policies that encouraged business interests or market competition and enacted policies that followed these conservative rationales. Unlike those of their left-of-center opponents, conservatives' political campaigns often highlighted and prioritized their progress in nonsocial policy arenas. In campaigns for reelection, for instance, Mayor Antônio Imbassahy in Salvador emphasized his administration's accomplishments in infrastructure projects, while Governor Joaquim Roriz in Brasília highlighted the construction of an award-winning bridge.

The different discourse of actors on the left and right could be easily dismissed as a rhetorical device were it not for the fact that left-of-center politicians were consistent in their follow-through and implementation of Bolsa Escola. In the case studies, emulation of Bolsa Escola and Renda Mínima occurred under left and left-of-center politicians: in Belo Horizonte under Célio de Castro (PSB), São Paulo under Marta Suplicy (PT), and Salvador under Lídice da Mata (PSDB).[31] Some politicians were so committed to the ideals behind Bolsa Escola and Renda Mínima that they implemented and defended the programs in ways that perplexed even their own allies.

Longtime advisers to Governor Cristovam Buarque and Mayor Lídice da Mata admitted they could not logically explain the actions taken by their candidates. For instance, Mayor Lídice da Mata implemented the Programa Renda Mínima Familiar in her last year of office even though it was clear that she would lose her bid for reelection and understood that her successor would most likely dismantle the program once his term began. She also faced criticism from her supporters and inner circle of confidants, who argued that a Renda Mínima program was feasible only for cities flush with resources; they argued that Salvador faced too many deficits for this type of specialized effort. Even so, she went ahead on principle because she was personally committed to the goals of the program (interview Mata 2004). Cristovam Buarque also deviated from instrumental political rationality in a way that could be understood only as grounded in his ideological commitments. During his campaign for reelection in 1998, he did not reach out to the mothers of Bolsa Escola, consistently telling his audiences that the social programs enacted during his administration were part of the state's obligations and constituted their social rights. Accordingly, he told beneficiaries of programs like Bolsa Escola that they did not owe him their votes and should feel free to vote for whomever they wished (interviews Buarque 2004; Ibañez 2003). The Buarque campaign staff admitted that his ideological speeches confused voters and contributed to his electoral defeat (interview Aguiar 2003). These examples of nonstrategic decision making by Lídice da Mata and Cristovam Buarque confirm the hypothesis that some politicians are indeed driven by their own deeply held values and will make decisions that go against their own electoral self-interest.

Right-of-center politicians and their senior staff also displayed their own ideological tendencies when it came to the social policy development. In general, right-of-center politicians and their politically appointed technocrats did not mention a "social deficit" when discussing their policy priorities. Rather, administrators and political appointees associated with the Imbassahy (PFL), Roriz (PMDB),[32] Maluf (PDS), and Pitta (PPB) administrations emphasized market-oriented priorities for economic development, including tourism, business development, and major public works. Given their ideological predispositions, it is not surprising that when left-leaning mayors lost their bids for reelection, their successors dismantled their education stipend programs. For instance, in Salvador, Mayor Imbassahy (PFL) simply dissolved the Programa de Renda Mínima Familiar. The city's secretary of social development, Raimundo Caires Araújo, noted that social policies were not among the mayor's top priorities and that the secretariat for social assistance had a limited budget (interview 2004). For this reason, their projects were small and often included sponsorship from private firms. For instance, under Mayor Imbassahy the city of Salvador administered federal programs (such as PETI, Bolsa Escola Federal, Agente Jovem), a few municipal social assistance programs,[33] and targeted projects such as a youth orchestra and small-scale cooperatives where participants developed arts-and-crafts goods for sale (interview Araújo 2004). Mayor da Mata's Renda Mínima program was so short lived and absent from the public memory that Secretary Araújo acknowledged he was unfamiliar with it. He also admitted that it had not occurred to him to institute a municipal Renda Mínima program. While staff in Salvador who worked on social policy were committed to their public assistance work, what was most striking was the frame they used to describe their work. The absence of a socially progressive rhetoric was notable. City officials never mentioned legacies of exploitation, social exclusion, racism, or lack of citizenship. Nor did they contextualize their work against the backdrop of democratization or empowering the poor. Rather, senior political appointees in this secretariat discussed their work in terms of assistance, charity, and responding to *pedidos* (requests) from the poor.

The administration of Governor Roriz (PMDB) from 1998 to 2002 in Brasília offers a parallel account. As in Salvador, when the right-of-center governor entered office in 1998 after defeating left-of-center Buarque, he moved quickly to terminate the Bolsa Escola program. His staff declared the program unnecessary because the district did not have problems with irregular school attendance but rather with low academic performance. The district suspended enrollment of new families in the Bolsa Escola program and designed an alternative program, Successo no Aprender (Success in Learning), which provided students with school uniforms, school supplies, eye exams, and extra classes on Saturdays, eliminating the cash grant altogether. In other words, the administration returned to a more traditional mode of public assistance. At the time, the administration's decision to suspend registration in the Bolsa Escola program drew considerable criticism from the news media, but officials pressed on with their intention to evaluate Buarque's Bolsa Escola and create their own education programs (interview Lima 2003).[34]

In 2001 the Roriz administration provided the only instance in this study of Bolsa Escola reinstatement. The city reintroduced a school grant program under a new name, Renda Minha (My Income), combining elements of both Bolsa Escola and Successo no Aprender. The director of the program, Lílian Carneiro Lima, downplayed the notion that politics or media pressures led to the decision to reintroduce the program; rather, she emphasized that the decision reflected policy evaluations and assessments of various programs (interview 2003). Unfortunately, it is difficult to disentangle these actors' motivations for reinstituting an education stipend program. Tracing the internal decision-making process of the Roriz administration is particularly difficult due to a lack of transparency. Public officials associated with the Renda Minha program were reluctant to discuss internal processes or the number of beneficiaries, or provide documents. Several technocrats explained that unless their supervisors granted approval, they were barred from providing "private internal documents" as these were not "public." Higher-level officials also refused requests for interviews. Nevertheless, it is possible to conclude that the decision-making process of reintroducing Renda Minha in 2001 was considerably different from that of Bolsa Escola in 1995. Renda Minha was not a major symbol of Governor Roriz's administration, as it was for his predecessor. The policy had less visibility both in terms of his politics and his personal discourse (e.g., in campaigns and in the media). One implication of this case may be that left-of-center ideology matters more for instances of first-time policy emulation than it does in the rare circumstances when policy reenactment occurs. This also suggests that all politicians, regardless of their ideological commitments, have learned that there are political consequences to reversing popular policies. Thus, once in place many of them are reluctant to reverse course.

Ideology offers an important lens for understanding why politicians and their senior staff implemented Bolsa Escola. Politicians and their politically appointed senior staff shared similar dispositions and views about the relative importance of social policy. They also shared commitments to prioritizing policies that would address long-standing social inequalities and persistent poverty. While left-of-center political actors generally shared similar partisan affiliations, such as the PT, PSDB, and PSB, they noted that their decision making was independent of partisan directives. As was discussed previously, early adopters of Bolsa Escola thought that their emulation decision preceded their party's decision to endorse the program (interview Buarque 2004; interview Mata 2004).

For most cities, the timing of Bolsa Escola and Renda Mínima emulation coincided with changes in administration as left-of-center mayors took office. The only instance where a city with a leftist administration did not adopt the program was in Belo Horizonte under the Patrus Ananias administration (1992–96). This suggests that although a left-of-center ideological commitment is necessary for emulation to occur, it may not be sufficient. Early adoption in particular requires that actors learn about innovations quickly. In this way, decision making might involve more than a self-regarding decision process by including a socializing process as well. The next section on social networks explores the extent to which emulation decisions reflected a process of social networking.

Social Networks

Civil society organization can serve a crucial function by creating opportunities for formal networking and learning. Education policy has been a central thematic interest among Brazilian associations; according to the Ministry of Justice, there are nearly two hundred public interest nongovernmental organizations whose primary focus is education.[35] Yet an important features of this sector is the way in which traditional corporatist interests, represented by teachers' unions, have retained their influence in larger policy debates. In practice, teachers have taken a narrower view of education policy, focusing on debates regarding curriculum development, pedagogy, textbooks, classroom conditions, teacher training, and teacher pay. Education stipend programs challenged the notion of what constituted an "education policy," as they integrated components of poverty alleviation with education goals. In other words, features of the policy itself created some cognitive dissonance for educators. But in addition to these conceptual policy differences, Bolsa Escola represented a political conflict over resources and funding priorities. Teachers' unions generally worried that the funds for the program would come from allocated set-asides for primary education, which federal law mandates, rather than from municipalities' general operating budget. Ironically, Bolsa Escola, Brazil's most internationally recognized education policy, was hardly a central issue among education professionals.[36]

Despite the low levels of interest in Bolsa Escola among education professionals, several avenues for learning proved to be important and linked domestic and international actors. Quasi-governmental associations such as Conselho Nacional de Secretários de Educação (CONSED) and União dos Dirigentes Municipais de Educação (UNDIME) were key institutions for UNESCO-Brasília officials who wanted to engage in education policy development (interview Cunha 2004). Other international organizations also sent important signals on the merits of the policy strategy. UNICEF awarded Brasília the Children and Peace Prize for Bolsa Escola in 1996. Then, United Nations Secretary-General Kofi Annan sealed international approval of the conditional cash transfer strategy when he endorsed Bolsa Escola at the World Education Forum in Dakar in April 2000 (Aguiar and Araújo 2002, 37).

One of the most important domestic organizations to contribute to the spread of education stipend programs in Brazil was not specifically an "education" association but a generalist policy entity: Programa Gestão Pública e Cidadania (Public Management and Citizenship Program), housed in the prestigious public management school of the Getúlio Vargas Foundation in São Paulo. As a UNESCO official explained, it should not be surprising that Bolsa Escola would first appeal to a generalist policy audience, rather than education specialists:

> Bolsa Escola appeals to a lot of different people . . . I think that as an idea, BE was most attractive to people in noneducation sectors: people who work on social policy, poverty, social assistance, et cetera. You see, I always consider education to be a very conservative field. There are three conservative institutions in society: the church, the military, and the schools . . . This phenomenon of being conservative, that is, slow to change, is very much present in education. (Interview Cunha, 2004)

Thus, the Public Management and Citizenship Program emerged as a particularly important organization among policy professionals by socializing them to follow the latest trends in their field. Part of its influence relates to its very institutional design, which included a dissemination strategy to publicize award-winning good governance programs. For example, it held public awards ceremonies so that national and local press could provide media coverage on the finalists. In addition, the program had a general outreach component that included working with the press, producing videos, and developing materials for municipal, state, and federal use. Since it was housed in a school of public management, the faculty and program staff also published books and case studies and held thematic conferences based on the award-winning entries for practitioners and scholars alike. From the perspective of public administrators, participation in the program's activities offered several benefits. First and foremost, when administrators submitted entries for the annual innovations competition they gained recognition and visibility for their work among their peers.[37] While some elected officials and their political appointees encouraged their staff to submit entries for the competition, more often policy professionals sought out the competition on their own, seeking to gain the professional legitimacy that the competition offers. Winning the award also creates the potential for applicants' programs to survive the turmoil that comes with elections and new executives.[38] The award provides civil servants with the affirmation they seek from their peers, that their work meets the profession's standards of excellence.

Both Brasília and Campinas received Public Management and Citizenship awards in 1996 for their respective education stipend policies. In partnership with the NGO Instituto Pólis, the Fundação Getúlio Vargas–São Paulo (FGV-SP) produced publications describing Bolsa Escola, and hosted conferences and meetings that featured officials from Brasília. As Marisa Pacheco, the coordinator of Bolsa Escola in Brasília noted, the Department of Education received many invitations to participate in conferences to talk about Bolsa Escola. Those invitations were normally divided among Governor Buarque, Secretary Ibañez, and herself. Nearly ten years after she started directing the program, Pacheco recalled that some of the most important venues for disseminating information about Bolsa Escola in Brasília were the seminars held by the FGV-SP (interview 2004). Civil servants in São Paulo, Belo Horizonte, and Salvador confirmed that they were familiar with the awards program, had attended a meeting, or had received publications from the Public Management and Citizenship Program.

In addition to the opportunities for formal socialization afforded by professional networks, elected officials and policy professionals cited "informal" social network contacts as crucial for convincing them to initiate change. Often these informal ties developed in highly idiosyncratic ways. Mayor Lídice da Mata decided to implement a Renda Mínima program after hearing the mayor of Campinas, a friend of hers, describe his city's program at a conference (interview Mata 2004). The mayors knew each other well, as they both were affiliated with the PSDB, where they sometimes attended the same events. In Belo Horizonte, the first efforts to institute Bolsa Escola originated in the city council, when Rogério Correia (PT) proposed replicating it in 1996. Correia reported that as a fellow "educator" he took special interest in seeing his education proposals developed by Buarque and had followed his campaign for governor in 1995 (interview 2004). Councilman Rogério Correia drafted legislation to initiate a Bolsa Escola in Belo Horizonte, emulating every feature of the Brasília program.[39] He also invited Buarque to testify before the city council to explain the program (interview Correia 2004). As a well-known politician in the Workers' Party, Marta Suplicy met Buarque on numerous occasions and learned about the well-publicized program, Bolsa Escola. But in Marta Suplicy's case, her informal socialization process occurred closer to home, as her husband, Senator Eduardo Suplicy, had been a major supporter of local Renda Mínima initiatives.[40] These examples serve to show that politicians—whether mayors, city councelors, governors, or senators—have their own informal social networks where they meet and learn about new ideas. Importantly, these politicians' political parties did not coordinate these exchanges. Rather, politicians and their senior staff characterized these interactions are highly personalistic and informal.

These informal network processes were important not only for elected officials, but also for their political appointees and senior staff. Horizontal learning was a major feature of Bolsa Escola emulation, as cities seeking to implement the policy visited innovating cities. The secretariat of education in Brasília frequently hosted visitors from other cities and states (interview Pacheco 2004; interview Ibañez 2003; interview Aguiar 2003). Officials in Salvador, for instance, traveled to Campinas to see how the Renda Mínima Familiar worked there. When Belo Horizonte took up the policy, Mayor Célio de Castro's wife, who served as secretary of public assistance, visited Campinas. The city's technical staff, however, visited Brasília to learn how officials there had determined eligibility for families and designed their registry (interview Leitão 2004). Although technocrats in Belo Horizonte conducted their own poverty assessment in anticipation of the program, they closely followed Brasília's plan, since Belo Horizonte's legislation essentially copied it. When Marta Suplicy enacted a Renda Mínima program of her own, she tapped Ana Fonseca to direct the program. As a scholar at UNICAMP, Fonseca had evaluated the Renda Mínima program in Campinas and was aware of similar programs in other cities (Fonseca 2001).

In the case of Bolsa Escola, social networks served two important, albeit separate, functions. First, formal and informal networks socialized actors on the latest developments and norms in their respective fields. Both technocrats and politicians wanted to demonstrate that they were aware of the latest trends and sought to gain legitimacy among their peers. Being a "follower" or "emulator" of cities such as Belo Horizonte, Salvador, or São Paulo was not perceived negatively. Technocrats and politicians would simply emphasize their city's unique features (e.g., high poverty rates, lower human development indicators) and accomplishments (e.g., program size and speed of implementation). Second, connectivity to social networks facilitated the learning process by providing policy makers with cognitive shortcuts that enabled them to emulate policies fairly quickly and with few adjustments. Even though the cities that adopted these programs had highly skilled technocrats who could have tailored these programs for local conditions, administrators largely engaged in wholesale replication of Bolsa Escola and Renda Mínima programs.

Conclusions

These case studies of Bolsa Escola adoption reveal the way left-of-center ideology and linkages to social networks both contributed to emulation decisions. Similarly, instances of administrations that failed to replicate the education grant program show that neither a mayor's leftist ideology nor the presence of professional networks was by itself sufficient to bring about diffusion. Both social norms and ideology mattered by shaping actors' motivations and reinforcing decision making.

Implementation of the education reforms required that executives seek policies consistent with their deeply held values. These politicians all wanted to remedy long-standing inequality and prioritize programs that would enhance citizenship by alleviating social exclusion. If a leftist worldview was a prerequisite for emulation decisions, it certainly was not sufficient to ensure adoption. For example, Mayor Patrus Ananias (PT) in Belo Horizonte chose not to implement the program in his last year in office, despite legislative efforts by leftist city council members. What also mattered in all these cases was not only the presence of a committed politician, but also his or her connection to a professional network. Municipal executives often met one another through formal events and informal contacts, both of which offered opportunities to share information about the latest development and highlight their administrations' accomplishments.

Similar network relationships matter for technical staff and high-level technocrats. Those individuals who worked on poverty and social development were often familiar with educational stipend programs and could name those cities that were ahead of the curve. But technocrats' desire to demonstrate their knowledge of professional norms was insufficient to lead to Bolsa Escola emulation. For instance, midranking civil servants in the office of Work and Social Development in the Antônio Imbassahy administration had publications from the Public Management and Citizenship office on their bookshelves. They also identified Porto Alegre and Campinas as cities in the vanguard for designing innovative social policies.[41] That Imbassahy's administration had abandoned an education stipend program was not for lack of technocratic socialization or knowledge, but rather reflected the absence of an ideological commitment on the part of the city's leadership.

The central role that ideology and social norms hold for Bolsa Escola emulation is surprising because it conflicts with so much of what we have come to expect about the politics of redistribution. Local governments in Brazil are well known for their history of local *coronels* who dominate the electoral arena through political patronage. Education stipend programs like Bolsa Escola and Renda Mínima could have had powerful electoral effects for politicians of all stripes. It would have been logical for calculating policy makers to emulate these programs as a vehicle for self-interested political behavior. Yet these ten case studies demonstrate that despite the logic of a political incentives explanation for policy emulation, it is actors' social justice commitments and connections to their peers that matter most.

CHAPTER 5

Health Reform

A Complex Idea Spreads

Like education, the provision of health care and the need to reform the health system have been long-standing priorities for a more equitable Brazilian state. Yet in this sector reform requires tackling a complex set of institutions and political legacies. The Brazilian health insurance system dates back to the Bismarckian social welfare state established during the Vargas era (1930–45) when medical care was tied to worker and employer contributions and based on an insurance principle of entitlements (Draibe 1994; Mesa-Lago 1978). From the beginning, President Getúlio Vargas established a two-tiered system; insured federal employees and workers in the formal sector had access to free medical care (hospitals, doctors, and complex medical interventions) through a centralized federal agency, Instituto Nacional de Assistência Médica da Previdência Social (INAMPS). A second federal agency, the Ministry of Health, was charged with managing preventive health care programs using federal budgetary allocations (Arretche 2004b, 160). Thus, in practice Brazil's two-tier health care system left the poor and informal workers with more precarious access to basic services.

For development specialists, infant and maternal mortality are telling indicators of a population's well-being. As Brazil entered the *abertura* period and politicians debated the democratic constitution, it was clear that the country faced serious challenges and would need to do much better. Estimates of infant mortality in Brazil in 1960 were as high as 115 per 1000, and although GDP per capita would rise at an annual rate of 4.8 percent between 1960 and 1980, infant mortality would fall at an annual rate of only 2.5 percent during this period (McGuire 2010, 150). As we will see, health reform in Brazil would require a commitment to alter the structure of health care delivery substantially to create more equitable access. In practice this would mean an end to the two-tiered system, acceptance of basic principles of universal care, and decentralized health care access for all citizens.

Today, the Programa Saúde da Família (PSF) is widely accepted as a new model for basic health service provision in Brazil. But to explain how and why it grew from a small project adopted by a few local governments to widespread health care reform across the country, this chapter explores the process by which policy makers came to emulate it. In the early 1990s it was not at all evident that PSF would come to represent a useful framework for all cities. After all, the program is based on innovative experiments in preventive health that were designed for unique Brazilian cities; the early precursors of PSF were community-based programs in the arid, poor state of Ceará in the northeast, and the large city of Niterói, which displayed high levels of human development. Yet despite the unique features of the program's earliest adopters, the policy eventually generated a tidal wave of emulations.

To explain why politicians and technocrats came to embrace PSF and were motivated to emulate it in their own municipalities, we will first examine national health reform efforts since the democratic opening in context. Central issues during this time period include real advances in social rights for health care access as well as stalled efforts to fulfill state obligations. Decentralization opened the door for municipal experimentation in health policy in the late 1980s and 1990s. The second section of the chapter provides an overview of state and local innovations, which laid the foundation for the family health program. The last section draws on twelve case studies to uncover the mechanisms that led to PSF emulation decisions. Qualitative evidence from interviews with policy makers reveals how their decisions reflected deeply held ideological beliefs and desires to seek legitimacy through professional affirmations, which come by following social norms. These findings are remarkable given that the clientelistic provision of access to basic health care has long yielded payoffs for Brazilian mayors.

National Context for Health Policy Reform

Brazil has a long history in the area of public health, as well as state involvement in the provision of health insurance, both of which shape some features of contemporary health reform debates. Prior to the 1900s most state activities aimed at curbing the spread of tropical and infectious diseases, such as yellow fever (N. Stepan 1976). An important turning point in the field of public health took place in the early 1900s in the city of Rio de Janeiro when its public health director, Oswaldo Cruz, launched vaccination and public health campaigns to control epidemic diseases (McGuire 2010, 158; N. Stepan 1976, chaps. 4 and 5). Oswaldo Cruz and his colleagues advanced knowledge by identifying insect-born parasites that could transmit diseases; further, Cruz's work spurred the development of a prestigious public health institute that bears his name, and contributed to advocacy surrounding the need for improvements in sanitation. As early as 1918, doctors, academics, scientists, and civil servants formed a Sanitarian League urging the government to initiate campaigns to fight against malaria, chagas disease, hookworm, and other endemic diseases (McGuire 2010, 159). So, early in the development of Brazil's public health system, networks of diverse professional actors sought to advocate for greater governmental involvement in bringing about improvements in basic health conditions.

The origins of Brazil's social security system also date back to the early 1900s, specifically the 1920s, when the state preempted an emerging working-class movement by granting social protections to selected sectors (Malloy 1979, 22–50; Weyland 1996, 89). In 1923 Brazil introduced the first social insurance program, the "Eloy Chaves law," which provided for the creation of a fund for retirement and survivors' pensions (Caixa de Aposentadoria e Pensão, or CAP) for each railway company (Malloy 1979, 40). The CAPs covered such benefits as burial, disability, funeral, retirement, and medical care to insured railway employees. In the late 1920s other firms and industries (such as those of dock and maritime workers) created similar retirement and pension funds. The logic of CAPs laid the foundation for Getúlio Vargas's (1930–45) extension of pensions to even more sectors of the economy into the state-corporatist system (Collier and Collier 1979, 972; Weyland 1996, 89). Like the Bismarckian social insurance system, the Brazilian state tied pensions and health care entitlements to worker, employer, and government contributions.[1] This corporatist policy favored formal sectors of the economy, such as organized labor and government workers, and excluded informal and rural sectors of the economy (Huber 1996). In so doing, Brazilian social policy not only left out those groups that were most in need of social protection, but also exacerbated social inequality (Hunter and Sugiyama 2009).

During the military regime (1964–85) the public social insurance system largely retained its Bismarckian characteristics.[2] INAMPS administered health care benefits in a highly centralized fashion and oversaw the management of public health care facilities, as well as contracts for services with private hospitals, clinics, laboratories, and doctors who provided state-funded medical services for federal and private sector workers (Arretche 2004b). The payment system for INAMPS, which included contracts for public and private service providers, created incentives to maximize services and focus on curative care to increase revenue (Arretche 2004b, 160). Basic medicine was left to two entities: the federal Ministry of Health, which drew on the general revenue budget, and state-level health agencies, which operated independently with their own budgetary resources. By the late 1980s, however, the federal government had largely abandoned basic health care altogether, and nearly all primary health care was managed by state and local governments (Arretche 2004b, 160–61).[3]

The INAMPS contribution scheme not only favored elite interests, but also exacerbated social exclusion through the geographic distribution of health care access. Lucrative contracts for hospitals and doctors concentrated in large cities where government officials and formal sector workers reside. Data on the geographic distribution of medical resources at the time is telling. For instance, in the mid-1960s, of the 3972 municipalities in the country, 2089 (53 percent) lacked a physician (Mello 1977, 107). Aggregate numbers, however, mask regional disparities. In the more industrialized southeast and south only 36.7 percent and 40.1 percent of cities lacked physicians, respectively. But figures for poor and agricultural regions had an even greater percentage of municipalities without doctors: central west (66.3 percent), north (75.7 percent), and northeast (70.8 percent) (Mello 1977, 108). Thus, Brazil's health care model had important consequences for both short-term access and long-term effects on the geographic allocation of medical infrastructure.

The transition to democracy ushered in the first stage of major health care reform. Some advocates for change noted that the existing social insurance system was expensive due to its focus on curative medicine, which benefited only a select few, and called for greater emphasis on prevention. Others noted that the social insurance system had left out informal sectors. The sanitarian movement (*movimento sanitário*), which represented a new generation of health professionals, local health authorities, and left-wing health experts, called for universal health coverage.[4] *Sanitaristas* (sanitarians) successfully allied with other social movement mobilizations for democratization to advance progressive health reform. These reformers found an audience for their advocacy at the VIII Conferência Nacional de Saúde (March 1986), which was convened by the presidency and the Ministry of Health. Their participation at the event allowed them to shape substantially the conference's final resolutions, which called for reorganization of national health care. The conference also declared it the state's obligation to fulfill objectives such as universalization, participation, and decentralization. The debate and outcomes of the conference laid the foundation for subsequent debates over health policy, which would take place during the Constituent Assembly.

The *sanitarista* movement made impressive strides in the late 1980s to enshrine progressive social rights in the constitutional text.[5] They successfully articulated their vision, including universal rights to health care, prioritization of basic health, and decentralization.[6] While the Constituent Assembly would water down some of their proposals, the venue proved particularly amenable to the movement's political strategies. In the end, Brazil's democratic constitution proclaimed a universal right to health and reinforced the state's obligation to fulfill those rights. Implemented in 1990, the unified health system (Sistema Único de Saúde, or SUS) was a comprehensive, fully financed system with free and universal entitlement. Importantly, financing for SUS would come from payroll deductions and general tax revenues, thus ending the formal distinction between the higher-quality services rendered by INAMPS and funded through contributory health insurance, and lower-quality health care funded through the federal budget (McGuire 2010, 162–63).

Although the constitution had articulated broad principles for progressive health care, many of the details on the unified health system were left unspecified, and reforms faltered through much of the early 1990s. Several factors contributed to delays in transforming the system. First, once Congress met to institute new legislation, opponents of progressive health reform (medical businesses, INAMPS bureaucrats, and conservative politicians) successfully resisted equalizing proposals (Weyland 1996). One of the most difficult political barriers advocates encountered was clientelist politicians who feared loss of access to "pork"; decentralization would undermine access to patronage, and preventive medicine, which targets whole communities, would undermine patrons' access to "selective incentives," which are individualized features of curative medicine (Weyland 1996, 165–66). As a result, decentralization efforts that would have prioritized primary care came to a standstill, and efforts to shift the ministry's resources for basic health care faltered as profit-seeking hospitals continued to benefit from contracts for mid- and high-level complex services.

Second, Brazil faced a fiscal crisis in the mid-1990s that made it difficult to increase spending for health care without cutting expenditures elsewhere. Health Minister Adib Jatene lobbied extensively to increase revenue for health and won legislative approval for a constitutional amendment creating earmarked revenue for health care. Yet the increase in revenue for the Health Ministry represented a short-lived victory. Minister Jatene lacked political clout in the cabinet; and Minister of Finance Pedro Malan opposed new taxes, especially those targeted for particular spending areas. Thus, the Finance Ministry simply cut the Health Ministry's resources to offset the gains from the new earmarked taxes (Arretche 2004b, 175). This conflict over budgetary allocations demonstrated the weakness of the Ministry of Health, which suffered under politically vulnerable ministers until President Cardoso selected José Serra, a close political ally, in 1998.

Third, while the *sanitaristas* had been effective in pushing for reforms during the democratic transition, their political influence diminished thereafter. Although decentralization had been a major goal of the sanitarian movement, to combat the influence of the medical industry at the national level, in practice it also had the effect of diffusing its attention from the national policy arena. *Sanitaristas* mostly focused on local problems rather than advocating for comprehensive overhaul of the inequitable national medical system (Weyland 1996, 181). Additionally, the sanitarian movement was unable to sustain its broad advocacy coalition. Not only did it lose the strength of partnership with other social movements, but internal coalitions began to splinter, reflecting the divisions among the movement's members (Cohn 1989, 132). As a result, many *sanitaristas* turned their attention to local initiatives for preventive medicine.

Despite all the political, administrative, and fiscal challenges for health reform in the 1990s, Brazil did manage to enact incremental changes. The second wave of reforms (1990–95) led to the consolidation of the unified system, including the "municipalization" of service delivery and implementation of financial mechanisms for allocationing federal funds (World Bank 2004, 157).[7] The third wave of reforms (1996–2001) focused on prioritizing basic care, specifying institutional roles, making legal and regulatory changes, and introducing alternative payment mechanisms (World Bank 2004, 157).[8] One of the most important changes for municipalities was the specification of federal transfers. Under new regulations, transfers would vary by program and the level of service delivered. Cities could opt out of the unified health system but doing so would require that local governments finance health care from their own budgets.

Overall, the movement for progressive health reform at the national level yielded mixed results. Without a doubt, *sanitaristas* won a major victory when the Constituent Assembly enshrined the right to health care and obligated the state to provide universal access. But other equity-enhancing efforts, such as prioritizing basic health, stalled under political and fiscal pressure. The ministry's efforts to foster decentralization of health services resulted in a shift in responsibility, as subnational governments took on the substantial job of prioritizing preventive and basic medicine. Next, we will turn from the national context to examine how subnational governments advanced health care access within their jurisdictions.

Local Experimentation and Innovation

While the Ministry of Health sought to advance national health reform and define intergovernmental responsibilities, many states and municipalities forged ahead by designing and implementing their own health care policies. In some instances, states shifted spending priorities and introduced new partnerships with local governments. In others, municipal governments took advantage of their newfound authority in the public health arena to experiment with new modes of health care delivery. We will start with an overview of some innovative local experiments in health care delivery during the late 1980s and early 1990s. As the cases reveal, in most instances policy makers sought to introduce progressive health reforms that would reach historically underserved populations and emphasize preventive and basic health care. The experience of São Paulo served as a notable counterpoint. During this period, local experimentation led to policy diversity, and programs typically addressed the unique challenges each jurisdiction faced. All in all, local governments would serve as "laboratories" that experimented with different models of health care. Their successes would inform and inspire the development of Programa Saúde da Família.

In the early 1990s, several Brazilian municipalities began experimenting with public health care models emphasizing preventive and basic health care and reversing the course of curative and doctor-centric approaches to medicine.[9] One of the most recognized efforts to emphasize community health occurred in Niterói, in the state of Rio de Janeiro, which instituted the Programa Médico de Família (PMF, Family Doctor Program). At the time, this large city had strong social development indicators, including high literacy rates, high median household incomes, and an average life expectancy of seventy years. Despite high levels of human development, aggregate figures masked social inequalities and pockets of deep poverty; city officials considered a quarter of the population to be at "social risk" and in need of specialized attention.

In 1991 Mayor Jorge Roberto Silveira (PDT) of Niterói visited Cuba, learned about its world-renowned health care model, and resolved to implement a similar system back home. The Cuban Health Ministry provided the municipality with technical assistance to implement its own Médico de Família program. In Niterói, doctors and nurse's aides worked collaboratively in clinics embedded in the communities they served. Each clinic included three or four teams; each team had a general practitioner and a nurse's aide and was responsible for a designated jurisdiction that included 200–250 families. This approach allowed PMF teams to resolve 70 percent of medical issues through clinical and home-based care. Unlike the Cuban model, however, officials in Niterói did not require that physicians reside in the communities, only their nurse's aides. The decision to deviate from the Cuban model was based on necessity: very few Brazilian doctors would have been willing to live in these impoverished neighborhoods (interview D'Angelo 2004). The family doctor program became one of the most highly regarded municipal public health efforts in Brazil.[10] For instance, in 1997 the Programa Médico de Família in Niterói won a national innovations award from the Gestão Pública e Cidadania program housed in the prestigious Getúlio Vargas Foundation in São Paulo.

Officials from Niterói were not alone in their desire to prioritize basic health problems and enhance prevention. However, Niterói was uniquely positioned to initiate a Cuban-inspired program: the city had the political, fiscal, and human resources it needed to develop a family doctor model. Health experts in small cities in the northeast also wanted to move from curative medicine to prioritize prevention but lacked the human and physical resources to replicate the Cuban model. The northeast faced high levels of poverty and had limited infrastructure; in general the region lacked sufficient clinics and hospitals, and physicians were in short supply. Given these structural challenges, officials sought an alternative to doctor-centric care that could emphasize community-based health.

In 1987 the state of Ceará in northeastern Brazil designed and implemented the pioneering preventive health program Programa de Agentes de Saúde (PAS). The program relied on two sets of actors: community health agents and nurses who would supervise them. As in the family doctor program in Niterói, state officials in Ceará wanted to promote basic health, emphasize prevention, and build ties with local communities. Health agents were selected from within communities to work directly with families. After receiving training, health agents would work with nurse-supervisors to register families' health care needs and encourage basic sanitarian practices such as water filtration, proper nutrition, and the promotion of vaccinations. Since the state also had particularly high levels of infant mortality, health agents also monitored the height and weight of children. In 1987 the rate of infant death in Ceará was 102 per 1000; this was double the national figure (Tendler 1997a, 21).[11]

Although the state of Ceará conceived and promoted the program, implementation still required municipal participation. Mayors who adopted the program had to find the funds to cover 15 percent of operating costs while also sharing administrative responsibilities with state officials.[12] Adoption of PAS across the state took several years and depended on mayors' willingness to opt into the program. But by 1992 basic health indicators across the state had improved dramatically, infant deaths had declined by a third, and vaccination coverage for measles and polio had tripled (Tendler 1997a, 22).[13] For these and other accomplishments, the state won the prestigious UNICEF Maurice Pate Award for child programs in 1993. In addition to Ceará, the southern states of Paraná and Mato Grosso do Sul also instituted their own community health agent programs.

The early experience of the PAS program stimulated the federal government to support its expansion in other states. In 1991 the Ministry of Health instituted the Programa de Agentes Comunitários de Saúde (PACS), which largely mirrored the PAS program from Ceará.

The objective of the PACS was to reduce infant and maternal mortality, primarily in the north and northeast, by extending basic health services to the poorest and most destitute areas (Viana and Dal Poz 1998, 18). The Ministry of Health started offering federal funds to stimulate the program's adoption across the northeast and provided guidelines detailing minimum requirements for health agents and their duties. For instance, health agents needed to be at least eighteen years old, proficient in reading and writing, and have a disposition for community health. These workers were responsible for registering families, assessing families' health and living conditions, collecting updated information for a national database, conducting home visits, identifying children for schooling, mapping community needs, and identifying at-risk areas, just to name a few of their activities.

An altogether different approach to basic health care during this time period was adopted by the city of São Paulo. Under Mayor Paulo Maluf (1992–96), a leader of the right-wing party PDS, city administrators sought to address several problems in public health services, including high costs, tremendous inefficiencies, and low quality of public services. Secretary of Health Getúlio Hanashiro, who shared Maluf's disposition for market-oriented solutions to public management problems, sought to reconfigure basic health services dramatically. The policy, the Plano de Atendimento à Saúde (PAS), integrated business sector principles into health services and represented a dramatic departure from mainstream public health strategies.[14] Although the Constitution ensured health care rights for all, city officials made it clear that their plan would prioritize service to the most indigent.

Under the PAS, municipal authorities planned to create market-based incentives for doctors and clinics and prioritized services for the neediest groups. Maluf proposed the creation of regional clinics that would serve a given area's designated population. To encourage greater efficiency, each clinic would operate as a doctor-owned cooperative.[15] Similar to private health care providers, each cooperative would in theory have an incentive to rein in costs and maximize efficiency of operations. The city would in turn provide per capita transfers for the cooperative, based on the number of registered beneficiaries assigned to each clinic.[16] Residents of São Paulo would have their own health care cards, similar to insurance cards provided by private insurers, and could visit their designated regional cooperatives for medical care. The PAS proposal endured stiff political opposition but was implemented in 1996 during Maluf's last year in office. Although the PAS is credited for its achievements in public management, such as improvements in work absenteeism, the plan has been widely discredited as financially unsustainable, and it was dismantled in 2000.

The Programa Saúde da Família (PSF, Family Health Program) was born out of various community health experiences, such as the Programa de Médico de Família, Programa de Agentes de Saúde from Ceará, and the nationally supported Programa de Agentes Comunitários de Saúde. On December 27–28, 1993, the Ministry of Health held a meeting of leading public health officials to discuss municipal health services and financing. As Viana and Dal Poz (1998) describe, the gathering was a response to demands from municipal secretaries of health, who sought greater financial support for basic health care. The meeting was sponsored by the minister's cabinet and included officials representing the ministry, as well as bureaucrats from municipal and state secretaries of health; also present were two officials representing international development organizations, namely UNICEF and PAHO.[17] An important feature of this technical meeting was that it included a broad spectrum of participants from throughout the country: technocrats involved in innovative experiences in the south and southeast engaged with officials from the northeast, who worked with PACS. The models from Niterói and Ceará were very influential in shaping the eventual design of PSF (Viana and Dal Poz 1998; interview Andrade 2004; interview Machado 2003). Health professionals liked the territorial organization of health services and the potential to focus on prevention rather than on demand-side service delivery. They also embraced the role of the community health agent but wanted to integrate other health professionals. To accomplish these goals, PSF drew on a larger team of workers, including a doctor, nurses, nurse's aides, and community health agents; nurses retained their central supervisory role over their aides and health agents.[18] In this way, the PSF program represented an upgrade to the PACS program; nurses were still central as administrators, and the community health agents' roles remained the same.

Over the years, the staff in the Ministry of Health nurtured the Programa Saúde da Família, protected it from administrative upheavals that came with ministerial turnover, and eventually championed its central role in the unified health system. While meeting participants such as Heloísa Machado and Luiz Odorico de Andrade had always envisioned the program as a central organizing model for basic health (interview Machado 2003; interview Andrade 2004), PSF started out with modest institutional support and limited fanfare. The program was one of many efforts in community health, a small project embedded among other larger ministerial programs. In its first year of operation (1994) the ministry signed limited *convênios* (funding agreements) with states and municipalities, which required that subnational governments contribute to the program's cost. Selection of eligible cities was restricted to those considered high priority based on a needs assessment conducted by IPEA.[19] In total, fifty-five municipalities signed agreements and instituted PSF in the first year of operation.

Over the course of several years, PSF program coordinators Heloísa Machado and Fátima de Sousa defended the program internally within the ministry. They weathered the restructuring that came with a constant stream of new health ministers, many of whom lacked the political support to initiate significant health reforms, and they eventually gained the support needed to institute and expand the program within the ministry.[20] A turning point for PSF came in 1995 when prominent heart surgeon Dr. Adib Jatene became the health minister for the second time in his career. As Jatene explained, he first learned about community health efforts and the role of the *agentes comunitários de saúde* when he was health minister in 1992. At the time, they were doing a wonderful job combating the spread of cholera in the north and northeast (interview Jatene 2003). Upon his return to that position in 1995, Jatene met with Machado and Sousa, who persuaded him that the PSF would work more broadly. After visiting cities that had instituted the program, such as Camaragibe in the state of Pernambuco and Sobral in the state of Ceará, Minister Jatene agreed to support it (2003).[21] In January 1996 PSF was transferred to the Secretaria de Assistência da Saúde (SAS), finding a more central home within the ministry and allowing for its institutionalization (Viana and Dal Poz 1998, 22).[22]

The administrative changes had several important consequences. First, the PSF gained broader visibility, and the staff started articulating the idea that it should move from an isolated project to represent an organizing principle for basic health care. Second, the ministry also moved toward integrating PSF with PACS and connecting it with broader efforts to decentralize health care and implement it within the Unified Health System. Eventually PSF would subsume the more modest Community Health Agent Program altogether.

Programa Saúde da Família sprang up at a moment when national health care reform was encountering some of its greatest political and fiscal difficulties. Local governments, on the other hand, were taking advantage of newfound authority to develop and implement new policies for better preventive health; these early experiments reflected a potpourri of approaches. As Judith Tendler observed in her case study of Ceará, decentralization of health policy has involved a mix of both central and local efforts (1997a, 23), as municipalities, states, and the federal government work collaboratively to deliver and finance health services. This observation certainly holds true for the PSF, which benefited from early municipal health policy experimentation, was conceived by a broad group of experts involved in all tiers of health care provision, and drew on federal financing offered through the Ministry of Health. Yet, to understand the evolution of the program's spread, from 55 municipalities in primarily small rural towns in the north and northeast, to extensive national adoption by 4944 cities in 2003, requires more than a simple tale of vertical pressures for diffusion. Although PSF did provide some political opportunities for mayors, such as the potential to dole out coveted health agent jobs to political cronies, the program was still highly complex and required restructuring health care services. Furthermore, some politicians and health policy technocrats would challenge the idea that PSF was a desirable policy for their cities. In practice, the adoption of PSF was not always guaranteed or automatic. Each city underwent its own policy-making process related to PSF. Thus, to uncover the adoption decisions for PSF, we must turn to the local dimensions of policy making and open the black box to reveal actors' motivations for policy emulation.

Explaining the Diffusion of PSF in Four Major Cities

Why did some cities adopt the Programa Saúde da Família quickly, while others lagged behind? Why would health policy makers emulate the program, particularly when many local governments had already experimented with alternative health care models? Also puzzling was that actors from large cities with sophisticated health infrastructure would emulate a program that largely drew its inspiration from areas that are far from typical: the poor rural northeast (with the PACS), and Niterói (with PMF), with high levels of human development and income per capita.

The case studies in this chapter examine the motivations behind PSF adoption in four research sites over three municipal administrations. These cities had great flexibility in determining their basic health models. Some administrations tailored health policy to suit the needs of their municipalities, while others adopted PSF. In other words, emulation of PSF was far from automatic or a foregone conclusion. Electoral competition varied across these cities, and the voters selected mayors representing various ideological predispositions, from rightists to leftists. In addition, health policy technocrats engaged in professional networking activities, but not necessarily the same ones. Table 5.1 provides an overview of the case studies: when PSF adoption took place, and the partisan affiliations of the mayors who adopted the family health program.

Political Incentives

Health care is an area of public policy particularly visible to the electorate because health policy affects the entire population, irrespective of age and income. For instance, the outbreak of infectious diseases, such as cholera, dengue, and HIV/AIDS, can affect an entire city's population, regardless of neighborhood and sociodemographic characteristics. The Programa Saúde da Família generated considerable public attention as its aims included prevention and basic health care. For beneficiaries of the program, PSF is also highly visible because it brings the state into the private sphere of domestic life through home visits and neighborhood

Table 5.1. Case Studies: PSF Adoption and Nonadoption

	Executive in Office and Party ID[a]	*Mayor's Ideology*	*PSF*
Brasília (DF)[b]			
1990–1994	Joaquim Roriz (PTR)	Right	n/a[c]
1994–1998	Cristovam Buarque (PT)	Left	Yes
1998–2002	Joaquim Roriz (PMDB)	Center-Right	No/Yes[d]
Belo Horizonte (MG)			
1992–1996	Patrus Ananias (PT)	Left	No
1996–2000	Célio de Castro (PSB)	Left	No
2000–2004	Célio de Castro (PSB)	Left	Yes
	Fernando Damata Pimentel (PT)[e]	Left	
Salvador (BA)			
1992–1996	Lídice da Mata (PSDB)	Center-Left	No
1996–2000	Antônio José Imbassahy (PFL)	Right	No
2000–2004	Antônio José Imbassahy (PFL)	Right	Yes
São Paulo (SP)			
1992–1996	Paulo Maluf (PDS)	Right	No
1996–2000	Celso Pitta (PPB)	Right	No
2000–2004	Marta Suplicy (PT)	Left	Yes

[a] Mayor's partisan affiliation at the time he or she ran for office.
[b] Brasília, the Federal District, operates under the gubernatorial electoral calendar.
[c] This period precedes the development of PSF; thus it does not constitute a case of diffusion.
[d] The program was suspended and then reinstated.
[e] Fernando Damata Pimentel (PT) assumed office in November 2001, after Célio de Castro suffered a stroke.

outreach. In addition, communities can determine whether a neighboring area has PSF while their own district remains underserved. The conventional wisdom is that health care can boost candidates' electoral prospects. For instance, it is thought that in the mid-1980s, politicians affiliated with the PMDB supported health care reform in order to boost their party's prospects with the electorate (Weyland 1996, 159). Later, some health ministry officials noted that the increased visibility of

PSF, with distinct uniforms for team members and logos for program materials, coincided with José Serra's presidential aspirations; Serra would invoke the PSF program during his 2002 presidential campaign (McGuire 2010, 179). Though he lost his bid for the presidency to Lula in 2002, Serra attributed his strong backing in the northeast to his support of PSF as minister of health (McGuire 2010, 179). Given the high visibility of PSF, it would certainly make sense for self-interested politicians focused on local electoral politics to embrace the program. In cities lacking PSF, candidates might campaign on implementing the program. Politicians in cities that already have a PSF policy might campaign on extending the program to new communities.

In addition to the general appeal that PSF holds among the poor, the program also has the potential to generate rent-seeking behavior as politicians have the ability to dole out particularistic benefits. Implementing PSF involves job creation as the program requires that *agentes comunitários de saúde* (ACS) reside in the communities they serve.[23] In a context where unemployment is high and the working poor encounter tremendous difficulties in making ends meet, a job as a community health agent is very attractive. The position does not require specialized skills in primary health;[24] the minimum requirements to qualify for the position include literacy, basic schooling, and "leadership" skills. In many ways, the ACS position is an extension of "women's work" in the domestic (private) sphere, which helps explain why the vast majority of the positions go to women.[25] The PSF also has the potential to generate a second type of political patronage. The geographical demarcation of neighborhoods served by the program offers a clear benefit for politicians who want to reach out to communities for electoral support. In other words, mayors who adopt the program can influence voters by deciding which neighborhoods will be served. This is particularly important as PSF typically targets economically and epidemiologically vulnerable areas, rather than extending the policy throughout the entire city. In practice, politicians can deviate from serving the neediest areas to fulfill their electoral agenda. For these reasons, savvy politicians who want to engage in traditional patronage politics can benefit tremendously from the family health program's design.

Mayors in each of the case study sites faced electoral competition and campaigned on issues of health care delivery. Given the electoral potential for enacting PSF, we might expect that all mayors, regardless of their ideology, would emulate the program. In cities with low levels of health infrastructure, PSF represented an important extension of new services to communities with limited access to health care. Thus, PSF represented the creation of new services. For cities with existing health services already in place (e.g., clinics and hospitals), the PSF program offered the potential to restructure health care to work with families and communities in a more integrated fashion.[26] In these instances, voters would benefit from higher quality services, greater interaction with health care providers, and easier access.

Despite the potential that PSF could offer, given the competitive electoral environment in the case study cities, the qualitative evidence reveals that mayoral candidates did not systematically endorse the program and instead sought a diverse set of health policies. Conservative politicians often advocated for market-oriented proposals, whereas leftist politicians tended to embrace PSF. Candidates' approaches to public health issues were certainly important to their campaigns and entered into the electoral debates in these cities. Of the four research sites, the city of São Paulo, where the PAS quasi-privatized system served as a counterpoint to PSF, offers the best proof that debates over health received widespread media attention (Cohn and Elias 1999, 67–94). All three mayoral campaigns dedicated considerable attention to health care issues, but candidates differed in their vision for the city. Some candidates, like Maluf and Pitta, argued São Paulo should institute private market incentives into its system. It was the leftist candidate, Marta Suplicy, who campaigned on health reform and announced she would implement the PSF if elected.

Even though PSF had the potential to gain electoral votes for Marta Suplicy, her advisers dismissed the notion that her favorable position toward the policy during the campaign represented a calculated electoral strategy (interview Manfredini 2003). The local media widely covered health issues in São Paulo, yet most residents were unaware of the technical dimensions of the various proposals under consideration. The groups that might benefit most from PSF, the poor and most vulnerable populations, were unfamiliar with the family health program. Once the administration moved to implement PSF, many citizen representatives who served on local health councils were skeptical of the program as they viewed clinics and hospitals, not PSF health teams, as appropriate places to go to for their health care needs. Moreover, several unions expressed deep concern about contract negotiations under PSF (interview Costa 2003; interview D'Agostini 2003; interview Oliveira 2003). In this light, Suplicy's emulation decision appears to reflect a calculated administrative risk rather than a clear-cut electoral strategy to win the election.

Brasília was the first of the case study cities to emulate PSF in the second half of Cristovam Buarque's administration. Although Buarque was a staunch leftist and often spoke about social rights and citizenship on the campaign trail, he was not a strong advocate for PSF and had not campaigned on a promise to implement the program. Rather, his focus was on Bolsa Escola and other educational policies. The decision to implement the family health program was largely delegated to his senior political appointees, notably his secretary of health, Maria José da Conceição (Maninha), who had learned about the program after receiving invitations from the Ministry of Health to see how PSF worked in Camaragibe in the state of Pernambuco (interview Conceição 2003; interview Arruda 2003). Although both Bolsa Escola mothers and PSF community health agents could have provided significant electoral support for Buarque's reelection campaign, his closest political adviser asserted that the governor refused to exploit beneficiaries of his social programs, and referred to these programs as "rights" rather than politicizing them by explaining that they were vulnerable to electoral turnover (interview Aguiar 2003). Political insiders in his administration lamented Buarque's approach, viewing it as a poor electoral strategy that contributed to reelection defeat.

In Belo Horizonte, where the political competition was concentrated to the left of the political spectrum, the decision to implement PSF was hotly contested among technocrats. Mayor Célio de Castro was said to have embraced PSF early in his first mayoral term (1996–2000) because of his own familiarity with the program; a physician by training, he had made health care a signature issue. Although he was an early proponent of the family health program, it nevertheless took him until 2000 to implement the program in the city. While the delay in emulating PSF gives the appearance of an electoral incentive, health experts in Belo Horizonte told a different story. Senior health policy technocrats in the municipal health department were familiar with the PSF program and were vocal opponents of it for Belo Horizonte. Most of the municipal health technocrats were trained in Saúde Coletiva at the prestigious Federal University in Campinas (UNICAMP). Members of this group shared similar views, and argued that PSF worked most effectively in settings that lacked a solid health infrastructure, such as regions in the north and northeast. Since Belo Horizonte had made important strides in the municipalization of health care services between 1992 and 1996, administrators preferred more integrated approaches to primary health care (interview F. Santos 2004). One of their concerns was that PSF would generate two separate administrative and in-take procedures, which would result in poor dialogue between PSF services and more complex levels of care (interview F. Santos 2004; interview Franco 2004). Thus, for several years the mayor encountered opposition from senior technocrats who favored other types of integrated health services. Ultimately, in order to implement PSF, the municipal Department of Health needed personnel changes. Some opponents of PSF left the secretariat, and new technocrats, who had adopted the program in the neighboring city of Betim, were brought in to administer the program in Belo Horizonte.

Like Belo Horizonte, Salvador was a late adopter of PSF. It took several years for Mayor Antônio Imbassahy to announce he would institute the health program. Health policy specialists, both inside and outside government, explained that the mayor was relatively uninvolved in the decision to implement PSF in Salvador and delegated these issues to his secretary of health, Aldely Rocha (interview Queiroz 2004; interview Nossa 2004). Technocrats in the city's Department of Health noted that the mayor was skeptical of the program, preferring that it expand slowly and expressing concern over the expense associated with it (interview Queiroz 2004; interview Nossa 2004). One observer of municipal health noted how it was ironic that the mayor initially failed to recognize the electoral potential behind PSF, and attributed the city's delays to the political elite's lack of imagination (interview Boa Sorte 2004).

In all these cases, mayors were rarely motivated to adopted PSF for electoral gains. Mayors' initial emulation decisions were largely delegated to senior political appointees, such as municipal secretaries of health, and technocrats, working as civil servants. Once PSF was in place, however, it was difficult to dismantle, and a few politicians found ways to use it for political gain. The administrations of two rightist politicians, Joaquim Roriz (PMDB) (1998–2002; 2002–6) and Antônio Imbassahy (2000–2004), are exemplary in this regard. Both are well known for their general use of political patronage, and those tendencies continued once PSF was enacted.

Joaquim Roriz of Brasília inherited Saúde em Casa[27] from Cristovam Buarque's administration. During his campaign, Roriz promised loyal partisans jobs as community health agents, a much coveted position among the lower classes, and handed out slips of paper indicating they would be in line for the jobs. Once the administration was in office and the health secretariat opened applications for the ACS positions, individuals began arriving with their letters showing that they were promised positions. As one informant noted, once in office Roriz installed an entirely new group of community health agents since he was unwilling to hire any of "Buarque's" people. While bureaucrats were reluctant to admit their own participation in this hiring scheme, they had all heard or seen evidence to this effect. Since the district's health secretariat had experienced several changes in leadership, technocrats felt free to say that their predecessors engaged in problematic hiring practices but that they were following proper rules.

The allegations of unethical recruitment practices for PSF were not limited to the community health agent position. One high-ranking health administrator in Brasília informed me that patronage was such a pervasive and ingrained part of the local political culture that upon announcing the resumption of the PSF program he received over a thousand personal requests from the politically connected for jobs associated with the program, including positions for doctors and nurses.[28]

Accusations were so pervasive that Brasília's Ministério Público (Public Prosecutor's Office), in collaboration with federal auditors, undertook investigations into allegations of widespread corruption and the misuse of funds. Overall, the administration of Joaquim Roriz in Brasília was especially notorious for irregularities related to the health sector (including PSF). The irregularities were so extensive that Jairo Bisol, a public defender with the Ministério Público, asserted that PSF in Brasília was synonymous with corruption (interview 2004).[29] Both federal and district audits of PSF concluded that the program was unoperational, that hiring practices had been based on political favoritism, and that many personnel were operating with incomplete teams (i.e., they lacked nurses or doctors). Investigations into allegations of fraud led the federal district to suspend the PSF program briefly. The suspension also coincided with the federal Ministry of Health suspension of PSF funds due to inquiries into improper use of health financing. When the program resumed, it did so under new leadership and with new personnel.

In Salvador, technocrats reported they faced very little interference when it came to hiring PSF personnel. But even so, "political interests" had impeded their ability to implement the family health program as they saw fit. Before establishing PSF in Salvador, staff members in the Health Department conducted a citywide epidemiological study and assessment of health services. Results from the study defined which districts should receive priority for PSF (i.e., which sanitarian districts should be served and in which order).[30] Though technocrats sought to follow their plan, they acknowledged that Secretary of Health Aldely Rocha, Mayor Antônio Imbassahy, and the "political leadership" had directed them to expand PSF territorially to include other parts of the city. So, it was not surprising that at an inaugural event for a PSF clinic in the neighborhood of Altos dos Coutos in June 2004, the ribbon-cutting event included dozens of the mayor's political allies. The mayor's political cronies (city and state officials, city council members, and candidates for elective office) gave speeches to the crowds massed near the health center.

That traditional conservative politicians, such as Roriz and Imbassahy, would continue to engage in "politics as usual" with PSF is not surprising; allegations of patronage and clientelism were certainly features of all their departments. But remarkably, PSF emulation decisions rarely came down to these electoral incentives. Most mayors who adopted the program delegated these policy decisions to their politically appointed senior staff. Cristovam Buarque gave his secretary of health, Maninha, wide latitude to emulate PSF (interview Conceição 2003). Mayor Imbassahy of Salvador was reluctant to embrace the program and did so only under pressure from health experts. Health policy specialists both inside and outside government asserted that Mayor Imbassahy was not involved in the decision to implement PSF in Salvador. Technocrats in the city's Department of Health noted that the mayor was skeptical about the program and preferred that the program's implementation proceed slowly. Marta Suplicy of São Paulo let her technical advisers decide how the city should recover from the debilitating experience with PAS. Even during the campaign for office her supporters were divided on whether to embrace PSF. In the early stages of the campaign, the PT-aligned think tank Instituto Florestan Fernandes sponsored meetings for health experts to debate the merits of PSF. Ultimately, key technocrats made the decision to endorse PSF for São Paulo (interview Manfredini 2003). Only Mayor Célio de Castro of Belo Horizonte was in the odd position of having embraced the program early on but without the administrative support to implement it (interview F. Santos 2004).[31] Since electoral incentives for PSF emulation offer a relatively weak explanation for the motivations behind policy enactment, we now turn to the two alternative explanations: ideology and social networks.

Ideology

Do actors' ideological commitments drive their emulation decisions? Do actors perceive this program to be "leftist" or "rightist," and if so, does the ideological meaning behind the program influence emulation decisions? While PSF does have equity-enhancing goals and reflects a reprioritization of basic and preventive services, actors' perceptions about the program and its ideological meaning changed over time. As the case studies reveal, mayors' ideological commitments mattered, as did those of their politically appointed technocrats and civil servants.

Mayors in each of the administrations had clear ideological tendencies, ranging from leftists to rightists (see table 5.1). In practice, mayors' ideological predispositions shaped the character of their administration. Senior appointed officials, such as municipal secretaries of health, were usually close political allies who shared the mayor's ideological views. Mayors also set the overall tone for their administration through budgetary allocations and championing their trademark programs. For instance, left and center-left mayors all championed education-related programs and emphasized the need to invert social spending to prioritize the needy and enhance "citizenship": Cristovam Buarque's trademark policy was Bolsa Escola, Lídice da Mata created the program Cidade Mãe, and Marta Suplicy created integrated "community schools" called Centros Educacionais Unificados (Unified Education Centers, CEU). Politicians on the right, on the other hand, emphasized business-oriented initiatives: Antônio Imbassahy highlighted tourism and business development, Joaquim Roriz championed construction of a bridge (Ponte Juscelino Kubitschek), and both Paulo Maluf and Celso Pitta defended the market-oriented health program PAS.

Although elected officials' ideological predispositions framed the range of options for health care, the most rampant ideological debates surrounding PSF occurred among technocrats and experts in public health. When PSF was first introduced in 1994, health policy specialists and activists associated with the *movimento sanitário* had mixed reactions to the policy. Their assessment of the program reflected broader debates in the international public health community over prevention, access, and prioritization of services. Many staunch leftists affiliated with the *movimento sanitário* in Brazil strongly embraced the goals asserted at the International Conference on Primary Health Care, held September 6–12, 1978.[32] The conference declaration, which was strongly influenced by a 1975 joint WHO/UNICEF report, *Alternative Approaches to Meeting Basic Health Needs in Developing Countries,* highlighted the limits of Western medicine and attributed the principal causes of morbidity in developing countries to "poverty, squalor, and ignorance" (Cueto 2004, 1866). The Alma Ata Declaration included the goals of "Health for All by the Year 2000" and reflected an ambitious effort to transform the entire health system. The holistic approach at Alma Ata linked public health issues with broader questions of development. It also challenged major assumptions about health care by emphasizing appropriate technology and calling for training lay health professionals. Implicitly, the declaration criticized advanced industrialized countries' approach to medicine with its emphasis on disease-oriented technology, overly specialized care, and elitist bias. The viewpoint articulated in the Alma Ata Declaration strongly resonated with many of the sanitarian movement's goals of prioritizing primary health care and engaging local communities.

While the Alma Ata Declaration provided a framework for many public health professionals worldwide, the international development community diverged in its approach to public health. The Rockefeller Foundation, along with UNICEF, articulated an alternative or "minimalist" approach in contrast to the Alma Ata Declaration. Instead of transforming the system, these actors favored small add-on programs. These institutions supported limited, short-term, and selective strategies best known as GOBI: growth monitoring, oral rehydration techniques, breast feeding, and immunization (Cueto 2004, 1869). From these international donors' point of view, this strategy offered the possibility of tracking measurable results through program monitoring and evaluation. Limiting efforts in selective primary care also helped these institutions avoid the political conflicts and the costs associated with the Alma Ata Declaration. In the Brazilian context, this approach certainly caught on: the PACS program in the northeast reflected modest GOBI strategies.

The international public health debate surrounding Alma Ata created two camps: one favored major transformation for universal primary care, while the other embraced complementary activities leading to selective primary care (Cueto 2004, 1869). Each set of approaches worked through long-standing linkages between international development organizations and Brazilian partners. For instance, the Rockefeller Foundation was one of the most important philanthropic organizations supporting public health, the control of epidemics, and medical research in Brazil during the twentieth century (Cueto 1990, 230–31).[33] Multilateral organizations such as the Pan-American Health Organization and UNICEF also established country offices in Brasília. The historic linkages between domestic public health officials and transnational actors were particularly strong because Brazil had made important advances in the study of tropical diseases; the country had established well-regarded schools of public health, most notably the Fundação Fio Cruz in Rio de Janeiro, and had a well-equipped school of medicine in São Paulo. For these reasons, the international debate about the proper scope of primary care was more than an abstract academic debate among international experts: the technical debate and ideological framework had a very strong effect on domestic public health experts who participated in these transnational networks.

As Brazilian public health experts debated the merits of PSF, their assessments often hinged on whether they saw PSF as reflecting the more radical universal primary care or neoliberal selective primary care. Many staunch leftists tended to embrace the holistic vision of Alma Ata and contested whether PSF was compatible with the declaration. Early critics of the program declared PSF a *programa pobre para pobre* (a poor program for the poor) and said it represented neoliberal policy (interview Junkeira 2003; interview La Forgia 2004). Staunch leftists initially opposed the program for several reasons. First, when the Ministry of Health introduced PSF it did so in a limited fashion, as one of several projects. Second, the program's design had been largely influenced by the PACS program—demonstrating a type of GOBI agenda—and had essentially served as an extension of it (Viana and Dal Poz 1998, 21). Since PACS was a predecessor of PSF, the earliest cities to adopt the family health program were in the northeast. This convinced some that PSF was intended as a targeted, rather than universal, approach to basic health. All this contributed to their belief that PSF was a "poor program for the poor." It would take years for the Ministry of Health to articulate its ambitious vision for PSF, namely that PSF could serve as a model to reorient primary health care for all.[34] Lastly, when José Serra led the Health Ministry (1998–2002), he made efforts to obtain supplemental funding for PSF from the World Bank. The implicit approval of PSF from the World Bank further convinced those actors that the program was a "World Bank program" representing Washington Consensus–style social policy.[35]

Nevertheless, other long-term public health experts associated with the *movimento sanitário* were quick to embrace the policy and argued that it was compatible with the Alma Ata Declaration. The policy coincided with their priorities to focus resources on primary care, centered on basic health and prevention. It also reflected previous sanitarian policy and public health initiatives that sought to build close community ties, dating back to the 1970s and 1980s.[36] Also important was that decentralization had created opportunities for many *sanitaristas* to put principles into practice. Those in the northeast were especially encouraged by the outcomes of both the PACS and PSF programs. Research suggested that these strategies could prevent the spread of cholera and lead to dramatic declines in infant and maternal mortality (Lima and Mangueira 2001; Mendonça et al. 2004; Mishima et al. 1999; Solla, Medina, and Dantas 1996). Leading participants who helped design the PSF also argued that the policy should be much more than an isolated program; actors such as Machado, F. Sousa, and Andrade wanted PSF to be the basis of a restructured primary health care system for all (interview Andrade 2004; interview Machado 2003).

Given these "mixed" signals about the program's broader aims, it is understandable that actors committed to universal primary care might balk at the PSF. But key actors, such as David Capistrano, Adib Jatene, and Luiz Odorico de Andrade, were crucial in convincing health experts that the program was compatible with full primary health coverage. Capistrano was a highly visible public health expert with ties to the Workers' Party. When he agreed to partner with Minister Jatene to implement a state-sponsored PSF program in São Paulo, he signaled his support for the model. In doing so, Capistrano recruited and converted skeptical leftists to believe the program was compatible with their values (interview Silveira 2003; Mattos 2003). Adib Jatene never affiliated with a political movement or party and had worked for both the rightist President Fernando Collor de Mello (PRN) and centrist President Fernando Henrique Cardoso (PSDB). As a result the former health minister enjoyed a solid reputation among technocrats for his deep commitment to Brazilian health care. His endorsement of the program carried special weight. Luiz Odorico de Andrade, a self-identified *sanitarista* who had formed part of the team to design PSF and later implemented it in Quixadá and Sobral in Ceará, also advocated for the program. Not only did he enthusiastically defend it within networks such as the National Council of Municipal Health Secretaries (CONASEMS), but he also created a training school for PSF and published the journal *SANARE: Revista Sobralense de Politicas Públicas* to showcase the program.[37] These individuals' activities caught the attention of many leftists and convinced them that PSF could represent a progressive transformation of Brazilian public health.

Surprisingly, rightist politicians largely stayed out of the ideological debate surrounding PSF. Some advocates of the program also sought to appeal to fiscal conservatives by suggesting that PSF could lead to greater economic efficiency given the rising costs of curative medicine in Brazil. The logic is that effective prevention can be more cost effective in the long term than expensive hospital-based treatment.[38] While publications by the World Bank (2004) support this general viewpoint, arguments for PSF based on potential cost-effectiveness gained little traction. Some advocates for the program were reluctant to promote it on economic grounds as they expected that full universal coverage of PSF would be costly (interview Andrade 2004). Though the actual cost of PSF is difficult to gauge, as operational costs are funded through federal transfers as well as municipal contributions, McGuire estimates that the per capita annual cost of PSF in 2000 was between US$34 and US$53, depending on the number and the composition of health teams (2010, 169).[39] However, it is difficult to place these figures into perspective for a cost-benefit analysis due to the lack of national data for comparing how PSF performs vis-à-vis the status quo (Macinko et al. 2007, 2079). Even so, neoliberal economic arguments based on the potential savings of preventive health care were largely absent from discussions, as most rightist politicians and technocrats declined to support PSF.

The development of health policy over three administrations in the city of São Paulo offers valuable insight into the ways ideology influenced emulation decisions. While most mayors delegated health policy issues to their secretaries of health, Mayor Maluf in São Paulo was unusually hands-on in selecting, advocating, and defending the PAS for the municipality. As was discussed earlier in this chapter, Mayors Paulo Maluf and Celso Pitta sought to implement their own public health policy for the city of São Paulo. The semiprivatized cooperative system was consistent with both mayors' conservative ideology, and Maluf held steadfast in defending the model against its earliest opponents.

From the outset, the PAS proposal fueled considerable debate and led to both legislative and judicial activity as various groups tried to block or support the implementation of the program. Various sectors, including some physicians, embraced the logic of doctor-controlled cooperatives and saw potential for greater financial and professional rewards. Others, including staunch leftists and activists in the sanitarian movement, were immediately critical of the plan. They preferred that municipal authorities seek universal coverage and access, as mandated by the Constitution; further, they argued that the nature of public health problems, such as communicable diseases, made private-sector solutions financially unsustainable.[40] Another concern among PAS opponents related to Maluf's electoral appeal with the public as someone who *rouba mas faz* (steals but gets things done). In other words, the mayor's widespread reputation for corruption led political opponents to anticipate that his health reform plan would serve as a vehicle for graft as well.[41]

Mayor Maluf announced the PAS on January 17, 1995, and moved to implement the program through decree in April of that year. However, the mayor encountered significant resistance to the plan, which delayed its start. City council members from the Workers' Party were among the most vocal opponents and sought to block the PAS through both judicial appeals and interventions in the city council. Ultimately, implementation of the PAS required city council approval, which it received, along partisan lines, on September 12, 1995.[42] Even though Paulo Maluf was nearing the end of his mayoral term and was ineligible for reelection, the city went ahead in instituting the PAS. When Celso Pitta, a political ally of Maluf's, won the 1996 election, he kept his campaign promise to maintain the PAS program during his administration.

Paulo Maluf's decision to adopt the PAS encountered resistance not only from actors within the city of São Paulo, but also from a host of external actors who appealed to him to reverse course. Minister Adib Jatene was personally interested in seeing the PSF program implemented in the city (interview Jatene 2003). Aside from the fact that the minister was a resident of São Paulo and took a special interest in it,

Jatene was also convinced that the program could have a positive effect; he had seen model PSF programs in northeastern cities and believed parts of São Paulo faced similar difficulties. He also wanted to see the program extended to the biggest metropolitan areas, such as Belo Horizonte, São Paulo, and Rio de Janeiro (Capistrano 1999). Therefore Minister Jatene reached out to Paulo Maluf on at least two occasions to appeal to him personally to enact PSF in São Paulo; but Maluf simply turned him down, citing other plans (interview Jatene 2003).

Minister Jatene refused to give up his goal of implanting PSF in São Paulo. Instead, he bypassed the municipal government and asked the governor of São Paulo state to install a state-run program within the city's borders. The center-left governor, Mário Covas (PSDB), agreed, and the state secretary of health, José da Silva Guedes, initiated a state-administered family health program within the city's borders called QUALIS (Qualidade Integral à Saúde). The program began in 1996 in the district of Itaquera, under a partnership agreement between the federal Ministry of Health, the State Department of Health, and the Santa Marcelina Hospital. In 1997 QUALIS expanded to São Lucas Park, Sapopemba, and the Nova Cachoeirinha district (Goldbaum et al. 2005).[43] To shepherd QUALIS, Adib Jatene selected a trusted advocate for public health with a solid reputation for commitment to primary health care: David Capistrano Filho. The selection of Capistrano was especially notable because of his high profile background and links to the leftist Workers' Party; he had been active in the *movimento sanitário,* was the former health secretary of the city of Bauru (1984–86), and was the former mayor of the city of Santos (1992–96).[44] As this episode suggests, Dr. Adib Jatene was firmly committed to PSF and was willing to work with politicians of all ideological stripes to get the program off the ground. But at least in the early years the minister found much greater receptivity for PSF among left and left-of-center politicians. Ultimately, it took the election of a leftist, Marta Suplicy, for the municipality of São Paulo to adopt the family health program.

In sum, the decision to implement PSF reflected the ideological beliefs of two sets of actors: mayors and their senior technical staff. Mayors who chose to implement the family health program were overwhelmingly leftist or center-left and had decided that the programmatic goals of working directly with patients in the community and of expanding access to primary health care were consistent with their core beliefs. In three of the four cities, PSF was introduced by left-of-center administrations, including Cristovam Buarque (PT) in Brasília, Célio de Castro (PSB) in Belo Horizonte, and Marta Suplicy (PT) in São Paulo. The only nonleftist to adopt the program was Mayor Imbassahy in Salvador, who according to technical staff did so unenthusiastically and with uncertainty about the program (interview Queiroz 2004; interview Nossa 2004).

A second set of key actors involved in emulation decisions was made up of politically appointed secretaries of health and their senior technical staff. In most instances, mayors selected secretaries who shared similar ideological beliefs and commitments. Leftist mayors were more likely to hire health secretaries and senior staff who self-identified as being part of the *movimento sanitário*. *Sanitaristas* adhered to similar leftist ideologies and used consistent rhetorical framing to discuss how they approached their work in health policy; these actors emphasized their identities, life experiences, and desire to "make a difference" through their work. They also described how the family health program reflected their values and beliefs by improving equity and access to health care and reversing the tide of government spending that had left out the poor. Even left-leaning administrators who initially opposed the PSF model on technical grounds, such as the senior health officials in Belo Horizonte, acknowledged that it was very difficult to oppose the program because the basic tenets of the program fit broader ideological appeals for equity, access, and meaningful linkages with the community (interview F. Santos 2004). Thus, left-leaning politicians and technocrats eventually embraced the family health program with the view that it was the best way for a democracy to deliver social policies that would address historic and long-standing inequality and create meaningful citizenship.

Social Networks

The health arena in Brazil has seen particularly robust civil society activity, which dates back to the mobilization efforts of the *movimento sanitário* during the 1970s and 1980s. The *sanitaristas* promoted the development of universal public health programs across the country, sent doctors far into the country's interior, published public health journals, promoted universal health care rights in the Constitution, and advocated for wider civic participation in policy making through decentralization. To broaden public debates and strengthen their agenda for public health (*saúde coletiva*), sanitarians founded the Centro Brasileiro de Estudos de Saúde (CEBES) in 1976. The organization was home to a wide array of different participants, including members of the sanitary movement, labor leaders in the health sector, women's groups, and individuals involved with other social movements. Importantly, CEBES members worked both within and outside of government. *Sanitaristas* would also create a second organization, Associação Brasileira de Pós-Graduação em Saúde Coletiva (ABRASCO), in 1979. While this organization had parallel origins, it was primarily academic and focused on postgraduate studies in public health. Institutionally ABRASCO served as a space for research, discussion of policy models, dissemination of information, and the generation of model reforms (Abrantes and Almeida 2002, 21; Escorel 1999). Though the sanitarian movement has since dissipated as a single entity, its legacy remains in these health care organizations and professional associations it helped establish. Given the vibrancy of associational life in the health arena and the central role that PSF took in primary health care debates, it is not surprising that these programs responded to proposed changes in primary health delivery. Both ABRASCO and CEBES have been at the forefront of the debate about the program's quality at conferences, meetings, and through publications.

Since the inception of PSF, health professionals in Brazilian municipalities have had frequent opportunities to assess the policy through the sector's numerous professional associations. Technocrats had access to official publications from the Ministry of Health but more often turned to other sources for the latest information in their field. PSF administrators, for instance, consistently identified ABRASCO and CONASEMS as important associations and cited the journal *Saúde em Debate,* published by CEBES, as a key reference.[45] The CEBES publication served as a forum for debate on the programs, including critiques, as well as case studies from the northeast, where authors detailed the merits of PSF. CONASEMS's annual conferences also became an important meeting ground for local health officials. When PSF was first introduced in the mid-1990s, most members were skeptical of the program. Yet within ten years most of the participants reported that they had adopted PSF. This turnaround also extended to academic circles, and by 2003 ABRASCO's annual meeting included fifty-nine paper presentations on PSF alone.

What brought about the turnaround of opinion on PSF? First, these organizations effectively brought together individuals from across the country and provided a forum for PSF promoters to advocate for the program. The regional diversity of professionals was crucial because so many proponents were from the northeast, and they might otherwise have been shut out of policy debates typically dominated by southeastern professionals.[46] They had been the most resistant to the family health model. Networks of professionals trained in Saúde Coletiva at UNICAMP, located in São Paulo, were also deeply skeptical of its appropriateness for the entire country (for example, see interview F. Santos 2004; interview Franco 2004; interview Junkeira 2003). This northeastern perspective was crucial because PSF had created obvious concrete benefits, convincing evidence of the policy's merits. Second, the health sector and its professional associations were composed of persons with different political affiliations, many of whom were willing to work across partisan lines. Formal networks, such as CONASEMS, ABRASCO, and the municipal, state, and national health councils, drew in participants across a broad ideological spectrum. Informal networks were also highly influential and operated through personal ties. A notable example of such collaboration applies to two leading figures in the medical profession, former minister Adib Jatene and David Capistrano Filho; both men worked for administrations with very different ideological profiles, yet they worked together to promote a pilot PSF program in São Paulo.[47] This partnership was highly influential, as Jatene drew on his extensive network in the specialized medical field, and Capistrano tapped his network of leftist public health officials. Lastly, several high-profile administrators began to show that PSF need not represent "a poor program for the poor." Several municipalities demonstrated that PSF could be an all-encompassing strategy for basic health services and could provide coverage for the entire population. In these ways, professional associations connected individuals, filtered information to their members, and shaped their views and professional norms.

Given the rich and overlapping networks associated with health policy, it is not surprising that administrators offered sophisticated and consistent analyses for why they wanted to adopt PSF. Technocrats frequently invoked similar explanations for the benefits of the program, including a belief that Brazil should focus on preventive medicine, a determination to engage directly with communities, and the conviction that basic medicine should move away from doctor-centric models. In some cases, albeit not all, technocrats specifically mentioned the Alma Ata conference as having articulated an important set of goals. Others mentioned the ground-breaking VIII Conferência Nacional de Saúde, held in March 1986, which demanded that the state provide universal health care as a basic social right. Although a few policy makers expressed skepticism about the program's applicability for their cities and even discussed the ways they tried to block the program, they acknowledged that in ten years the PSF model had become the professional norm in their field (interview Franco 2004; interview F. Santos 2004). This helps explain why eventually cities like Salvador and Belo Horizonte adopted PSF. In Salvador, city health administrators acknowledged with some discomfort that they were relatively "late" in adopting PSF and that several nearby cities were ahead of them in implementing "model" programs (interview Queiroz 2004; interview Nossa 2004). The sheer density of health care associations and their ability to shape professional norms thus helps explain the phenomenal spread of PSF across the country.

Although formal overlapping networks tell us a great deal about professional socialization, it is also important to acknowledge the ways in which informal networks provided individual policy makers with wide-ranging connections and convinced them to initiate change. Often the informal networks revolved around personal relationships. For instance, Adib Jatene first met David Capistrano Filho in 1979 when he served as state secretary of health in São Paulo and Capistrano was a *sanitarista* working for the state's public health agency (Jatene 2000).[48]

Over the years, Jatene had taken note of Capistrano's accomplishments in Bauru and Santos, and quickly identified him as a natural choice for director of QUALIS. In selecting Capistrano, Jatene chose someone who held tremendous influence within the political left and the movement. Capistrano became an important spokesperson for the PSF program, persuading many skeptical colleagues of the merits of the policy and arguing that PSF was not a "poor program for the poor."[49] On an individual level, Capistrano connected informally with countless actors in the health policy arena and convinced them that PSF was an appropriate model for primary health delivery, even in the largest metropolitan areas (interview Silveira 2003; interview Gouvea 2003; interview Manfredini 2003; interview R. Santos 2003).[50]

In addition to the personal contacts that drew actors to learn about PSF, other informal opportunities arose for learning and socialization. For instance, when technical staff at the Ministry of Health wanted to promote PSF, they strategically identified influential staff members in different cities and invited them to visit a "model" city. They believed that once visitors saw how effective the program was, they would be motivated to adopt it in their own hometowns and would advocate for it with their supervisors (interview M. F. Sousa 2003). For instance, around 1995 and 1996 the ministry sent key actors in the federal district to the northeast to visit model PSF programs (interview M. F. Sousa 2003). One of these individuals went to Recife in the state of Pernambuco to see how city administrators had adopted PSF; she later advocated for it with Health Secretary Maninha (interview Peixinho 2004). This type of experience was also crucial for São Paulo's Secretary of Health Eduardo Jorge Martins Alves, who credits his enthusiasm for the program to having seen PSF firsthand in the northeast as a member of Congress (interview Martins Alves 2004).

In these ways social and professional networks, both formal and informal, played an important role in transmitting ideas and shaping new norms. When individuals were socialized to believe that a particular policy represented "the model" in their field, they were especially eager to adopt a similar approach, lest they fall behind their peers. This dynamic was particularly true for the family health program, which was embraced by the dense and overlapping health networks. Interviews with Brazilian policy makers in all four cities revealed that social and professional networks prompted individuals to influence the policy agenda by proposing new programs. Social network connectivity was thus a necessary component for policy diffusion to occur.

Controlling for Fiscal Transfers

Though the Ministry of Health had an important role in promoting the Programa Saúde da Família, the impact of its fiscal transfers on diffusion is mixed. Thus, these transfers cannot rightfully be seen as a motivating cause for actors' desires to adopt PSF. Starting in the mid-1990s, a few administrators in the ministry began advocating for a preventive health approach, represented in PSF. Programa Saúde da Família eventually evolved from a small isolated project embedded precariously in the bureaucracy to an established division in the ministry that would eventually reorganize basic health care policy around the program's design. By the late 1990s, the ministry began providing line-item fiscal transfers for cities that chose to adopt the program.[51] Funds from the ministry constituted partial financing, essentially matching grants on a per-team basis, and were structured to encourage small municipalities to achieve total coverage of their population quickly (World Bank 2002, 46).

Despite the opportunity to gain access to resources through PSF, many mayors and city administrators refused to institute the program. In São Paulo, Mayor Paulo Maluf rejected federal funds and a personal appeal from Minister Adib Jatene to introduce PSF (interview Jatene 2003). Throughout the 1990s, health administrators in Belo Horizonte were skeptical of the PSF model and refused to implement it, despite losing federal resources. Ironically, technocrats affiliated with both the Cristovam Buarque and Joaquim Roriz administrations in Brasília reported that they implemented PSF despite *not* having received regular earmarked funding from the federal government; both sets of officials claimed that political rivalries between officials in the federal and district governments led to irregular funding.[52] As for other city administrations, officials from Belo Horizonte, Brasília, and São Paulo all explained that, once they chose to adopt PSF, they appreciated the "extra" PSF financing. However, they also emphasized that the program was still very expensive to operate; the fiscal transfers alone were insufficient to motivate them to adopt the program because the costs far exceeded the transfers.[53] Officials from Salvador were the only program administrators to cite their policy choices as a reaction to "directives from the federal Ministry of Health." Though partly responding to the transfers, they also acknowledged they were "behind" other neighboring cities and needed to respond to the new paradigm.

Conclusion

Throughout much of the 1990s, when the federal government struggled to define health care reform, municipal governments became laboratories for experimentation and innovation in basic health. Cities like Niterói and Londrina were inspired by leftist primary health care models and drew on Cuba's family doctor model. In São Paulo, the mayor favored a more conservative approach that integrated public-private partnerships. Others embraced a nascent model that integrated community health with teams of health care professionals, called Programa Saúde da Família. Most importantly, this period of experimentation demonstrates that for municipalities across Brazil, issues of basic health care delivery were far from clear or automatic. Rather, politicians and technical health policy staff debated the merits of different programs and made calculated decisions about which policies to adopt.

Contrary to conventional wisdom in political science, which emphasizes neoclassical behavioral assumptions that individuals pursue their own self-interest, the actors in this study did not emulate PSF for electoral gain. In other words, there is no evidence that mayors adopted the family health program for the purpose of winning an election. Instead, most emulation decisions were delegated to politically appointed staff and highly specialized health experts capable of assessing the ideological and technical merits of the program. In the few instances where rightist politicians came to embrace PSF for its political benefits, they did so belatedly and after staff members had initiated the policy's emulation. This finding is remarkable given that PSF easily lends itself to clientelism and patronage politics on the part of mayors.

As this chapter argues, actors' motivations in adopting PSF were largely driven by two factors: ideological commitments to social justice, and desires to keep up with evolving professional norms. Although these factors were consistently important for all the case studies, actors' ideological interpretations of PSF changed over time. Staunch leftists had to analyze and interpret the PSF to determine whether it was consistent with their ideological commitments, and in many cases their assessments evolved. Professional and informal social networks were often important features of this process because they reinforced actors' ideological commitments. In other words, professional networks such as CEBES, ABRASCO, and CONASEMS created opportunities for professionals in different jurisdictions to learn about PSF and debate the program's merits and meaning. Informal networks and friendship ties were also important among leftist politicians and technocrats. When key opinion leaders such as David Capistrano Filho and Eduardo Jorge Martins Alves embraced the family health program, it served as an important signal for others that the policy was consistent with their leftist ideological commitments. Next, we will further explore how ideology and social norms operate together to spur emulation decisions, drawing on evidence from PSF and Bolsa Escola.

CHAPTER 6

Conclusion

Ideology and Social Networks

In Brazil, democratization and decentralization ushered in an era of experimentation by local governments that sought to address long-standing challenges in education and health care. Many politicians and policy experts throughout the country embraced equity-enhancing reform and thereby participated in new diffusion processes. What drives the spread of model reforms among Brazil's local governments? This research tests three distinct approaches to understanding individuals' motivations for emulating innovative social policies in Brazil. Each corresponds to distinct analytic research traditions found in political science and sociology and reflects the disciplines' paradigmatic response to questions of what drives political behavior. Do actors follow conventional rational choice assumptions about electoral self-interest and pursue social policies to win elections and political influence? Or do politicians make policy choices regardless of self and others and emulate policies because of their deep-seated ideological commitments? Alternatively, do actors respond to a community of shared norms and emulate policies to demonstrate to their peers that they are in line with their profession's latest trends? To answer these questions, this study draws on both statistical and qualitative evidence to uncover the process by which actors make emulation decisions for social sectors reforms.

This chapter unifies the statistical and case study analyses presented earlier to provide a theory for the motivational determinants of local social sector diffusion. First, we will consider how actors in the case study cities and in the larger statistical sample drew on ideological and sociological motivations for emulation. By comparing trends in education and health care reforms, we see how these factors worked both in isolation and together to provide mutually reinforcing effects. Next, we will explore the policy consequences of the diffusion of local social sector models from the 1990s. As programs like Bolsa Escola and PSF gained recognition as good governance models, both within Brazil and internationally, the federal government made strides to expand in these areas. We will examine recent trends in poverty relief and health care access and potential implications for the gendered construction of citizenship in Brazil. Finally, we will consider the implications of this research for the development of theories of diffusion.

A Motivational Approach for the Diffusion of Social Sector Reforms

The diffusion of education and health reforms across Brazil demonstrates similar causal mechanisms that explain why actors are motivated to emulate them. Remarkably, the statistical and case study evidence reveals similar findings, despite differences between qualitative and quantitative research designs. Figure 6.1 provides a visual representation of the theoretical findings of this study. A more in-depth analysis of each factor, as well evidence from Bolsa Escola and PSF emulation, follows.

A political self-interest approach offers an intuitively appealing explanation for the spread of social policies in Brazil. This rationale speaks directly to rational choice assumptions about actors' determination to pursue their electoral aims to gain reelection and increase their political power; it thus represents both the theoretical and instinctive conventional wisdom. In political science, the assumption of rationality is one of the principal ways researchers have sought the regularity nec-

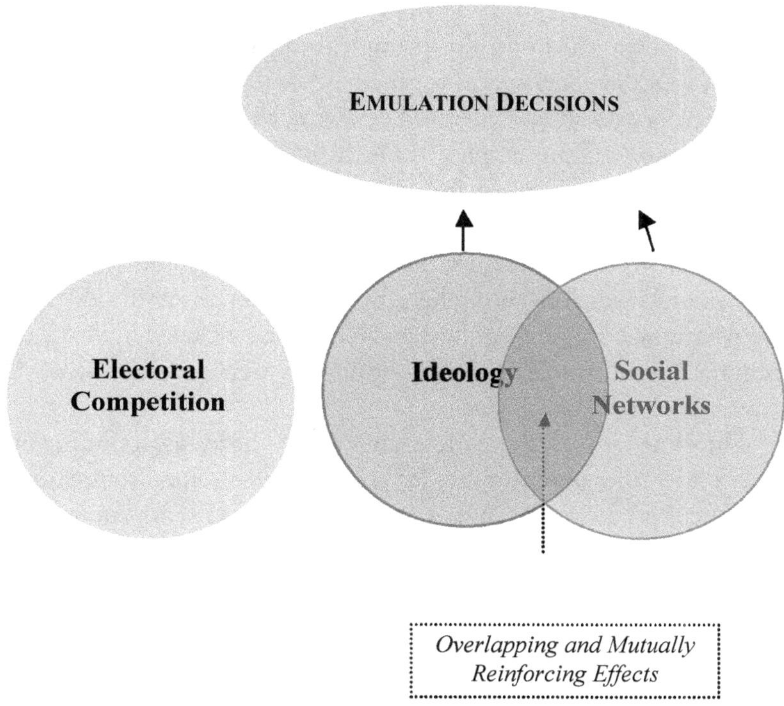

Figure 6.1. Explaining Social Policy Diffusion: A Motivational Approach

essary for generalization (Riker and Ordeshook 1973, 11). So, a surprising finding is that electoral competition fails to explain actors' motivations for social policy emulation.

As we saw in chapters 3, 4, and 5, politicians rarely make emulation decisions as vehicles to advance their electoral political agenda. Certainly, the pressure to win elections and distinguish oneself from one's competitor is crucially important in the Brazilian municipal arena. Campaigning on the provision of these social programs can offer a clear opportunity to gain votes. Mayors Cristovam Buarque, Marta Suplicy, and Célio de Castro all campaigned on their intention to implement either Bolsa Escola or PSF. Once in place, these programs offer the potential for significant electoral payoffs. Mayors and their staffers can, if they so desire, target benefits to those voters more likely to support them in future municipal elections. For example, campaign staffers could seek out Bolsa Escola beneficiaries for their votes. In the case of health reform, mayors who adopt PSF could designate which neighborhoods are served by the program or who will be hired to fill sought-after posts. Do some neighborhoods get full coverage of PSF while others do not? Which neighborhoods get new PSF facilities? Some executives do indeed use these electioneering strategies. For instance, under the administration of Mayor Antônio Imbassahy in Salvador, the political leadership determined which neighborhoods should be included in the health program. Often the favored neighborhoods were not those with the greatest epidemiological needs.

For some mayors, these programs can be politically appealing not because they offer opportunities for policy-based electoral competition, but rather because they can perpetuate "politics as usual" through patronage and corruption. Of the two reforms examined in this study, the family health program is the most vulnerable to corruption and electoral machinations, because PSF includes the hiring of new personnel and the power behind job creation offers the opportunity for significant political payoffs. The community health agent job under PSF is an especially desirable position among the lower classes because it requires relatively little education or background in health care; often the only requirements are residency in the neighborhood served and demonstration of leadership skills. Community health agents also have tremendous access to potential voters because of their jobs. Thus, they can serve as important conduits between politicians and voters.[1] Other jobs, for nurse's aides, nurses, and doctors, are also highly coveted, with decent pay scales. At the time of this research, most cities hired health care professionals for PSF on an ad hoc basis and with temporary contracts that lacked the protections offered through the civil service. Since this approach offers tremendous potential for patronage, I fully expected political mayoral interference. Of the cases of PSF adoption, the administration of Joaquim Roriz in Brasília was the most notorious for irregularities related to the PSF, as investigations into widespread corruption and the misuse of funds unveiled (interview Bisol 2004). This suggests that while the expectation that political self-interest drives policy decisions is reasonable, there is very little evidence to support it across the board.

Despite some of the electoral benefits that Bolsa Escola or PSF entail, there is a wealth of evidence that for the most part mayors and their political staff did not seek to replicate these programs for self-interested electoral or economic gains. As the event history models reveal, greater electoral competition does not explain the likelihood that Bolsa Escola or PSF will diffuse. Moreover, the degree of electoral competition does not explain differences in adoption for the 224 largest cities. The case studies reinforce these findings in several ways. Politicians in this study rarely used these programs to leverage votes and or other forms of political support. For instance, I found no evidence that politicians engaged in targeted campaigning of mothers who received a conditional cash transfer. Nor was there widespread patronage and clientelism with the family health program. Citizen watchdog groups and public prosecutors did investigate accusations of malfeasance with the PSF program under Governor Roriz in 2003–4, but blatant corruption was not a common feature of the program in other cities.

If politics as usual—patronage, corruption, and other vote-buying practices—was not the motivation for social sector reform, were politicians responding to general demand from the electorate? Here the evidence suggests that elected officials did not appear to enact Bolsa Escola and PSF as part of a electoral response from voters. Though Bolsa Escola received widespread media coverage, none of the cities had citizen groups demanding that candidates or incumbent mayors adopt Bolsa Escola. In addition, citizen delegates who served on local health councils rarely advocated introducing PSF; if anything they were resistant to the program and wary that it would not result in improved services. The populations served by PSF were unfamiliar with the program, and they still viewed clinics and hospitals—not PSF health teams—as appropriate places to go to for their health care needs. This general tendency certainly makes sense. For the poor and most vulnerable voters who are dependent on the state's provision of basic social services, it would be challenging for them to propose specific policy solutions from elsewhere. Instead, citizens would call for improvement in the quality of schools or better access to health care. City officials responsible for adopting PSF would often have to persuade citizens and local health councils that the program would be an improvement. Thus, the adoption of Bolsa Escola and PSF often took place in the absence of electoral "demand."

A final set of actors to consider includes those who served as senior political advisers and politically appointed technocrats who served as high-ranking experts in the fields of education and health. My interviews with secretaries of education and of health and other senior program administrators revealed that few identified their emulation decisions as reflective of an electoral political agenda. Policy experts instead focused on the merits of the reform and the technical challenges they faced in implementing the program. For instance, Bolsa Escola could increase school attendance, but technocrats were also concerned that by incorporating previously marginalized and failing students into the system, other performance indicators could decline. The complications were even greater for those administrations that adopted PSF because doing so required reorganizing health services, updating facilities, conducting new training, and formulating new relationships with patients. For many cities, adopting PSF also involved assuming responsibility for services that were previously in the hands of state governments. Technocrats thus focused on the details of implementing reforms given the unique realities of their cities. The process was often complex, and health experts would often report that they had not yet reached their operational goals because of difficulties related to training, recruiting personnel, and retaining staff. From a technocratic point of view, emulation of these programs involved great administrative complexity. A further challenge included the potential that political interference through patronage and clientelism could hinder their administrative goals. For these reasons, many experts did not advocate for these reforms to politicians as a sure bet for winning elections.

Electoral competition thus provides a deficient explanation for understanding social policy diffusion. These cities had competitive municipal elections with hotly contested campaigns, but mayoral campaigns did not drive the selection of the public policies or the speed at which policy replication occurred. Mayors adopted these policies when there was little demand even knowing that there was a chance the policies could fail to provide positive results by the next election.

Since electoral interests cannot convincingly explain emulation decisions, we need to turn to other motivational explanations. If conventional rational choice explanations based on electoral competition cannot account for the diffusion of social sector reforms, what role, if any, does ideology play in motivating individuals into action? Did policy innovations spread across cities governed by mayors on both the left and right? Or do only individuals with certain ideological commitments feel compelled to adopt programs such as Bolsa Escola and PSF? Do political actors make decisions to implement programs because they are strongly motivated by their ideological beliefs, even when these choices appear politically inexpedient?

As the case studies and event history analyses reveal, leftist politicians were much more likely to adopt Bolsa Escola and PSF, whereas both centrist and right-wing mayors were unlikely to do so. Leftist ideology mattered not only to mayors, but also to technocrats and political appointees, such as secretaries of education and health. Staff members regularly displayed their ideologically driven preferences and discussed their policy choices in relation to their values and beliefs. In nearly every case of program adoption, technocrats, political appointees, and elected officials who self-identified as leftist discussed these programs with similar rhetoric. These individuals invoked comparable themes and concepts to explain program emulation; one common description was their desire to address a "social deficit" and prioritize funding to alleviate social inequality. Another theme was the construction of "citizenship" and the view that education and health care were important social rights. In other words, for these actors, full citizenship rights in democratic Brazil included the state's obligation to fulfill basic social services.

Though ideology played a central role in emulation decisions, ideological interpretations of these programs were not static. Bolsa Escola was quickly embraced by left-of-center politicians who found the policy consistent with their own ideological convictions and priorities. This was very different with respect to PSF; many leftist health policy specialists were initially skeptical about the program and wondered whether the PSF was really aligned with their ideological commitments. In this case, many health policy experts consistently expressed their leftist beliefs, but it took time for them to assess whether PSF was consistent with their commitment to universal primary care. Over time, the family health program emerged as the new professional norm and "late adopting" cities with rightist mayors, such as Mayor Imbassahy, also came to replicate the program.

As we saw in chapter 5, health policy specialists on the left found PSF's mission laudable, but they had to reconcile its potential with other information that caused cognitive dissonance. For instance, although the program sought to advance health care access for the poorest, most vulnerable, and socially excluded groups, other features of the policy seemed to be inconsistent with leftist values. Some actors identified signals that the policy might reflect more conservative neoliberal values. Since the family health program had followed in the footsteps of an earlier program targeted to the poor, rural northeast, some leftists described PSF as a "poor program for the poor." During Fernando Henrique Cardoso's administration, Health Minister José Serra also approached the World Bank about financing for the program. That the World Bank was open to supporting the program's expansion served as evidence to some that the policy was a Washington Consensus project. On the other hand, well-known leftist David Capistrano Filho supported PSF by prominently advocating for it. Many progressive health policy advocates had to sort through these mixed messages and interpret the policy for themselves. In practice, this meant that the PSF program was subject to a longer review process by politicians and their technical advisers to determine whether it was consistent with their ideological beliefs. Left-of-center ideological commitments mattered for both policy domains and were consistently important. Yet actors' leftist ideology alone fails to account for an all-inclusive explanation of social policy emulation. Rather, networks were crucial in making leftists see PSF as compatible with their ideology. To uncover how education and health policy experts came to embrace the program, we now turn to the role that social networks played in shaping professional norms, socializing actors, and motivating them to seek legitimacy in relation to their peers.

Social networks played an important role in motivating actors across Brazil to emulate Bolsa Escola and PSF. At the most basic level, they provide actors with knowledge about their profession's latest trends. In this sense, networks operated as conduits of information. But more importantly for a study that focuses on actors' motivations, networks also socialized actors. When professional networks provided space for debate, evaluated policies, and declared those policies successful or "innovative," they went beyond "information exchange" to place a value on that information. Interviews with politicians and technocrats in Brazil revealed that most actors were embedded in various forms of associational life. These actors often discussed their work with their peers—that is, they stated whether they were proudly ahead of the curve, were quick to notice the latest developments, or were embarrassed to be behind their peers and were thus late adopters. Municipal policy makers in both Bolsa Escola and PSF policy domains consistently referred to their peers, suggesting that they sought to keep up "with the Joneses," especially when the Joneses were highly regarded innovators. In framing their work in this manner, actors sought the legitimacy to be gained from their colleagues; when individuals were linked to social networks, their emulation decisions were driven by social norms and other-regarding motivations.

Social networks mattered in shaping actors' quests to gain legitimacy. First, professional associations were crucial for most technocrats and a few politicians who held close ties to their profession. These associations were fundamental conduits for socialization and information exchange across geographical space. As Friedkin notes (as cited in Kilduff and Tsai 2003, 58), professional networks are important because they link people who have similar functional roles but who might otherwise be isolated and lack peers within their jurisdiction. Second, informal associations such as neighborhood and friendship ties also mattered, but these sprouted up in more idiosyncratic and less predictable ways. Differences between education and health policy arenas explain how the structure, scope, and density of professional networks can influence emulation decisions. So, we turn next to uncovering the differences in social network activity, both formal and informal, related to Bolsa Escola and PSF emulation.

As chapter 4 explains, Bolsa Escola represented a hybrid program that embraced both educational achievement and poverty alleviation. As a result of these complementary aims, the program never found a home in a single policy domain. Some cities housed their programs in departments of education, such as Brasília and Belo Horizonte; others did so in departments of public assistance, as in, for example, Campinas; yet others created new agencies, as in the case of São Paulo; or they entered into private-public partnerships, as was the case with Salvador. While the program had clear links to education and set goals related to increasing school attendance and decreasing grade repetition, it never captured the center of the education sector's professional agenda. Rather, Bolsa Escola's main advocates were general policy practitioners interested in innovative public policies, not education specialists. In general, the professional associations in education were lukewarm toward the education grant program, and traditional teachers' unions were uneasy about losing resources. For these reasons it took a generalist network of policy practitioners associated with the Gestão Pública e Cidadania network to stimulate actors' desires for emulation.

Even if professional organizations in the education sector had formally embraced Bolsa Escola, there would still be important differences between the education and health sectors. Unlike the situation in the field of public health, advocates for progressive socially inclusive education had never formed a large-scale social movement during the democratic transition. While university students did join prodemocracy movements, their activities did not serve as the foundation for primary and secondary educational reforms. Nor would student groups plant the seeds for long-standing education associations, as was the case with the sanitary movement. Much of the depth and breadth found in today's health sector associations, including organizations such as ABRASCO, CEBES, and CONASEMS, dates back to early organizing by *sanitaristas*. Today, these public health associations serve an important role in bringing together influential health policy technocrats, creating opportunities for learning, socialization, and informal exchanges.

The evidence from the event history analysis and case studies also reveals that informal networks promoted policy diffusion, albeit in less consistent and more idiosyncratic ways. In the case of PSF, strong regional effects influenced adoption decisions; states farthest from the early adopting region of the northeast were least likely to emulate PSF. In interviews, technocrats also identified which neighboring cities were ahead of the curve, and many technocrats who promoted the program said they did so after personally visiting innovative programs (see, for instance, interview Martins Alves 2004; interview Peixinho 2004). Although regional effects did not promote Bolsa Escola diffusion, informal relationships did. Policy makers involved with Bolsa Escola often mentioned learning about the program through colleagues and meetings. One notable example offered by Mayor Lídice da Mata is illustrative: she first learned about Renda Mínima at a meeting where the mayor of Campinas made a presentation (interview 2004).

In these ways, politicians and especially technocrats responsible for social policy development were strongly influenced by their informal and professional associations. PSF spread quickly because of the health sector's dense social and professional networks, which shaped experts' desire to keep up with new professional norms. The education sector, by contrast, has far fewer formal organizations, explaining the relatively slow pace of Bolsa Escola and Renda Mínima diffusion. Though informal networks mattered, their effects were more haphazard and weaker than those produced through formal professional channels. As the analysis shows, social policy diffusion at the municipal level was strongly influenced by two motivational factors: first, actors' ideological commitments and deep-seated desires to enact policies that were consistent with their leftist worldviews; and second, actors' quest for professional legitimacy and desire to demonstrate to peers that they were keeping up with professional norms. Each of these motivational approaches is treated separately in this study for conceptual clarity. Yet these motivational factors need not operate in isolation; in fact, the case studies reveal that at times ideology and social networks work together and display mutually reinforcing effects. For a select number of politicians and politically appointed technocrats, both these motivations operated together and in complementary ways. The analysis of Bolsa Escola and PSF emulation offers clarification in this regard.

On occasion, like-minded leftist politicians participated in meetings that not only introduced them to new social policy ideas, but also helped them interpret these policies as progressive solutions to social exclusion. This type of serendipitous event was important for Bolsa Escola diffusion; Mayor Lídice da Mata in Salvador met with Campinas's mayor, Magalhães Teixeira, at an event and there learned about the Renda Mínima program (interview Mata 2004). Similarly, Belo Horizonte city councilman Rogério Correia said that as a former educator and Workers' Party representative, he took an interest in Cristovam Buarque's education proposals in Brasília (interview 2004). Partisan meetings created opportunities for social networking among officials who shared ideological beliefs. These meetings also gave mayors a sense of trends in local governance as their colleagues presented information on their most innovative practices. These networking events served a similar function as professional network meetings for technocrats, except that it was mayors who sought to gain legitimacy and recognition from their peers.

In the case of PSF, social networks and ideology worked together in slightly different ways; in this instance, health policy technocrats and politically appointed health secretaries found that professional networks could assist them in evaluating the merits of the policy in ideological terms. Many leftist health experts rejected the family health program in the early years of its enactment in Brazil. It was not that they were unfamiliar with it, but rather they experienced cognitive dissonance between their ideological commitment to expanding universal primary care and PSF's more limited design. For example, left-leaning technocrats working in Belo Horizonte and São Paulo wanted universal access for primary health care and worried that PSF was a poor program for the poor—that is, a bandage approach to offering services in areas that lacked basic health infrastructure rather than a full coverage program with similar strategies across class lines (interview Junkeira 2003; interview F. Santos 2004; interview Franco 2004). They argued that their cities had already made important strides in the municipalization of health care services and needed to concentrate on strengthening the existing health care network rather than adopt PSF and create parallel points of entry for services (interview F. Santos 2004; interview Franco 2004). While these individuals retained their doubts about PSF, they also acknowledged that the left had not identified and articulated an alternative to PSF that was consistent with their values and beliefs. Crucial to the ideological debate surrounding PSF were discussions of its coverage. PSF advocates noted that the program was part of a broader strategy and should cover the entire population, not just residents in poor neighborhoods. Thus, discussions over universal territorial coverage helped convince many committed leftists that the program could further their goals of universal primary care.

Both informal and formal networks operated in reinforcing ways to persuade technocrats of the merits of the family health program. First, professional networks, such as CEBES, ABRASCO, and CONASEMS, became venues for debating the merits and limits of the family health model and its integration into the public health system. Journal publications and meetings sponsored by these organizations were consistently cited by technocrats in the adopting cities as influential in the evolution of their thinking around PSF. As a national organization, CONASEMS helped shed light on the innovations from the northeast and brought together municipal health secretaries from across the country. Second, informal networks through interpersonal ties among actors proved to be critically important. When well-traveled and nationally recognized public health experts such as Adib Jatene, David Capistrano, and Luiz Odorico de Andrade endorsed the program, the larger public health community took notice. Many technocrats cited these individuals as important opinion-makers and said they were more willing to evaluate the merits of this approach after hearing that these individuals were strong advocates. Another form of person-to-person contact that reinforced the socialization process took place through field visits. For instance, the Ministry of Health invited key municipal actors as well as members of Congress to visit well-regarded PSF programs in the northeast—for example, Camaragibe in the state of Pernambuco—so they could see for themselves how the program worked; the ministry's view was that the program would sell itself once people had a chance to see it in practice (interview M. F. Sousa 2003). This type of personal exposure was crucial in persuading São Paulo's secretary of health under Marta Suplicy, Eduardo Jorge Martins Alves, that PSF could work (interview Martins Alves 2004). Finally, as the event history model would suggest, weak ties among individuals who operate in geographic clusters were also important. For instance, program directors in Salvador referenced learning from experiences in Camaçari and Vitoria da Conquista (interview Queiroz 2004; interview Nossa 2004); in Belo Horizonte administrators referenced neighboring Betim (interview Franco 2004); and Santos was an important point of reference in São Paulo (interview Gouvea 2003). Field research thus reveals the importance of multiple and overlapping types of social networks; formal associations provided venues for information gathering and socialization while informal personal ties reinforced the legitimacy of new approaches. Thus, we see that the dense and overlapping networks in the public health field played a significant role in convincing technocrats that PSF was the new "norm" and helped them persuade reluctant mayors, especially leftists, that the reform would further their ideological commitment to progressive health care.

To summarize, the conventional political incentives approach, which assumes rationality and emphasizes individuals' pursuit of their electoral self-interest, failed, surprisingly, to explain social policy diffusion in Brazil. Many early adopters of these models embraced the programs for technical reasons, and senior health administrators had to persuade elected officials that doing so was consistent with their values and beliefs. Thus, the central theoretical finding of this study is that ideology and socialized norms drove individuals' decision making and their desires to replicate new policy models in Brazil. Technocrats with strong professional ties, on the other hand, consistently cited their profession's norms and their commitment to following the latest trends and models, regardless of partisan politics.[2] The speed and extent of policy diffusion were tied to the density of professional networks.

This study draws on two diffusion traditions to examine the spread of social policies across Brazilian municipalities. Although research on diffusion extends to multiple social science disciplines, there is a notable divide between those scholars who employ qualitative methods and those who use advanced statistical analysis. Researchers who draw largely on qualitative methods and process tracing tend to embrace more constructivist, or interpretative, approaches to diffusion that emphasize emulation, learning, "policy transfer," and norms (see, for instance, C. Bennett 1991; Evans 2004; Finnemore 1996; Weyland 2007;

Mossberger 2000). By contrast, scholars who employ statistical analyses with a large number of cases tend to embrace more rationalist assumptions about actors' strategic behavior in making adoption decisions (see, for instance, Berry and Berry 1992; Mooney 2001; Simmons and Elkins 2004). Event history models can also analyze broader trends, including the ability to understand the risks or likelihood that a given jurisdiction will adopt a policy.

While Mahoney and Goertz (2006) suggest that qualitative and quantitative research should be undertaken separately because each is marked by its own values, assumptions, and presuppositions, this work embraces the view that these methods can be complementary in explaining policy diffusion processes. The large-n component of this study not only captures diffusion trends in social policy adoption, but also allows for greater generalization of causality (King, Keohane, and Verba 1994). The event history findings provide a probabilistic interpretation of the likelihood that a jurisdiction adopts either Bolsa Escola or PSF. The qualitative case studies offer in-depth analyses of the mechanisms that lead to diffusion. Process tracing also allows for the possibility of causal heterogeneity and importantly clarifies policy makers' motivations for emulating Bolsa Escola and PSF. Although both methods produce similar explanations for the motivations that drive policy makers' adoption of these social policies, it is worthwhile to explore the differences and similarities between the qualitative and quantitative findings.

An important distinction between the two methods employed in this work relates to how we understand diffusion processes. The event history findings focus on the likelihood that diffusion will occur; once a jurisdiction has adopted a program, the city is dropped from the analysis. The assumption underlying this method is that once a policy is implemented, it will remain in place. For many governments, this notion about the nature of public policy is reasonable. Once a new policy is enacted, it can be difficult to reverse course because actors and institutions have a vested interest in maintaining the status quo.[3] However, as the case studies reveal, the Brazilian public policy environment is more unstable; some municipalities make symbolic name changes whereas others undergo more serious alterations as policies are suspended or reversed altogether when new executives take office. For instance, the renaming of programs is fairly common as politicians seek to place their own stamp on public policy. In Brasília the family health program has been called Saúde em Casa and Programa Saúde da Família, and Bolsa Escola has also been called Renda Minha and Renda Mínima. For the most part, the renaming of programs by city mayors remains a symbolic gesture that does not interfere with the programs' administration or continuity. But a more serious phenomenon for diffusion research is policy suspension or reversal. The case study evidence from Brasília reveals that turnover does occur and corresponds with electoral shifts from a leftist to a rightist mayor.

By incorporating two research methods that examine diffusion processes that can capture emulation, nonemulation, and reversal, this study is able to uncover the importance of ideology in decision-making processes. Both the large- and small-n studies offer remarkably consistent findings on the role that ideology plays in social policy emulation: Left-of-center politicians are more likely to adopt Bolsa Escola and PSF; while reversal is relatively rare, those instances also inform the general findings of the importance of mayors' ideological commitments as only rightists chose to reverse course. In addition, the case studies of the Buarque and Roriz administrations show that ideology also matters when it comes to policy reversal. In other words, when a rightist comes into office and lacks the same ideological predisposition to address social inequality, this mayor is more willing to suspend a program he identifies as "leftist." In this way, the qualitative research, which includes an in-depth analysis of "outlier" cases, can contribute to a more nuanced understanding of diffusion processes as well as the role of ideology in motivating politicians' decisions.

Given that large- and small-n research draws on different types of data, it is only natural that differences in measurement for the theoretical variables of interest could also contribute to meaningful insights. Both qualitative and quantitative approaches test the extent to which electoral competition, ideology, and social networks matter in driving emulation decisions, but these causal factors are conceptualized slightly differently. The data-intensive requirement for the event history analysis necessitates in some instances imperfect measures for the theoretical variables of interest. Assumptions about ideology, for instance, are based on an actor's partisan affiliation, but that partisanship might not truly capture his or her worldview. By contrast, process tracing allows for "thick description" that can reveal interpretive accounts such as the meaning an actor ascribes to her ideological beliefs.

The measures of social network connectivity and their effect on stimulating social policy emulation serve as a clear example of how both methods draw on slightly different measures to test the theoretically driven hypothesis that policy makers who are part of networks will seek to "keep up with the Joneses." Recall, for instance, that the measure of formal network connectivity is based on membership and participation data provided by CEBES and the Public Management and Citizenship Program. The data from the Public Management program is of better quality because it includes more information on who participated and it accounts for annual fluctuations. In the case of CEBES, however, administrators had not kept annual databases on membership but rather continuously updated a single list.[4] Since staff members emphasized that the geographical distribution of members was fairly constant over time, values were simply repeated for every year in this study. Nevertheless this solution to a shortcoming in the data likely leads to a less powerful network effect for the PSF model. The case study analyses enhance understanding of socialized norms by allowing subjects to identify which networks matter to them. The interviews also uncover how actors view different associations and engage in various professional and informal networks. In this way the qualitative cases show how participation in the Public Management and Citizenship Program and CEBES networks mattered for policy makers. In addition, the case studies also shed light on the unique features of civil society activity in the health sector, to explain PSF emulation. Debates on the merits of PSF extended beyond CEBES to fora organized by ABRASCO and CONASEMS, among others, and emphasized the nature of the field's dense professional network space.

On the face of it, both the qualitative and quantitative methods examine ideology similarly: elected officials and their senior political appointees are classified as leftists, centrists, or rightists. The statistical models reveal that the presence of a leftist mayor has a statistically significant impact on the likelihood of Bolsa Escola and PSF emulation.

Also important is that centrists and rightists behave alike in the large-n study; in other words, centrists and rightists adopt these policies at similar rates. But what is it about leftists that makes them so eager to emulate these social policies? As the case studies reveal, leftists who adopted these programs shared similar commitments, beliefs, and desires to govern in a way that fitted their worldview. They were driven to address historic social exclusion and reverse decades-old spending priorities that benefited the elite and middle class. Interestingly, most of the leftists interviewed for this study framed their policy choices as driven by their belief that Brazil needed to construct "citizenship." Pro-poor and equity-enhancing policies like Bolsa Escola and PSF were a means for expanding those citizenship rights. Since questions regarding actors' motivations are fundamentally about how they interpret social policy and attribute meaning to their actions, research must go beyond the statistical correlates to include qualitative approaches that explore individuals' motivations.

Finally, the methodologies employed in this study examine the potential impact that electoral competition has on policy diffusion. Capturing electoral competition is one of the most challenging issues for a longitudinal study of Brazilian municipal elections because of irregularities in electoral data collection during the early 1990s.[5] Thus, the case studies provide an opportunity to fill in information where data is lacking. At the same time, the case studies provide "texture" on the nature of electoral competition for the research sites. For instance, when left-of-center Mayor Lídice da Mata won the executive office of Salvador in 1992, her rise reflected a brief political opening caused by the declining influence of the conservative politician Antônio Carlos Magalhães (ACM). The political break was especially notable as ACM and his political allies had controlled Bahian politics, at the state and local levels, for decades and he was well known as a conservative clientelist powerbroker.[6] By 1996 ACM once again reigned supreme in both state and municipal politics, and his candidate for office, Antônio Imbassahy, won handily. In this way knowledge of specific local elections not only elucidates the nature of the campaign debates and election, but it also reveals how political contexts sometimes reflect broader political dynamics tied to state and national-level alliances.

Scholarship often focuses on a single policy or political phenomenon to explore the determinants of policy diffusion (for recent examples, see Brinks and Coppedge 2006; Mossberger 2000; Orenstein 2003; Simmons and Elkins 2004). By contrast, this project has examined two distinct policies, one related to health and the other to education. There are important theoretical rationales for selecting two social policies. First, this study seeks to avoid the problem of a pro-innovations bias by examining only those programs that diffuse broadly and rapidly. Both social sector reforms analyzed here diffused but did so at dramatically different rates: PSF spread more extensively than Bolsa Escola. Second, research on public policy tends to emphasize differences across issue areas, rather than similarity. Conventional policy studies highlight the distinct features of each policy domain, examining entrenched interests, class conflicts, and the unique actors and institutions involved in each sector. However, it is also possible that distinct policies are driven by similar causal processes when it comes to emulation. To explore some of the unique and shared features of Bolsa Escola and PSF, this section draws on the analysis presented in chapters 4 and 5, specifically highlighting the degree of policy design complexity, policy "flexibility," and the gendered political appeals of these programs.

A striking difference between the two social policy issues in this study is their degree of complexity. Bolsa Escola represents a straightforward and simple idea with the goals of improving educational access and addressing the intergenerational transmittal of poverty.[7] Key policy entrepreneurs such as Cristovam Buarque made the analogy that Bolsa Escola was just like college-level grants for needy students, the only difference being that the school grant targets needy children. The simple comparison made it easier for many Brazilians to relate to the program, even though the policy's design seeks to address more complex issues of intergenerational poverty, child labor and the opportunity costs of education, and the need to induce attitudinal and behavioral changes among parents. Administratively, implementation of Bolsa Escola was also uncomplicated; it merely required the city to create a database of beneficiaries with corresponding school attendance information. Teachers needed to submit information to the city, but Bolsa Escola did not otherwise change the core of their job duties.

The clear-cut features of education reform were in marked contrast with the complex nature of primary health reform. Unlike Bolsa Escola, PSF represented a highly sophisticated re-visioning of health care delivery. The health program encapsulated decades of domestic and international debates on how to structure primary health care (see chapter 5). Not only did it require that municipal health agencies shift resources in public health, it also called for many health professionals to embrace the new model. Unlike Bolsa Escola, PSF implied a dramatic change in the nature of health workers' day. For instance, many doctors and nurses who had existing civil service employment with city governments had to renegotiate contracts.[8] To hire community health agents, whose job description conflicted with traditional civil servant job contracts, city officials established partnerships with local nonprofit associations.[9] The sheer complexity of the program's administration offered a striking contrast to Bolsa Escola. Many policy makers viewed PSF as a "big idea" that involved substantial commitment to reorganizing health care delivery in Brazil. For these reasons, it would seem that these two policies reflect dramatically different types of social policy.

These differences in complexity (both ideational and administrative) did have an impact on policy makers' acceptance of these social policies.[10] Key policy entrepreneurs associated with Bolsa Escola and PSF experimented with how to frame their policies to maximize their acceptance. For instance, Cristovam Buarque at one point described Bolsa Escola as a policy that paid mothers for the work they already do; this characterization did not sit well with feminists or conservatives, so he quickly abandoned it to describe the program instead as a school scholarship (interview Almira 2003). In the case of PSF, the framing issue did have substantive implications. Did the program represent "primary health care" or "selective primary care"?[11] While framing issues were important to both social policies, the simplicity behind Bolsa Escola was especially important to facilitating its acceptance.[12]

Policy flexibility was another element of Bolsa Escola and PSF that a few technocrats found attractive. While most cities adopted these programs wholesale and made few modifications to their policy design, in a few cities technocrats found ways to build upon these policies once they were in place. Bolsa Escola and PSF served as the foundation for additional program elements.[13] For instance, in Belo Horizonte, administrators responsible for Bolsa Escola had previous professional experience in public assistance and social work. The staff could simply have created a registry and made cash payments to beneficiaries, but they decided to institute monthly meetings for the mothers in the program. Mothers were invited to select topics for discussion; among the issues Bolsa Escola beneficiaries were most eager to address was how to search for employment. In this way, Bolsa Escola in Belo Horizonte became more than a school grant program and served as an outreach and development program for poor mothers as well.

Though the Ministry of Health set clear rules for how the PSF program ought to be implemented in order for cities to qualify for federal grants, many cities enhanced their PSF program with complementary services or distinct approaches.[14] For instance, Sobral in the state of Ceará was an early adopter of the family health program. But one of the modifications city officials embraced was the expansion of services to include oral hygiene by dentists as part of the system for primary medicine. In São Paulo, administrators affiliated with PSF created a birthing center for women as an alternative to hospital deliveries. Sometimes these local experiments with PSF were viewed with skepticism by federal health administrators who preferred a unified approach, while at other times, new ideas "trickled up" and the addition was embraced by national policy makers.

A central question in diffusion studies is whether adoption decisions truly reflect emulation of an existing policy. Do policy makers adapt an innovative policy before implementing it, thus rendering it different? Or do actors simply apply a "policy label" without adopting the specifics of policy design?[15] In this study, both Bolsa Escola and PSF were largely emulated wholesale by policy makers: few politicians and senior technocrats tweaked these programs before adopting them. Rather, it was after cities adopted these policies that technocrats experimented by adding different components. That Bolsa Escola and PSF were perceived as useful foundations for complementary activity speaks to their general appeal. It can also help explain why technocrats were willing to buy into these programs and why these policies may have "stuck" as city administrators established vested interests in these programs.

In summary, this study brings together two different research traditions to uncover actors' motivations for social policy emulation. Employing distinct approaches in a single study makes up for the inherent weaknesses of each method, clarifying the mechanisms that drive diffusion while also allowing for greater generalization. A second analytic characteristic of this project is its comparison of two different types of policy issues. Bolsa Escola is a relatively small program with specific aims geared toward a particular constituency. Programa Saúde da Família, on the other hand, has broad goals to redefine an entire class of health care services to all families. These differences might suggest that these programs are not comparable. However, both social sector reforms also share characteristics that make them similarly attractive to administrators seeking to make their mark. Ultimately, both policies appeal to leftist politicians and technocrats who embrace them for their social justice and citizenship goals.

Consequences of Local Social Sector Reforms

The local social sector reforms that began in the mid-1990s have contributed to further diffusion and changes in social policy reform. For instance, the family health model is now entrenched in the primary care system, and cities have adapted the program further. In addition, the federal government has continued to draw on lessons from the emulation of local Bolsa Escola and has made significant advances of its own for poverty relief. A prominent feature of social policy today is the targeted focus on women and mothers, thus reinforcing the idea that social inclusion comes about through gender-sensitive social policy design. At the same time, the Brazilian models have had lasting consequences beyond that country's borders and have contributed to the worldwide diffusion of conditional cash transfer programs. This section briefly describes the most recent policy implications of the social sectors analyzed in this book, examines some of the larger consequences for the construction of citizenship in Brazil, and ends by discussing Brazilian contributions to the international diffusion of CCTs.

National Trends in Health and Poverty Relief

This project has focused on the politics behind social sector reforms and on the mechanisms that drive diffusion at the local level. I have taken it as a given that the programs, Bolsa Escola and Programa Saúde da Família, are innovative strategies, well regarded by policy experts. However, it is less clear whether these programs will be effective elsewhere. Can an educational cash grant program produce the desired results if implemented in a city that lacks other educational resources for school achievement? Should cities with complex health infrastructure, where residents prefer clinician-based services, adopt a family health program? As we have seen, many of the cities adopting these policies did so without undertaking research to determine whether these programs are indeed appropriate solutions to their social problems. The issue of efficacy is important, especially since actors who adopt these policies assume they will address problems of social exclusion, poverty, and inequality. Since the publication of the first case studies evaluating these programs (e.g., Jacobo Waiselfisz, Abramovay, and Andrade 1998; Bava et al. 1998) there has been growing agreement that conditional cash transfers and community-based medicine are good ideas. For instance, in a longitudinal ecological analysis of panel data from 1990 to 2002, Macinko and coauthors find that PSF is associated with reduced infant mortality rates in Brazil; their analysis reveals that, when controlling for other factors, a 10 percent increase in the program population coverage contributes to a 4.5 percent decline in infant mortality (2006).[16] Finally, there is emerging evidence that PSF has other positive health effects by reducing costly hospitalizations for ambulatory care-sensitive chronic disease, such as stroke, asthma, and cardiovascular disease (Macinko et al. 2010). These findings not only help support the expansion and coverage of PSF, but also suggest that this reform can produce cost-effectiveness in the long term.

Local governments have continued to embrace the PSF model, and many late adopters have taken on the program while others have deepened their commitment to the model. First, the family health model has continued to spread throughout the country. With consensus surrounding the program and the encouragement provided by the Ministry of Health, cities that had "resisted" the family health model have now mostly adopted the program. According to the latest data from the Ministry of Health for 2008, 5325 municipalities have adopted PSF; this figure represents 94 percent of all municipalities (see appendix B, fig. B.1). While the southeast of Brazil still lags in adoption when compared with the northeast and central-west regions, the diffusion process in Brazil has clearly reached the near maximum saturation rate (see appendix C for additional data). Second, the family health model has evolved in other important ways. This analysis has focused on the emulation decision itself rather than on the features of implementation. But many local governments have not only adopted the model but also deepened their commitment to the family health program by expanding the total population covered. In 2003 approximately 36 percent of Brazil's total population had access to a family health team, whereas by 2007 nearly 47 percent had access (Ministry of Health 2009). The expansion of coverage suggests that the model is slowly moving from a model of selective primary care to universal primary care. For this reason, the Ministry of Health now refers to the model as Estratégia Saúde da Família (Family Health Strategy, or ESF), as a reorientation of the public assistance model by offering integrated care through family health teams.

At the same time that the primary care model has spread throughout Brazil, many cities have adapted the program by expanding services and modifying the composition of the personnel who make up the family health teams. One notable example in this regard is the small city of Sobral in the state of Ceará which was one of the earliest adopters of PSF in the country. By the early 2000s the Department of Health had decided to expand services beyond the traditional model by adding complementary services to their program (e.g., social workers, therapists, and dentists). The city's poor were woefully underserved by dentists, and Sobral's coordinated program, Saúde Bucal (Oral Health), has served as an important point of access. Officials in Sobral published case studies of their approach to organizing PSF to publicize their accomplishments and help spur adaptations elsewhere (interview Andrade

2004; for example, see the journal *Sanare* 2003). By 2007 over four thousand municipalities had added dentistry to their PSF programs with the assistance of fiscal transfers from the Ministry of Health (Ministry of Health 2009). These trends and adaptations suggest that the PSF program is the standard model for primary health care delivery in Brazil. The task in the immediate future is to continue to offer expanded coverage and integrate complementary activities, while also ensuring quality care.

When it comes to education and poverty relief, even greater transformations have taken place in the form of a significant large-scale conditional cash transfer programs. The road to establishing Bolsa Família, the country's largest poverty program, had its twists and turns. As Fernando Henrique Cardoso's presidency was coming to a close in 2001, the Ministry of Education (MEC) launched a federal Bolsa Família program. The federal version largely emulated programs designed by cities: it provided very modest grants to poor mothers on the condition that their children go to school. During the presidential campaign, Lula sought to highlight the social policy issues, such as the problem of persistent hunger. Later during the transition period he addressed food insecurity more broadly and pledged to assist citizens so that they would be able to have three square meals a day. While his "Fome Zero" (zero hunger) program generated considerable interest both in Brazil and abroad, the policy would falter as experts debated how best to reach nutritional gains (e.g., through subsidies, cash grants, or other agricultural strategies). In the end, Lula's efforts with Fome Zero would be short lived as technocrats within the federal government pushed to consolidate small and disparate poverty relief programs into a single unified program.

In 2003 Lula launched a "new" federal conditional cash transfer program called Bolsa Família.[17] Bolsa Família unified several existing programs that provided targeted benefits in the form of a CCT or subsidy—Bolsa Escola, Bolsa Alimentação, and Vale Gas—into a single policy. One objectives was to improve efficiency by avoiding duplication of benefits. In addition, a single registry of applicants and beneficiaries enabled technocrats to target the neediest, track compliance, and, eventually, evaluate policy outcomes. Bolsa Família is effective at targeting the neediest; nearly two-thirds of beneficiaries live in extreme poverty earning under R$70 (approximately US$35) per capita on a monthly basis. A second group of poor who can also participate are those earning a monthly income between R$70 and R$140 per capita. The size of the cash grants provided to families depends on a number of factors, including whether family is classified as extremely poor or poor, monthly income, family size, and the ages of the children in the household; the grants range from as little as R$22 (US$11) per month to a maximum of R$200 (US$100) (Ministry of Social Development 2009). In return for these grants, mothers of poor children are required to comply with certain rules. Initially, the program's conditionality related to education and required children's regular school attendance. Later, Bolsa Família would include health requirements, such as the monitoring of children (e.g., vaccinations, height and weight monitoring) and checkups for pregnant women and nursing mothers. Overall, the Bolsa Família program has made tremendous inroads across the country. More than 11 million families (approximately 44 million individuals) have received the benefit of the conditional cash grant; this number represents nearly a quarter of Brazil's population. This program has the potential to provide a minimum living standard for all Brazilians by lifting millions out of abject poverty.[18] At the same time, the program has not been a financial burden on the Brazilian state. Bolsa Família constitutes only 2.5 percent of all government expenditures (about 0.5 percent of GDP), which is a small share of overall social spending (Lindert 2006).

Although the structure of social spending in Brazil, including significant commitments to social security, health care, and education, has remained fairly constant since democratization,[19] Bolsa Família nevertheless represents a significant departure from traditional poverty relief strategies. Like municipal Bolsa Escola and minimum income programs, Bolsa Família aims to provide a minimum level of protection to the poor while also seeking to increase human capital formation. Arguably, the federal government is best positioned to design a conditional cash grant program as it has the fiscal resources and administrative capacity to take on a large-scale poverty program. A national program can also compensate for regional inequality and the differing levels of fiscal capacity across the country's approximately 5500 municipalities.

Uncovering the motivations for implementing a national CCT by the Cardoso and Lula governments falls beyond the scope of this book. Though Melo (2008) argues that intense electoral competition between the PSDB and the PT for the presidency drove the Cardoso administration to scale up local programs, elsewhere (2011a) I argue that national policy making was actually part of a more complex diffusion process that included "bottom-up" domestic pressures, "horizontal" pressures from cross-national competition, and "top-down" pressures from international financial institutions. Specifically, the emulation of Bolsa Escola Federal (National Bolsa Escola) resulted from bottom-up processes that reflected professional norms among municipal officials as well as intergovernmental competition; once federal officials embraced the policy, development norms and financing from international development institutions helped ensure that these programs would endure (2011a). For our purposes, a particularly interesting feature involving Bolsa Família is that the experiences of local governments were crucial in providing early stimulus for a national program. Municipal innovation and diffusion led the way for federal emulation by both President Cardoso and President Lula. Further, there are indications that Bolsa Família has retained many of the "good governance" features that were present in the municipal programs. Brazil has a long history of federal public policies being diverted to support clientelist politics at the local level, yet Bolsa Família appears to be insulated from traditional patron-client practices that reinforce clientelism, and it may strengthen citizenship for the poorest and most vulnerable groups (Hunter and Sugiyama 2009).

Gendered Dimensions of Citizenship

A second implication of social sector reforms has to do with the ways Brazilian social policy since the mid-1990s has made women and children the primary beneficiaries of state services. With health and education reforms defining who is worthy of assistance and determining the behavioral obligations of mothers, the state has also been defining gender roles within the family and community. Mothers were the targets of Bolsa Escola grants and continue to retain a focus under Bolsa Família. Women also make up the bulk of PSF health agents and team members, and these programs have the potential either to transform gender relations or reinforce traditional family norms. Thus, both these social policy arenas define the way motherhood and "family" serve as focal points for organizing social services. In many ways, these programs reflect what Maxine Molyneux (2006) describes as the new neoliberal poverty agenda where motherhood is at the service of the state. These socially "neutral" themes do not challenge mainstream constructions of gender and family values in Brazil, which likely enabled their adopters to see them as generally acceptable.[20]

The gender politics surrounding Bolsa Escola was particularly explicit in that mothers were identified as the most responsible adults in children's lives: only mothers could be trusted to spend their children's grants to further their education and basic living needs. Fathers were largely dismissed by policy makers as either impractical to work with or less likely to fulfill their paternal roles. Some administrators pointed to pragmatic concerns such as the large number of female-headed households and noted potential problems that could arise if men fathered children with several women. A few others embraced progressive discourse about empowering women, but these viewpoints were rare and largely absent from the public discourse on the program. Nonspecialists and politicians were more likely to revert to stereotypes to explain the gendered appeal of Bolsa Escola; that fathers might use the grants to drink alcohol was the most common dismissal. In practice, Bolsa Escola's political appeal was tied to these traditional social norms surrounding motherhood and the prioritization of family.[21]

In some ways, the gendered dimensions of the PSF program were more ambiguous. On the face of it, the PSF program seemed at odds with the broader trends in the field of public health of making sex and gender explicit in organizing health services. Public health in Brazil has included a focus on women's health issues, particularly as they relate to reproduction, and infant and maternal health.[22] In the last decade, public education campaigns on domestic violence also shed light on the health effects of violence against women. These larger trends in public health of providing specialized care for women and acknowledging gender relations in Brazil were less explicit under the family health program. The family, rather than the individual, was the "unit" to receive attention.[23] Special attention to girls and women would require that health care professionals mainstream gender in their work. In general, it is possible for an integrated family approach to result in better care, as health workers are able to contextualize health problems and see patients' home environment. But successful integration of women's health depends on the quality of training programs and the sensitivity of nurse supervisors. Yet these concerns were rarely expressed by administrators of the program in research sites I visited. Politically, PSF has a gender-neutral facade and appeals to traditional constructions of nuclear family life. The logo that accompanies the program in posters, clinics, and brochures includes the image of two parents with two children within a house. Unlike specialized health programs based on women's reproduction or disease-centric care, the PSF image has a broad appeal that everyone can relate to while also reinforcing notions of family life embraced by social conservatives.

The gendered features of these new social policy models rarely entered into policy debates among high-ranking officials. For instance social policy technocrats hardly ever highlighted issues of gender norms when discussing these programs. Rather, it was the street-level bureaucrats[24] who worked with program constituents on a daily basis who would point out the practical implications of working with women or mothers. These individuals were much more knowledgeable about gender and family relations and were more likely to discuss the ways in which these programs either reinforced mothering duties or addressed the traditional roles that women undertake within the family. What are the implications of Brazil's new social sector regimes for constructing gendered citizenship? Has social policy sought to advance women's status, or has it reinforced traditional family roles?

The low levels of gendered discourse on social policy making is surprising because Brazil is home to a women's movement that made significant strides in pressing for democratization (Alvarez 1990; Jacquette and Wolchik 1998) and has since formed professional nongovernmental organizations to press the women's rights agenda (Alvarez 1990, 1999). Although Brazil has made efforts to create spaces for women by instituting a women's ministry and gender quotas for political parties, these avenues for women's formal political participation have not translated into policy debates over women's roles in the new social sector models. What does it take to mainstream gender into social policy debates in Brazil? This question speaks to central research questions in comparative feminist scholarship, including recent studies on feminist policy in the European welfare state, as well as in developing countries (see, for example, Ewig 2010; Jordan 2006; Mazur 2002; Molyneux 2006). The implications of these social sector reforms for the construction of gendered citizenship and the gendered policy debate are for now left unanswered and await future research.

Transnational Diffusion of Conditional Cash Transfer Models

In an increasingly globalized world where policy makers operate in domestic, cross-national, and international networks, it should come as no surprise that innovations might spread across country borders. Nevertheless the rapid convergence around the conditional cash transfer model is considered remarkable in the international development community. Within a decade, nearly every Latin American country has adopted a conditional cash transfer program (see appendix D, table D.1). The appeal of CCTs extends beyond the region, and increasingly countries in Africa and Asia have also adopted them. To what extent did Brazilian models contribute to this worldwide trend?

Brazilian policy makers were not alone in their attempts to address poverty alleviation and human capital development in the mid-1990s. While Brazilian cities such as Campinas and Brasília developed municipal conditional cash transfer models in 1995, the Mexican government also designed a new poverty program, Programa de Educación, Salud, y Alimentación (Program for Education, Health, and Nutritrion, or PROGRESA), in 1997. Like Brazil's Bolsa Escola, PROGRESA was viewed by technocrats as a significant departure from previous poverty alleviation models. Prior to PROGRESA's development, Mexico's major poverty alleviation program, Pronasol, was widely criticized for serving as a vehicle for patronage politics and vote-buying practices by the ruling Institutional Revolutionary Party (PRI) (Dion 2010).[25] In response to criticisms surrounding Pronasol, President Ernesto Zedillo (1994–2000) launched PROGRESA, which was designed to support poor households with small children in rural areas. In 2000 Zedillo expanded the program to reach semiurban beneficiaries, as well as a few urban families. Shortly thereafter, under President Vicente Fox, the program underwent a name change, to Oportunidades (Oportunities), and rapidly expanded throughout the country. Oportunidades included a cash transfer with three components: a household nutrition component, a school subsidy for school-age children (with differential payments to encourage girls' educations), and an annual transfer to cover school costs (Barrientos and DeJong 2006, 547). The conditional requirements of Oportunidades were extensive, including regular school attendance, parenting sessions, and health monitoring for mothers and infants. By 2004 approximately 5 million families (25 million individuals) were participating in the program (Cohen, Franco, and Villatoro 2006, 87). To put this figure in perspective, this means that nearly a quarter of the Mexican population was a beneficiary of this poverty strategy.

From the start, the PROGRESA was designed with the goal of facilitating program evaluations, and technocrats in Mexico City worked closely with international specialists, including the International Food Policy Research Institute (IFPRI) and independent researchers, to provide evaluations of the program's outcomes (Potter 2009; Skofias and McClafferty 2000; Teruel and Davis 2000). According to President Zedillo, he sought to insulate the program from politics and provide technocrats with the latitude to design, implement, and evaluate the strategy on its merits (Zedillo 2009). With positive program evaluations that revealed improvements in household nutrition, health, and educational attendance, PROGRESA quickly gained widespread recognition within the international development community. It also enjoyed some political insulation, allowing the program to endure despite significant political turnover when President Fox of the competing National Action Party (PAN) took office in 2000.

Municipal Bolsa Escola models and PROGRESA thus emerged nearly simultaneously and largely independently in the mid-1990s,[26] and each program attracted considerable attention within the international development community. For instance, Mexico's improved outcomes on nutrition and health appealed especially to the World Bank and the Inter-American Development Bank. Bolsa Escola's focus on education and its effect of reducing child labor generated interest among officials within UNICEF, UNESCO, and the International Labour Organization. Since PROGRESA was a larger federal program with more beneficiaries, Mexico gained more visibility by serving as the country host to the World Bank's first international conference on conditional cash transfers in May 2002. Brazil served as host for the second World Bank conference in April 2004. As one might expect, attributing credit for the origins of CCTs is politically sensitive. Perhaps for this reason, many publications cite both the Brazilian municipal programs and Mexico's PROGRESA as innovative (see, for example, Fiszbein et al. 2009).

Like the diffusion of Bolsa Escola across Brazilian municipalities, the transnational spread of CCT programs around the world reflects complex processes. In a large-n cross-national study of Latin American CCT diffusion, I have argued that the emulation of CCTs is largely caused by international forces rather than domestic preconditions. Specifically, I found that neighbor emulation, professional norms among the development community, and financing from international financial institutions explain the adoption of this new social policy model in the region (Sugiyama 2011b). Innovative programs such as Bolsa Escola/ Bolsa Família and PROGRESA/Oportunidades have clearly emerged as a new development norm through hundreds of publications, international conferences, and funding support by key international financial institutions such as the World Bank and the Inter-American Development Bank. Another key contribution to the development of consensus surrounding this new poverty alleviation strategy has been high-profile endorsements by world leaders. For instance, during the "Dakar World Education for All" forum in April 2000, UN Secretary-General Kofi Annan suggested that Bolsa Escola should be considered around the world (Missão Criança 2001, 7). A few years later James

Wolfensohn said, "Bolsa Família has already become a highly praised model of effective social policy. Countries around the world are drawing lessons from Brazil's experience and are trying to produce the same results for their own people" (World Bank 2005b). These specific mentions of Bolsa Escola and Bolsa Família have been tremendously influential in the diffusion of CCTs.

Although international organizations have been active promoters of CCTs, it is also important to acknowledge the contributions of Brazilian policy makers and institutions in the promotion of CCTs elsewhere.[27] Personal direct contact has provided an important source of information for foreign governments. In some instance, Brazilians such as policy entrepreneur Cristovam Buarque and the organization he founded, Missão Criança, have been active promoters of Bolsa Escola for other countries. For instance, Lana and Evans (2004) argue the nongovernmental organization Missão Criança was an influential "knowledge institution" that contributed to the policy transfer of Bolsa Escola to Ecuador's Beca Escolar program. The organization has also worked closely with Portuguese-speaking countries in Africa to assist in their implementation of Bolsa Escola (interview C. Silva 2003). Since the development of the federal Bolsa Família, the Ministry of Social Development (MDS) even set up a special office to interact with international visitors and organizations and hosted many international visitors wanting to learn how the program is designed and administered (interview V. Sousa 2011). While officials note that they are very careful to explain that "one size does *not* fit all" and that each country should set up CCTs according to its domestic needs and institutional dynamics (interview Modesto 2011), Brazil's improvements in poverty reduction have inspired many queries for information and technical exchanges (interview V. Sousa 2011).

In sum, municipal Brazilian innovations in the mid-1990s reflected a new global trend in conditional cash transfer models for addressing poverty alleviation and human capital development. Together with Mexico's PROGRESA, Bolsa Escola captured the attention of the international development community. The dramatic spread of CCTs around the developing world represents a significant paradigm shift in addressing poverty today. Though neither Brazil nor Mexico *caused* the dramatic spread of CCTs, both countries' officials deserve credit for their innovations and contributions to the development of new professional norms among the technocratic development community. Remarkably, what started out as a small-scale municipal experiment fueled trends in Brazil and beyond.

Theoretical Implications of Policy Diffusion in Brazil

The findings presented in this book speak to several research communities as well as to practitioners in the field of social policy. For scholars of Brazilian politics, this work challenges long-held assumptions about patronage, clientelism, and the politics that shape reform efforts. Practitioners with policy expertise who care about shielding their programs from political interference can also gain insights from the Brazilian case. Also important for those with a particular interest in poverty alleviation and equity-enhancing public policy, this project informs practitioners of the mechanisms that enable innovative strategies to diffuse. Finally, this book addresses key disciplinary debates on actors' motivations in political decision making and challenges conventional assumptions about rational decision making and electoral competition as the main motivators for policy making.

Most research on social policy in Brazil has emphasized the role of institutions or sector-specific features of health and education (see, for instance, Affonso and Barros Silva 1996; Arretche 2000, 2004a, 2004b; Arretche and Marques 2002; Draibe 2004). But with greater municipal authority in decision making, local governments have proved capable of innovation and experimentation in a number of policy domains. The trends toward emulation and diffusion are relatively new for Brazil and merit greater attention. Policy diffusion research can provide a new analytic lens for understanding both the horizontal and vertical processes that drive the spread of similar policies across the country. The replication of social policy in Brazil also offers a unique opportunity to explore diffusion; it has occurred in a country with thousands of local governments which is better known for its vast contrasts than its similarities.

As this book reveals, emulation and diffusion are now important new features of the policy-making process in Brazil, and the trends identified in social sector reform are likely to occur in other policy arenas in the near future.

Those familiar with Brazil's political landscape, with its legacies of *coronelismo,* political clans, patronage, and clientelism,[28] will also note just how little politics as usual influenced the diffusion of model reforms. As in many other Latin American countries, education and health have traditionally served the clientelistic distribution of small-scale benefits designed to gain electoral support. Since the education and health sectors can provide local politicians with avenues for corruption, policies such as Bolsa Escola and PSF constitute the most likely cases for the electoral incentives argument. The absence of widespread political interference stands in marked contrast to common assumptions that politicians simply desire to "buy" electoral support and do not care about helping the poor. Rather, it appears that policy-making decisions fall outside the scope of electoral politics. These findings suggest that we need to move beyond simplistic assumptions about politics as usual to understand the complexity of decision making among Brazilian politicians.

For those concerned with the practice of democratic politics in subnational Brazil, there is much to be optimistic about. While the findings here differ from conventional assumptions that greater electoral competition contributes to adoption of policy innovations, we should not infer that elections do not matter in practice. To the contrary, mayoral elections hold important political meaning as we see that ideological differences between politicians on the right and the left have real implications for defining policy priorities. As the analysis shows, left-leaning politicians are more likely to embrace poverty-reducing and equity-enhancing social reforms. Right-leaning politicians are less likely to adopt model reforms and more likely to maintain the status quo in sectors such as education and health. Thus, while electoral competition has not *motivated* social policy reforms among local politicians, ideological preferences clearly have important *consequences* for politicians and voters. To date there is reason to believe that democracy in Brazil has helped to bring about meaningful local elections with ideologically substantive debates and outcomes for its citizens. As citizens have greater opportunities to observe the implications of mayors' ideological discourse on their governance approaches and policy priorities, they will more likely be able to evaluate candidates in the future.

This study also has important implications for those concerned with the practice of social policy development and poverty relief. By contrasting two distinct policy arenas of central concern to local governments, we see that the motivations that drive policy emulation can result in different outcomes. Not only did policies diffuse at different rates, but the likelihood that a policy experienced "longevity" also differed. When ideology was the predominant motivation for policy makers, as was the case with Bolsa Escola and Renda Mínima, the programs were much more vulnerable to policy reversal once there was a turnover in government. Municipal Bolsa Escola never became a standard model for education reform that encompassed new norms across education and public assistance associations. Rather, supporters of the educational grant program were socialized through the generalist Public Management and Citizenship network. This contrasts significantly with the family health program, which became defined as the new professional standard. In this case diffusion was extensive, and PSF was much more likely to remain in place once implemented. If we consider "good governance practices" to be those that encompass some measure of policy regularity across administrations, then there is reason to believe that the existence of a professional society really does matter. By investing in social networks that can cross ideological divides and socialize individuals into shared professional norms, advocates of social policy innovation can go far to promote diffusion.

An important question in social science has been, what motivates individuals' political behavior? Different disciplinary traditions have emphasized such divergent factors as self-interest, socialized norms, or the power of ideas. While fields such as political science and sociology have pursued theory-building exercises based on these underlying assumptions, diffusion research that crosses disciplinary divides has tended to leave motivations unspecified and untested. In other words, diffusion scholarship in political science has emphasized the importance of rationality and electoral competition to explain policy making, while similar research by sociologists has emphasized the role of social networks (see, for instance, Berry and Berry 1992; DiMaggio and Powell 1983; Granovetter 1973; Walker 1969). Recently researchers have begun to address the mechanisms of diffusion by drawing on competing research traditions (Shipan and Volden 2008; Simmons, Dobbin, and Garrett 2008; Weyland 2007, 2010b). This book engages with these recent works by focusing on the motivations for emulation and by adding new insights into the role of ideology for policy emulation, by bringing actors to the forefront of the analysis and uncovering the microprocesses that lead to diffusion.

In testing three competing explanations for emulation decisions, this research reveals that electoral self-interest fails to explain the diffusion of Bolsa Escola and PSF. This finding is particularly noteworthy considering that the motivation to win electoral competition is one of the basic behavioral assumptions in political science. Instead actors can be driven to emulate innovative policies for principled and other-regarding reasons. This surprising result suggests that future research on diffusion should take care to avoid embedding behavioral assumptions. For this reason, research designs should make sure to assess the mechanisms that drive emulation decisions. While statistical techniques such as event history analysis can facilitate generalization for a larger number of cases, case study approaches and process tracing are necessary to uncover the mechanisms that drive emulation decisions.

This study sets an agenda for future scholarship on policy diffusion. The findings underscore the need to test actors' motivations in political decision making. When diffusion research embeds disciplinary and paradigmatic behavioral assumptions about political behavior, scholars run the risk of misinterpreting political activity and the mechanisms that drive diffusion. For these reasons, future diffusion research should specify and test assumptions about the motivations for emulation. In this way, diffusion scholarship may shed light on broader political science debates on the manifestations of political self-interest. This project bucks the conventional wisdom that self-interest, as demonstrated through electoral competition, drives resource allocation decision making. Though these findings are drawn from the local Brazilian political arena, it is also possible that similar trends exist elsewhere and for other diffusion phenomena. In order to integrate diffusion studies with larger theory-building exercises in political science, future research will need to explore the explanatory power of electoral competition, ideology, and social networks for other country studies and transnational cases of diffusion.

APPENDIX A

Table A.1. Cities Included in Survey of Municipal Managers of Conditional Cash Transfer Programs

State	Municipality	State	Municipality
AC	Rio Branco	ES	Vitória
AL	Maceió	ES	Vila Velha
AL	Arapiraca	ES	Serra
AM	Manaus	ES	Linhares
AP	Macapá	ES	Colatina
BA	Vitória da Conquista	ES	Cariacica
BA	Teixeira de Freitas	ES	Cachoeiro de Itapemirim
BA	Salvador	GO	Rio Verde
BA	Lauro de Freitas	GO	Luziânia
BA	Juazeiro	GO	Goiânia
BA	Jequié	GO	Aparecida de Goiânia
BA	Itabuna	GO	Anápolis
BA	Ilhéus	GO	Águas Lindas de Goiás
BA	Feira de Santana	MA	Timon
BA	Camaçari	MA	São Luís
BA	Barreiras	MA	São José de Ribamar
BA	Alagoinhas	MA	Imperatriz
CE	Sobral	MA	Codó
CE	Maracanaú	MA	Caxias
CE	Juazeiro do Norte	MG	Varginha
CE	Fortaleza*	MG	Uberlândia
CE	Crato	MG	Uberaba
CE	Caucaia	MG	Teófilo Otoni
DF	Brasília	MG	Sete Lagoas

State	Municipality	State	Municipality
MG	Santa Luzia	PE	Jaboatão dos Guararapes
MG	Sabará	PE	Garanhuns
MG	Ribeirão das Neves	PE	Caruaru
MG	Pouso Alegre	PE	Camaragibe
MG	Poços de Caldas	PE	Cabo de Santo Agostinho
MG	Patos de Minas	PI	Teresina
MG	Montes Claros	PI	Parnaíba*
MG	Juiz de Fora	PR	São José dos Pinhais
MG	Ipatinga	PR	Ponta Grossa
MG	Ibirité	PR	Pinhais
MG	Governador Valadares	PR	Paranaguá
MG	Divinópolis	PR	Maringá
MG	Contagem	PR	Londrina
MG	Conselheiro Lafaiete	PR	Guarapuava
MG	Betim	PR	Foz de Iguaçu
MG	Belo Horizonte	PR	Curitiba
MG	Barbacena	PR	Colombo
MG	Araguari	PR	Cascavel
MS	Dourados	PR	Apucarana
MS	Campo Grande	RJ	Volta Redonda
MT	Várzea Grande	RJ	Teresópolis
MT	Rondonópolis	RJ	São João de Meriti
MT	Cuiabá	RJ	São Gonçalo
PA	Santarém	RJ	Rio de Janeiro*
PA	Marabá	RJ	Resende
PA	Castanhal	RJ	Queimados
PA	Belém	RJ	Petrópolis
PA	Ananindeua	RJ	Nova Iguaçu
PA	Abaetetuba*	RJ	Nova Friburgo
PB	Santa Rita	RJ	Niterói
PB	João Pessoa	RJ	Nilópolis*
PB	Campinha Grande	RJ	Magé*
PE	Vitória de Santo Antão*	RJ	Macaé
PE	Recife	RJ	Itaboraí
PE	Petrolina	RJ	Duque de Caxias
PE	Paulista	RJ	Campos dos Goytacazes
PE	Olinda*	RJ	Cabo Frio

State	Municipality
RJ	Belford Roxo
RJ	Barra Mansa
RJ	Angra dos Reis
RN	Parnamirim
RN	Natal
RN	Mossoró
RO	Porto Velho
RO	Ji-Paraná
RR	Boa Vista
RS	Viamão*
RS	Uruguaiana
RS	Sapucaia do Sul
RS	São Leopoldo
RS	Santa Maria
RS	Santa Cruz do Sul
RS	Rio Grande
RS	Porto Alegre
RS	Pelotas
RS	Passo Fundo
RS	Novo Hamburgo
RS	Gravataí
RS	Caxias do Sul
RS	Canoas
RS	Cachoeirinha
RS	Bagé
RS	Alvorada
SC	São José
SC	Palhoça
SC	Lages
SC	Joinville
SC	Jaraguá do Sul
SC	Itajaí
SC	Florianópolis
SC	Criciúma
SC	Chapecó
SC	Blumenau
SE	Nossa Senhora do Socorro

State	Municipality
SE	Aracaju
SP	Taubaté
SP	Taboão da Serra
SP	Suzano
SP	Sumaré
SP	Sorocaba
SP	São Vicente
SP	São Paulo
SP	São José dos Campos
SP	São José do Rio Preto
SP	São Carlos
SP	São Caetano do Sul*
SP	São Bernanrdo do Campo
SP	Santos
SP	Santo André
SP	Santa Bárbara d'Oeste
SP	Rio Claro
SP	Ribeirão Preto
SP	Ribeirão Pires
SP	Presidente Prudente
SP	Praia Grande
SP	Piracicaba
SP	Pindamonhangaba
SP	Osasco
SP	Moji das Cruzes
SP	Mogi Guaçu
SP	Mauá
SP	Marília
SP	Limeira
SP	Jundiaí
SP	Jaú
SP	Jacareí
SP	Itu*
SP	Itaquaquecetuba*
SP	Itapevi
SP	Itapetininga
SP	Itapecerica da Serra

State	Municipality	State	Municipality
SP	Indaiatuba	SP	Carapicuíba
SP	Hortolândia	SP	Campinas
SP	Guarulhos	SP	Bragança Paulista
SP	Guarujá	SP	Botucatu
SP	Guaratinguetá	SP	Bauru
SP	Franco da Rocha	SP	Barueri
SP	Francisco Morato	SP	Barretos
SP	Franca*	SP	Atibaia
SP	Ferraz de Vasconcellos	SP	Araras
SP	Embu*	SP	Araraquara
SP	Diadema*	SP	Araçatuba
SP	Cubatão	SP	Americana
SP	Cotia	TO	Palmas
SP	Catanduva	TO	Araguaína

* Denotes cities where municipal authorities declined to participate in the phone survey; thus they are excluded from the statistical analysis.

APPENDIX B

National Data on the Adoption of Programa Saúde da Família

Figure B.1. National Cumulative Adoption of Programa Saúde da Família

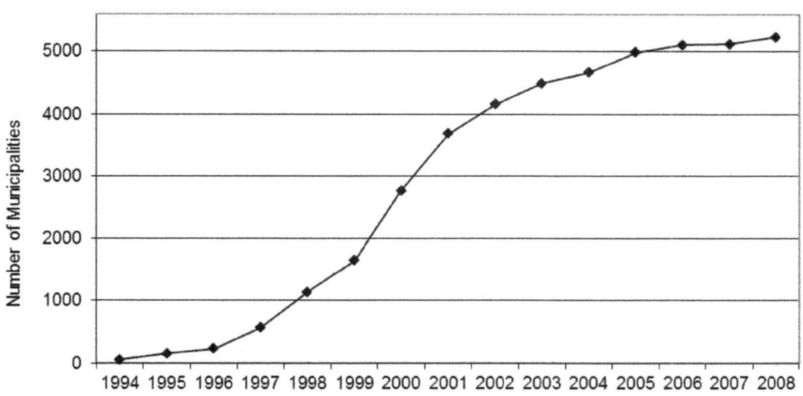

Source: Ministério da Saúde, Departamento de Atenção Básica e Saúde da Família, online.

Table B.1. PSF Coverage of Regions' Population over Time (%)

Region	*1994*	*1995*	*1996*	*1997*	*1998*	*1999*	*2000*	*2001*	*2002*	*2003*	*2004*	*2005*	*2006*	*2007*	*2008*
Central West	0.2	0.2	0.2	4.6	10	9.4	19.8	34.3	39	39.9	41.6	45.8	44.7	45.9	48.2
North	0.2	0.4	0.4	0.4	4.9	11.7	15.9	23.8	30	31.3	34.2	40.4	41.8	42.5	70.6
Northeast	1.4	3	3.4	4.2	9.3	13.7	26.4	39.1	45.3	50.5	54.9	64.3	67.2	67.4	47.2
Southeast	0.3	0.9	1.2	3.5	5	6.1	12.5	17.4	22.6	26.5	29	32.1	34	34.5	36.9
South	1.1	2.2	2.3	3.3	5	6.4	17.2	25.5	30.7	34.6	38.9	43.2	44.6	44.9	47.9
Total	**0.74**	**1.6**	**1.86**	**3.51**	**6.57**	**8.95**	**17.87**	**26.35**	**31.87**	**35.69**	**39**	**44.4**	**46.2**	**46.6**	**49.5**

Source: Data for 1994–97 provided by the Ministry of Health, Departamento de Atenção Básica and Population Estimates and CAPSI, IBGE, Sistema de Captação de Dados para Pagamento. Data for 1998–2008 from Ministério da Saúde, Departamento de Atenção Básica e Saúde da Família, online.

Table B.2. Percentage of Municipalities Adopting PSF by State and Region (1998–2008)

Federal Units	*1998*	*1999*	*2000*	*2001*	*2002*	*2003*	*2004*	*2005*	*2006*	*2007*	*2008*
DF[a]	100	100	100	100	100	0	100	100	100	100	100
GO	2	11	52	85	95	97	93	99	99	98	99
MS	10	18	46	68	94	95	97	97	97	97	99
MT	14	18	59	81	96	98	93	98	99	94	100
Central West	**7**	**14**	**53**	**81**	**95**	**97**	**94**	**98**	**99**	**97**	**99**
AL	75	88	99	96	97	96	96	99	99	100	99
BA	4	7	15	32	46	57	67	89	94	95	97
CE	81	90	88	98	95	96	96	99	99	100	100
MA	1	8	22	40	62	74	85	98	100	99	99
PB	9	16	63	89	94	96	100	100	98	100	100
PE	38	56	81	92	93	95	96	98	100	99	100
PI	7	53	86	92	98	98	98	99	100	100	100
RN	12	30	51	83	84	93	93	99	99	99	100
SE	29	43	41	89	92	93	92	96	97	100	100
Northeast	**22**	**36**	**55**	**71**	**79**	**84**	**88**	**97**	**98**	**98**	**99**
AC	23	64	68	77	77	77	82	91	95	100	100
AM	2	32	48	68	71	71	74	82	89	89	92
AP	0	13	13	13	19	25	69	88	94	94	100
PA	13	29	46	50	59	55	68	78	83	86	91
RO	12	87	96	79	85	83	79	94	92	90	100
RR	0	13	33	60	73	87	80	87	93	93	93
TO	44	57	50	66	90	94	92	94	96	96	96
North	**21**	**45**	**53**	**61**	**73**	**74**	**79**	**87**	**90**	**91**	**95**
ES	20	18	48	72	82	81	86	94	94	95	97
MG	45	46	55	70	72	83	84	90	95	95	98
RJ	22	34	62	79	85	87	87	92	93	92	97
SP	12	17	43	54	64	68	70	70	72	73	75
Southeast	**30**	**33**	**50**	**64**	**70**	**77**	**79**	**83**	**86**	**87**	**89**
PR	17	24	53	71	77	83	84	91	92	93	96
RS	5	7	22	34	49	62	73	77	79	80	83
SC	12	23	50	78	92	97	96	96	98	98	99
South	11	17	40	57	69	78	82	86	88	89	91
Brazil	**21**	**30**	**50**	**66**	**75**	**81**	**84**	**90**	**92**	**92**	**94**

[a] The Federal District is composed of Brasília (n = 1).

Source: Ministério da Saúde, Departamento de Atenção Básica e Saúde da Família, online.

Table B.3. Number of Municipalities Adopting PSF by State and Region (1998–2008)

Federal Units	*1998*	*1999*	*2000*	*2001*	*2002*	*2003*	*2004*	*2005*	*2006*	*2007*	*2008*
DF[a]	1	1	1	1	1	0	1	1	1	1	1
GO	4	27	125	210	233	238	229	244	244	240	243
MS	8	14	35	52	72	73	75	76	76	76	77
MT	17	22	74	113	133	136	129	138	139	133	141
Central West	**30**	**64**	**235**	**376**	**439**	**447**	**434**	**459**	**460**	**450**	**462**
AL	76	89	100	98	99	98	98	101	101	102	101
BA	16	28	63	134	190	239	280	370	394	395	405
CE	149	166	161	180	175	176	177	183	183	184	184
MA	1	18	48	87	135	160	185	213	216	214	215
PB	21	36	140	199	210	214	222	223	218	222	223
PE	70	103	149	170	172	175	178	182	185	183	185
PI	16	118	189	205	217	218	217	221	222	222	222
RN	20	50	84	138	141	155	155	166	166	165	167
SE	22	32	53	67	69	70	69	72	73	75	75
Northeast	**391**	**640**	**987**	**1278**	**1408**	**1505**	**1581**	**1731**	**1758**	**1762**	**1777**
AC	5	14	15	17	17	17	18	20	21	22	22
AM	1	20	30	42	44	44	46	51	55	55	57
AP	0	2	2	2	3	4	11	14	15	15	16
PA	19	42	66	71	84	79	97	112	119	123	130
RO	6	45	50	41	44	43	41	49	48	47	52
RR	0	2	5	9	11	13	12	13	14	14	14
TO	61	79	70	92	125	131	128	131	133	134	134
North	**92**	**204**	**238**	**274**	**328**	**331**	**353**	**390**	**405**	**410**	**425**
ES	15	14	37	56	64	63	67	73	73	74	76
MG	382	390	467	595	614	704	720	767	809	814	835
RJ	20	31	56	73	78	80	80	85	86	85	89
SP	79	111	278	351	413	436	452	454	466	474	485
South East	**496**	**546**	**838**	**1075**	**1169**	**1283**	**1319**	**1379**	**1434**	**1447**	**1485**
PR	69	95	213	283	308	331	334	365	368	373	382
RS	21	31	104	169	241	306	362	382	394	397	413
SC	35	66	147	227	268	285	281	280	287	286	291
South	125	192	464	679	817	922	977	1027	1049	1056	1086
Brazil	**1134**	**1646**	**2762**	**3682**	**4161**	**4488**	**4664**	**4986**	**5106**	**5.125**	**5235**

[a] The Federal District consists of Brasília (n = 1).
Source: Ministério da Saúde, Departamento de Atenção Básica e Saúde da Família, online.

APPENDIX C

Phone Interview Protocol:

Research assistants introduced themselves and the research study. After identifying the municipal official responsible for socioeducative programs for the city, researchers asked the following questions:

A. Does your city administer a *municipal* conditional cash grant for educational purposes? Some cities call these programs Bolsa Escola or Renda Mínima.

If yes:

What is the program called?
When was it instituted?
If respondent cannot recall the year it was enacted, inquire about any legislation or decrees that preceded the program's start.
What department is responsible for the program?
Does the program include conditionality, e.g., regular school attendance?
Please describe the main features of your city's program.

If no:

Was there such a program in the past?

B. Is there anything else you would like to share about your city's socioeducational programs?

C. Thank you for your time in answering these questions.

APPENDIX D

Table D.1. Adoption of Federal/National CCT Models in the Americas

1997	Mexico (PROGRESA/Oportunidades)
1998	Honduras (Programa de Asignacion Familiar)
1999	
2000	Colombia (Familias en Accion)
	Costa Rica (Superemonos)
	Nicaragua (Red de Proteccion/Social Atencion a Crisis)
2001	Brazil (Bolsa Escola Federal/Bolsa Família)
	Jamaica (Program of Advancement through Health and Education)
2002	Chile (Chile Solidario)
2003	Ecuador (Bono de Desarollo Humano)
2004	Argentina (Programa Familias)
2005	Dominican Republic (Solidaridad)
	El Salvador (Red Solidaria)
	Paraguay (Red de Promocion y Proteccion Social)
	Peru (Juntos)
	Uruguay (Plan de Asistencia Nacional a la Emergencia Social)
2006	Bolivia (Bono Escolar–Juancito Pinto)
	Panama (Red Oportunidades)
	Trinidad and Tobago (Targeted Conditional Cash Transfer Program)
2007	
2008	Guatemala (Mi Familia PROGRESA)

Source: Sugiyama 2011b, 7.

NOTES

Chapter 1. The Politics of Social Sector Reforms, Subnational Governance, and the Prospects for Policy Diffusion

1. All Brazilian cities are called *municipios,* regardless of size and location. I use the terms *municipalities* and *cities* interchangeably throughout.

2. According to the Constitution (1988) education is the right of all and the duty of the state and of the family; free public education shall be provided with equal conditions of access (title VIII, chapter 3, section 1, articles 205 and 206). "Health is a right of all and a duty of the state and shall be guaranteed by means of social and economic policies aimed at reducing the risk of illness and other hazards and the universal and equal access to actions and services for its promotion, protection and recovery" (title VIII, chapter 2, section 2, article 1996).

3. See Grindle (2007, chap. 1) for an excellent overview of theoretical and practical debates on the merits of decentralization.

4. In the U.S. Supreme Court case New State Ice Co. v. Liebmann, 285 U.S. 262 (1932), Justice Brandeis's dissent notes: "It is one of the happy incidents of the federal system that a single courageous state may, if its citizens choose, serve as a laboratory; and try novel social and economic experiments without risk to the rest of the country." This introduced the metaphor of states as democratic laboratories.

5. According to data from the World Bank, Brazil's income inequality is the highest in the region. Countries with greater income inequality included Swaziland, Central African Republic, Sierra Leone, Botswana, Lesotho, and Namibia (2005, table 2.7).

6. This term was coined by Brazilian economist Edmar Bacha in the 1970s.

7. Antônio Carlos Magalhães (ACM) began his political career in the 1950s and served in a number of electoral positions—governor, senator,

congressman, and mayor—as well as political appointments throughout his career. ACM died in July 2007, but his political clan continues to run for office in local, state, and federal elections.

8. Secretaries in turn hire their senior management. The staff of the bureaucracy is largely composed of career civil servants.

9. Local governance in Brazil is similar to the "strong mayor" model found in large cities (e.g., Chicago and New York) in the United States.

10. The federal government had a limited experiment with Renda Mínima in 1997, when it provided select cities with matching grants if they established the program. This program was short lived and is widely viewed as a policy failure.

11. Unlike the well-regarded model from Cuba, Niterói modified the residency requirements for doctors due to the challenges of staffing. Cuba's primary health model required that doctors live in the communities they served and actively promoted relocation of doctors to rural areas that had been underserved prior to the revolution. Niterói's family doctor program did not require physicians to live in the community and instead relied on community health agents to build linkages with the community. The modification was due to practical limitations in staffing; the city would not have been able to staff the program had it included a residency requirement (interview D'Angelo 2004).

12. As Rogers notes, most studies of diffusion have not asked such "why" questions about actors' motivations (2003, 115). Recent examples of researchers who are filling this void include Finnemore 1996; Mossberger 2000; and Weyland 2007.

13. According to an analysis by the Ministry of the Treasury (2004), municipal spending in education and culture, along with health and sanitation for the period (1998–2003), constituted an average of 49.4 percent of the gross municipal revenues (16).

14. Cities that administer Bolsa Escola and PSF have won good governance awards from the Gestão Pública e Cidadania program in São Paulo.

15. As Lieberman (2005) notes, mixed-methods research can include various analytic strategies to leverage synergistic value. While Lieberman advocates for a nested design, where statistical analysis informs the selection of small-n cases, this study uses a different logic in selecting cases.

16. See Tarrow (2010) for a rich discussion on combining quantitative and qualitative research, which he describes as Triangulation (107–10).

Chapter 2. Theoretical Debates on Policy Diffusion

1. One of the most influential studies on diffusion has been done on the spread of hybrid corn in Iowa; see Ryan and Gross (1943); Gross (1942); and Ryan and Gross (1950).

2. First developed for typewriters, the QWERTY keyboard was designed to limit jamming. It is less efficient than an alternative keyboard designed by Professor August Dvorak in 1932. Although the Dvorak keyboard is more efficient, it never caught on (Rogers 2003, 8–11).

3. For a review of different treatments of the concept of diffusion—process versus outcome—see especially Elkins and Simmons (2005, 36–38).

4. For greater elaboration on this issue, see Collier and Messick (1975) and Box-Steffensmeier and Jones (2004a; 2004b).

5. Event history analysis is also referred to as "survival analysis" because it allows for assessment of "risk" or "failure" in considering whether an event will take place over a given period of time. For an updated analysis of quantitative methods for diffusion studies, see Box-Steffensmeier and Jones (2004a; 2004b).

6. For a discussion on the uses and limits of counterfactual analysis, see McKeown (2004).

7. To date, there are no studies of diffusion within Brazil or a developing country.

8. Both Brazil and the United States share a similar federal structure. Both countries also share presidentialism and executive control over the bureaucracy. The most substantial distinction between the two countries is that Brazil, unlike the United States, explicitly recognizes the role of municipalities for governance and social policy provision in its constitution (1988).

9. Lowi's (1995) seminal classification of public policies combined an analysis of policy content with associated costs to explain why some are easier or harder to pursue. The heart of his analysis lies in the tensions between long-term policy goals and actors' shorter-term political goals. Lowi classifies policies into three categories: distributive, regulatory, and redistributive.

10. Rogers uses *rational* in relation of efficiency—that is, "the most effective means to reach a given end" (2003, 116).

11. Walker uses rationality in terms of competition but also as *bounded* rationality where decision makers use cues and shortcuts to make decisions. Rather than seek all the information possible, individuals who operate on limited time seek to "satisfice" by seeking only some of the available information.

Ultimately, Walker argues that researchers should aim to predict this behavior (1969, 889).

12. See also Weyland (2007, 2010b) for analyses that draw on social psychology to uncover heuristic shortcuts in decision making.

13. Shipan and Volden (2008) use the term *imitation* rather than *emulation* but essentially treat these concepts comparably.

14. For a particularly notable example of research that incorporates process tracing and includes discussion of the policy process, see Kingdon (1995).

15. See Brady (2004) for a useful discussion on the limits of statistical analysis.

16. As Elkins and Simmons note, research on diffusion has taken on numerous definitions, each of which has distinct underlying assumptions about decision makers' behavior. This study borrows elements from their definition of diffusion, which considers governments as independent in terms of decision making but allows for uncoordinated interdependence. My conceptualization allows for the testing of numerous causal mechanisms that drive diffusion (2005, 25).

17. Anthony Downs's (1957) seminal work, which applies economic theory to explain political competition and government action, established many of the rationality assumptions that were later adopted by his successors. His model follows the axiom that "every individual, though rational, is also selfish . . . Thus whenever we speak of rational behavior, we always mean rational behavior directed primarily toward selfish ends" (1957, 27).

18. Riker and Ordeshook make clear that their ideas about rationality play a fundamental role in social science, and provide the regularity for generalization (1973, 11).

19. North's assertion is particularly remarkable as he is widely known for his application of neoclassical economic principles for a theory of state and institution building; he shares a Nobel Prize with Robert W. Fogel for their work in the field of new economic history.

20. See especially Sartori (1969).

21. This definition of ideology is a substantively different from Downs's view, which argues that the development of ideologies is a means to political power for social classes or groups, rather than a representation of actual goals (1957, 96). Downs argues that in the American context, ideologies represent cues or shortcuts for voters who face uncertainty and information costs. Ultimately, ideologies are functional in that they are used by parties to obtain votes.

22. Michael Taylor (2006) offers an interesting analysis that contrasts incentives-based rational choice explanations for human behavior with a

more holistic approach to understanding people's decisions, which emphasizes meaning, feelings of connectivity, and narratives; see especially chaps. 2 and 3.

23. Although Keck and Sikkink do not specifically address diffusion, their work on transnational advocacy networks offers valuable insights on how cross-border networks that link actors with shared norms are key to explaining policy advocacy on issues such as human rights, women's rights, and the environment (1998).

24. DiMaggio and Powell (1983) refer to this as "normative isomorphism."

25. The ministries of education and health have played an inconsistent role in supporting the spread of municipal Bolsa Escola and Programa Saúde da Família. None of the municipalities in this study benefited from federal financing to spur the adoption of municipal Bolsa Escola programs. Funding for PSF adoption has changed over the time period in this study; at first very few municipalities qualified for any incentive grants.

26. There are multiple reasons for the dominance of capital cities in the political landscapes of Latin American countries. One is simple demographics. In many Latin American countries, nearly 50 percent of the population resides in the capital city. Brazil, on the other hand, has many large cities throughout the country; at least thirty-one had populations over half a million in the census year 2000.

27. See Martins and Libânio (2005).

28. According to Transparency International (2004), the global anticorruption watchdog organization, a survey of Brazilians revealed that 7 percent of respondents reported that they were offered money for votes in the March 2001 elections. Interestingly, their studies indicate that vote buying is not limited to the poor.

29. There has been considerable research on the effects of partisanship on macroeconomic policy. Garrett and Lange (1989), who examine economic policy choices by OECD countries, argue that rather than policy convergence across parties, governments dominated by the left and right differ considerably (676). Boix (2000) also finds that partisanship has effects on macroeconomic policy making in OECD countries, though he argues that partisanship and institutional differences matter and are heavily constrained by the international context in which they are embedded (67).

30. In contrast, surveys by Power reveal that leftist politicians are much more willing to present themselves in public in highly ideological ways (Mainwaring, Meneguello, and Power 2000, 183).

31. This view differs from that of Lucas and Samuels (2010), who argue that the main ideological distinction in Brazil is the PT versus the rest, suggesting that other parties lack ideological differentiation.

32. The *abertura* period consisted of a slow, gradual, and insecure political liberalization begun by the Geisel administration in 1974. The slow transition from military rule to democracy took over fifteen years to complete.

33. According to the Ministry of Justice, Brazil has 455 organizations classified as public interest organizations (Ministry of Justice Website, accessed February 18, 2007).

34. Recent exceptions include Shipan and Volden (2006); Simmons, Dobbin, and Garrett (2006, 2008); and Weyland (2005, 2007).

Chapter 3. Diffusion Trends in Education and Health Policy Reforms

1. However, only cities with below their state's average income per capita were eligible (Lavinas and Barbosa 2000).

2. While Elkins and Simmons (2005) argue that the definition of diffusion should be restricted to uncoordinated activity, this study embraces a broader view of diffusion to include both coordinated and uncoordinated events. This allows for a broader understanding of the effect federal initiatives have on local governments that must still decide whether to follow new opportunities or funding streams. The uncoordinated features of diffusion do have implications for data collection, as there is more data available once the health ministry undertakes a coordinated effort.

3. State-based record keeping on municipal adoption of PSF from 1994 to 1997 is uneven; despite concerted efforts to retrieve information on the earliest adopters it has been impossible to obtain this information. In cooperation with this study, staff members from CONASEMS initiated a state-based inquiry to retrieve this historic data. Unfortunately, many states had not maintained records from that time period or had never systematically tracked the municipal adoption of PSF.

4. Research assistants Francisco Marques, Ana Paula Karruz, and Evelyn Chaves carried out phone interviews between November 2003 and October 2004. In some instances, these researchers made repeated calls to reach those civil servants responsible for educational social programs.

5. Noncooperation included instances where respondents explained they needed a supervisor's permission to provide information. Some administrators asserted they needed formal requests for information. When inter-

viewers sent formal letters of inquiry with follow-up phone calls, staff still declined to provide information.

6. Cities dropped as missing cases in Model 1 included Fortaleza (CE), Abaetetuba (PA), Olinda (PE), Vitória de Santo Antão (PE), Parnaíba (PI), Magé (RJ), Nilópolis (RJ), Rio de Janeiro (RJ), Viamão (RS), Diadema (SP), Embu (SP), Franca (SP), Itaquaquecetuba (SP), Itu (SP), São Caetano (SP).

7. For instance, aggregate state data provided from the Ministry of Health for 1994–98 confirmed that several municipalities in the study had not adopted PSF during that time period. A few other state health departments, including Goiás and Ceará, made their municipal-level data available for this study. In addition, a few municipalities had websites that specified the date PSF began in their cities.

8. Regardless of size and location, under federalism municipalities share the same legal authority and responsibilities as stipulated in the Constitution.

9. The entire database includes annual observations for each city, from each policy's start-year to 2003. For the purposes of this analysis all cities are included in the sample (i.e., cities that previously adopted the program are not dropped from the data set). I select 1998 as it is the first year of the second administrative period in this study.

10. The sample size is 223 because the municipality Timon (MA) was not incorporated in 1998. Timon is included in the analysis for later years.

11. Data for the 1992 municipal elections are very difficult to obtain. The federal government had not imposed guidelines for how states should collect and distribute election data. Some states, such as Minas Gerais, collected systematic and detailed information on election results, while other states did not. In subsequent elections voting was electronic, facilitating the distribution of election data.

12. Brazilian election law requires that mayors win 50% + 1 of the valid votes when cities have more than 200,000 electors. A few cities in this sample held second-round elections for mayor. However, for even comparison across the cases, this measure examined only first-round results.

13. Left parties: PT, PC do B, PSB, PPS, PDT, PMN, and PV; center parties: PSDB, PMDB, PTB; right parties: PFL, PL, PDS/PPR/PPB, PRONA, PSC, PSL, and PSD. The relatively new party, PV, is included in the left category as its members are often former party members of other left parties.

14. Party switching is relatively common in Brazil, although, mayors from well-established and institutionalized parties (e.g., PT, PSDB, PFL) typically retain their partisan affiliations through the course of their term.

15. In tracking Gestão Pública Award applications, I did not include those cities that had applied only for an award for a Bolsa Escola/Renda Mínima program, so as to avoid the problem of autocorrelation.

16. Central west: Goiás, Mato Grosso do Sul, Mato Grosso, and Distrito Federal (Brasília); north: Acre, Amapá, Amazonas, Pará, Rondônia, Roraima, and Tocantins; northeast: Alagoas, Bahia, Ceará, Maranhão, Paraíba, Piaui, Rio Grande do Norte, and Sergipe; southeast: Espirito Santo, Minas Gerais, Rio de Janeiro, and São Paulo; south: Paraná, Rio Grande do Sul, and Santa Catarina.

17. In lieu of a Cox Proportional Hazard model, I use a logistic model with time controls to capture the expected effects of federal health care financing on the adoption of PSF. I omit the variable T1 and include controls from T2 until the last yearly observation available for two reasons: first, the neighborhood effect variable is lagged by a year, rendering observations for T1 incomplete; second, the data is right censored, which means that the analysis terminates before all possible adoptions have taken place.

18. For further details on event history methodology for the social sciences, see Allison 1984; Box-Steffensmeier and Jones 1997, 2004a, 2004b.

19. The Ministry of Health does have a sophisticated online database, Datasus, with information on health financing; however, this data is available only for the most recent periods, from 1998 to the present.

20. Small cities: population less than 150,000; medium cities: population between 150,000 and 300,000; large cities: population greater than 300,000 (IBGE/Ipeadata).

21. Martins and Libânio (2005) provide IDH-M data for 1991 and 2000. I assume municipal trends for annual observations from 1992 to 1999 and extend the trends for later years.

22. In the sample, 2.9 percent adopt Bolsa Escola.

23. In the sample, 13.8 percent adopt PSF.

Chapter 4. Education Reform

1. In the case of education, municipalization involved the transfer of schools and their related administrative apparatus from state to municipal control.

2. The constitutional amendment passed in September 1996 and went into effect on January 1, 1998.

3. Up to 60 percent of the fund can be used for teacher salaries; no minimum salary is stipulated.

4. In 2004 the minimum was R$564 per pupil in first through fourth grades, and R$595 in fifth through eighth grades (Presidential Decree 5.299, December 7, 2004).

5. For more on the problem of assessing the origin of ideas, see especially Kingdon 1995, chap. 4.

6. For instance, Antonio Maria da Silveira in 1975 and Edmar Bacha and Roberto Mangabeira Unger in 1978 published on this topic. For discussion on the contribution of these early scholars, see Fonseca 2001, 99–109; Aguiar and Araújo 2002, 31.

7. Suplicy's interest in a cash-based minimum income program dates back to his graduate training in the United States, where he learned about Milton Friedman's ideas for a negative income tax, and policies such as Aid to Families with Dependent Children (AFDC) and later the Alaskan Permanent Fund Dividend Program.

8. Suplicy was a firm supporter of a universal program geared toward individuals, not families.

9. At the time, a minimum income was approximately C$45 thousand. The bill specifically called for a supplement for the difference between the minimum income threshold and actual income. In the event an individual had no income, the supplement would not exceed 50 percent of the threshold to encourage people to work.

10. An amended version of the Renda Mínima legislation was finally passed and signed by President Lula on January 8, 2004. However, even at the bill's signing Lula and others noted that they were uncertain whether the legislation could ever be implemented.

11. Although local governments would take up programs with the name Renda Mínima, these often differed from the original proposed by Suplicy. He nevertheless "consulted" with cities and "welcomed" modifications, suggesting they represent a single idea (interview Suplicy 2003).

12. The city is also home to nationally renowned UNICAMP (the University of Campinas), which has a well-known center in social policy evaluation, lending to both interest and ease for studies of the city's Programa de Garantia de Renda Mínima.

13. Lei No. 8.261, dated June 6, 1995, and regulamentado pelo Decree No. 11.471 of March 3, 1995.

14. Families had to have a per capita income of R$35 or below to meet eligibility requirements.

15. Heads of households signed a "Termo de Responsabilidade e de Compromisso," which required the following: the children's regular school attendance and regular attention to health care, and children could not reside on the streets. In addition, families were required to participate in monthly meetings.

16. Decree 16.270 on January 22, 1995, and regimented by Portaria 16 on February 9, 1995.

17. At the time, a minimum salary was approximately $76 US dollars. The benefit was fixed, regardless of the number of children in the household.

18. In 1996 the Campinas program received a semifinalist award, and the Brasília program received the top finalist award. Bolsa Escola also won the award Criança e Paz (Children and Peace) from UNICEF.

19. Interestingly, of all the organizations to evaluate and support the earliest Bolsa Escola efforts, only UNESCO was a truly education-oriented institution; all others are generalist organizations that focus on "good governance," poverty alleviation, and development.

20. See, for instance, Assunes 1997; Ibañez 1996, 1997; Dimenstein 1997; Geraldes 1999; Fernandes 2001; Lago 2001; Silva 1996; Steck 1997; Bolsa da sobrevivência 1997; Villaméa 2001; Mello 2000; Crianças darão nota à Bolsa-Escola 1997; 98% das pessoas 1997; Rossi 1997; Husseini 1996.

21. See, for instance, Becker 1999; Brazil: Schooling the Multitudes 1997; LaFranchi 1998.

22. In practice, Pacheco and Conseição Zotta Lopes had strong theoretical and administrative reasons for directing the cash benefit to mothers. In their previous work in public housing, they noticed how problematic it was when women were not included on deeds with their husbands. They noticed that without explicit attention to their status, women could become even more vulnerable. In addition, there were practical considerations: women were more likely to have custody of children and were often heads of households (interview Pacheco 2004).

23. The politics related to São Paulo's enactment were particularly intense as it became a battleground between two prominent politicians, Mayor Marta Suplicy (PT) and Education Minister Paulo Renato Souza (PSDB). Each politician defended the merits of the program. Mayor Suplicy offered a "compromise" that included an integrated program and the municipal government's logo on the Federal Bolsa Escola debit card. MEC officials took that as a sign of clear partisan politics and dismissed the idea decisively. Bill-

boards later went up across the city detailing how much money low-income citizens were losing because of the Suplicy administration's delayed enactment of the Federal Bolsa Escola.

24. Rocha noted that cities such as Belo Horizonte and Belém replicated the Brasília program wholesale; there were few adjustments made to target the particularities of those cities (interview 2003).

25. This figure represents half a minimum monthly salary (in 2000).

26. In my informal conversations with Bolsa Escola beneficiaries, it was clear that participants understood which politician was responsible for the program.

27. For an alternate analysis of the national adoption of Bolsa Escola Federal see Sugiyama (2011a).

28. Merilee Grindle offers a useful analysis of the ways in which teachers' unions have perceived themselves as "losers" when it comes to education reform in Latin America (2004).

29. Ana Fonseca, the director of Renda Mínima in São Paulo, has conducted evaluations of similar programs in Belo Horizonte, Brasília, Campinas, and Salvador. At the time, she held an academic post at UNICAMP.

30. None of the cities that adopted municipal Bolsa Escola or Renda Mínima programs benefited from federal funds. Vertical diffusion—such as that caused by federal inducements through financing—was not a feature of municipal Bolsa Escola replication. Belo Horizonte, São Paulo, and Salvador all created their own municipal programs without federal subsidies, demonstrating that horizontal diffusion across cities does take place. Surprisingly, even when the federal government later initiated its own program, many cities, including Belo Horizonte and São Paulo, balked at the chance to integrate their municipal program with the federal one, which would have allowed them to reduce municipal expenditures. They also maintained their own municipal programs even after their cities began administering the federal program.

31. According to Coppedge (1996) the PSDB is a centrist party. Lídice da Mata's own ideological dispositions place her to the left of center. After her term as mayor of Salvador, she joined the leftist party, PSB.

32. According to Coppedge (1996) the PMDB is a centrist party. Joaquim Roriz's own ideological dispositions place him on the right.

33. For instance, in 2000 the city provided needy citizens with a *cesta básica* (food basket), containing basic goods such as rice, beans, noodles, and so forth. Shortly thereafter, the municipality began working with grocery stores to enable beneficiaries to use supermarket cash cards for food purchases.

34. Officials disregarded the evaluations by the Fundação Getúlio Vargas–São Paulo, UNESCO, and the World Bank and commissioned their own study. The study the Roriz administration commissioned was not made available.

35. The Ministry of Justice monitors public interest civil society organizations in Brazil and provides a directory of these organizations on its website (2007). http://www.mj.gov.br/snj/oscip/default.htm.

36. When Cristovam Buarque lost his bid for reelection, rather than work with an existing education organization, he established his nongovernmental organization. Missão Criança was created to promote the spread of Bolsa Escola in Brazil and worldwide.

37. All applicants receive a certificate from the program, and all entries are included in a public database, available on the Internet.

38. Policy continuity across different mayoral and gubernatorial administrations is relatively rare in the Brazilian context.

39. The legislation for Belo Horizonte is a replica of the program in Brasília, including defining eligible families, the stipend, and targeting of women as beneficiaries. When it came time to implement the program, municipal administrators retained these program features (interview Rocha 2003; interview Leitão 2004; interview L. Castro 2004).

40. The couple separated in 2001 and divorced in 2003.

41. Porto Alegre in Rio Grande do Sul is well known for the Orçamento Participativo (Participatory Budgeting).

Chapter 5. Health Reform

1. CAPs were to be funded by workers (3 percent of monthly income) and employers (1 percent of company's annual gross income), and the government contributed in the form of taxes levied on users of the railway system. Later the "Triple Contribution" to *previdência social* would be enshrined in the 1934 constitution (Malloy 1979, 42).

2. A notable change was the expansion of benefits to agricultural workers. To curb the swell of rural-urban migration and preempt rural opposition and mobilization, the repressive government of General Emílio Médici (1969–74) created a social security scheme for agricultural workers (FUNRURAL) and delegated its administration to the National Confederation of Rural Workers (CONTAG). This strategy sought to create a positive constituency for ARENA (Stepan 1978; chaps. 2–3 would call this "inclusion-

ary corporatism"). The rural workers' benefits would be subsidized by the urban sectors since these workers often lived in conditions of extreme poverty and could not afford a contribution scheme (Weyland 1996, 90). This arrangement would later lay the foundation for incorporating other marginalized workers.

3. Subnational governments were responsible for 93 percent of all primary care.

4. From 1960 to 1970, there was a dramatic increase in the number of schools of medicine, from twenty-nine to seventy-three, representing an average increase of five university programs per annum (Mello 1977, 179). The 1970s also constituted an important turning point for the burgeoning field of collective health (*saúde coletiva*). Previously, medical schools emphasized social medicine (*medicina social*), which Cohn (1989) argues is conceptually different from a collective health (*saúde coletiva*) framework. In substituting "medicine" for "health," reformers sought to broaden the objective of their field. Further, in replacing "social" with "collective," this area would become more vague, requiring tracking of the entirety. At the same time, collective health maintains the relationship between the biological and the social (Cohn 1989, 126, translated and paraphrased by the author).

5. According to Cohn, in formulating their political strategies the sanitarian movement collaborated with various sectors, including other social movements (1989, 129).

6. Although the SUS includes principles of universal coverage and access, the *sanitaristas* fell short of some of their more ambitious goals. For instance, early constitutional proposals called for the state to create a "unitary health system" in which public and nonprofit facilities would have priority, and medical business would be contracted only as a last resort (NEPP 1989, 154–60, as cited in Weyland 1996, 168).

7. New administrative rules were codified in the 1993 *Norma Operacional Básica* (NOB), which specified the rules for decentralization and allowed municipalities to choose the degree of health care complexity they could offer. Municipalities were required to demonstrate their capacity to deliver the level of service they wanted to provide, and the majority of local governments were quick to participate in health decentralization. By 1997, 3127 of 4973 municipalities would participate in decentralization (Arretche 2004b, 174).

8. These changes were codified in the 1996 *Norma Operacional Básica* (NOB). Although NOB was published in 1996, it did not go into effect until 1998.

9. These experiments include Porto Alegre, Curitiba, Londrina, Marília, São Paulo, Botucatu, and Fortaleza (Terra and Malik 1998).

10. Jatene (1999) as cited in Ministry of Health (1999b, 13). For more on this program, see Terra and Malik (1998) and Hübner and Franco (2007).

11. As McGuire (2010, 167) notes, there is disagreement over the infant mortality rate in Ceará in 1987, with estimates ranging from 102 per 1000 to 77 per 1000 (Tendler 1997a, 21; Tendler 1997b, 110).

12. State officials sought to minimize rent-seeking behavior and traditional clientelism on the part of mayors by retaining control over the hiring of community health agents (Tendler 1997a, 24).

13. Given the disagreements over the baseline infant mortality rate in Ceará in 1987, it should not come as a surprise that there is disagreement over the improvements over time. Terra de Souza et al. (1999) report more modest declines, from 102 to 80 per 1000, for the period 1986–94 (see also McGuire 2010, 167).

14. The World Bank has cited the PAS as an experiment with innovative forms of organization and management (World Bank 2004, 178).

15. This model required that civil servants, who had been employed in municipal health care, depart from the public system and opt into the semi-privatized cooperative clinics. Approximately 35,000 civil servants (88.3 percent of all workers) were removed from their original positions when they declined to integrate into PAS cooperatives. Of those, 17,705 found positions in other municipal agencies, accepted demotions, or accepted positions in the municipal health secretariat (Gouveia and Palma 1999, 143).

16. Under the plan, the municipality would pay cooperatives approximately US$15 (or R$15) per capita per month. This figure was based on estimates of costs for similar services offered by the private sector (Cohn and Elias 1999, 19).

17. According to Viana and Dal Poz (1998), meeting participants included Eugenio Villaça Mendes (PAHO), Oscar Castillo (UNICEF), Halim Antônio Girade (UNICEF), and Luiz Odorico de Andrade (municipal secretary of health for the city of Quixada in the state of Ceará) (1998, 19).

18. Programmatic details were conceived at the December meeting but were elaborated by staff from the Ministry of Health in 1994 (Viana and Dal Poz 1998, 20).

19. The federal research agency, IPEA, produced a report, *Mapa de Fome,* which identified the poorest cities. This report served as the basis for determining eligibility for PSF participation (Vasconcellos 1999, 156).

20. Since December 1993 the Ministry of Health has been under the leadership of Henrique Antônio Santillo (August 1993–January 1995), Adib Domingos Jatene (January 1995–November 1996), José Carlos Seixas (November–December 1996), José Carlos de Albuquerque (December 1996–March 1998), José Serra (March 1998–February 2002), Barjas Negri (February 2002–December 2002), and Humberto Sérgio Costa Lima (January 2003–July 2005).

21. Minister Adib Jatene was so enthusiastic about the program that he took it to the president's cabinet and introduced it to the president and first lady, Ruth Cardoso. They traveled together to the northeast to see it on the ground (interview 2003).

22. Several government documents illustrate the evolution of PSF institutionalization within the ministry; see, for example, Ministry of Health (1997, 1999a, 2002b, 2009, 2011).

23. From the very beginning, the staffing of PSF teams has required creative human resource solutions that differ from conventional hiring associated with civil servant contracts (Viana and Dal Poz 1998, 29). Part of the human resource challenge comes from the difference between existing civil servant positions for professional staff and the longer number of work hours (forty hours full time) required of professional PSF team members. An additional challenge is the residency requirement for community health agents, which is unusual among competitive civil servant positions. As Viana and Dal Poz (1998) note, municipalities found different subcontracting solutions for staffing health teams, including contracts made between municipal health secretariats and neighborhood associations or cooperatives (29n24). While Tendler's study of PACS in Ceará highlights the important safeguards put in place to reduce the possibility that patronage and clientelism would trump meritocratic criteria for selecting personnel (1997a, 28–29), in practice local governments have discretion over the selection of PSF personnel and practices vary.

24. ACS training in sanitation and preventive medicine occurs after they are hired.

25. Women in Latin America often face a triple burden of paid work, unpaid family care, and community care. The job of an ACS blends traditional gender roles that delegate to women responsibility for family life and domesticity and for their community.

26. Adib Jatene argued that even in cities like São Paulo, with sophisticated health infrastructure, PSF represented a new "add-on" service because there were territories of the city that were underserved by clinics and

hospitals. In his view, the conditions of urban poverty in the city's periphery are similar to those of underserved rural communities in the northeast (interview Jatene 2003).

27. The Buarque administration gave the PSF program its own name, Saúde em Casa.

28. Professional staff within the PSF health teams, including nurses and doctors, earn more than their respective municipal civil servant colleagues, in some instances twice as much (Viana and Dal Poz 1998, 29n24).

29. As Bisol (interview 2004) explained, the entire health care system was the source of a lot of money (for services, medication, operational expenses, etc.) and represented an opportunity for graft. He estimates that R$40 million (approximately US$20 million) in health funds went to the construction of the district's bridge. In 2004 the Ministério Público was planning to investigate new allegations into clientelistic practices with health care delivery, including a scheme in which doctors on the government payroll offered preferential services to patients with political connections. The new allegations involved doctors paid by the federal district but contracted through the Instituto Candango de Solidariedade, a nonprofit association, which had ties to Wesliam Roriz, Governor Roriz's wife.

30. Initially technocrats in the city government wanted to build off of the existing ACS program. They also favored complete PSF coverage for the health district Subúrbio Ferroviário, which has some of the worst health indicators. But nearly four years after the program's start, only about 50 percent of that district's population was covered by PSF (thirty-five PSF teams). Rather than extend full coverage within that district, the city started extending PSF with teams in districts 2 (Itapagipe), 3 (São Caetano), and 12 (Cajazeiras).

31. Mayor Célio de Castro suffered a massive stroke in November 2001; his vice-mayor, Fernando Pimentel, served the rest of his term. Mayor de Castro died prior to the start of field research.

32. As Cueto (2004) explains, the international situation surrounding the Alma Ata conference was highly politicized given the context of the Cold War. Despite early difficulties selecting an appropriate location for the event, the conference included three thousand delegates from around the world, with seventy participants from Latin America, 97 percent of whom represented public health ministries (Cueto 2004, 1867). The conference and its proceedings had a lasting effect on Brazilian public health officials, who often refer to Alma Ata goals during interviews (e.g., interview Machado 2003; interview Andrade 2004).

33. As Cueto notes, Brazil was the largest country recipient of Rockefeller Foundation donations in the Americas from 1913 to 1940. The vast majority of those funds went toward research for disease control (e.g., yellow fever). After 1946 the foundation focused grant making on physiological research through support for schools of medicine in São Paulo and Bahia (1990, 230–32).

34. Adib Jatene, who became health minister in 1995, was supportive of the PSF and argued that it was not a "poor program for the poor." In 1997 the ministry published *Saúde da Família: Uma estratégia para reorientação do modelo assistencial.* In 2000 the ministry framed the PSF program as the principal model for basic health (World Bank 2004) and encouraged municipalities to hire enough PSF health teams to cover 100 percent of their jurisdiction's population.

35. This viewpoint was expressed by the researcher and state health policy analyst Virginia Junkeira (interview 2003). However, World Bank health policy program officer Jerry La Forgia asserted that the idea that the bank-imposed PSF was misguided; bank staff follow Brazilian government ministers' lead (interview 2004).

36. For example, the Programa de Interiorização de Ações de Saúde e Saneamento (PIASS) was first introduced in the northeast in 1976 and lasted until 1979. From 1980 to 1985 the PIASS was extended to other areas, including São Paulo. For a history of sanitarian policy and community health, see J. Silva and Dalmaso (2002).

37. The first volume of *SANARE* focuses on the PSF as a strategy to restructure public health (vol. 1, no. 1, Oct.–Dec. 1999).

38. At the time this was a theoretically based discussion without significant evidence. In recent years, scholars of public health have begun tracking the effects of PSF on health outcomes. Macinko et al. (2010) find that municipalities with high PSF enrollment have lower rates of chronic disease hospitalization rates. This suggests that PSF may in fact improve system performance by reducing unnecessary hospitalization.

39. Macinko et al. note that in 2005 municipal contributions range from 0 to nearly 100 percent of program costs. They estimate of the cost of PSF is US$30 per capita (2007, 2079).

40. It is worth noting that while PT city council members opposed PAS, they were also skeptical of implementing PSF.

41. Paulo Maluf has consistently asserted his innocence against accusations of corruption. Nevertheless, in 2005 he spent forty days in jail on

accusations of racketeering, tax evasion, and money laundering. In March 2007 the New York City district attorney's office indicted him in a corrupt kickback scheme at the expense of Brazilian taxpayers. According to District Attorney Robert Morgenthau, Maluf and four coconspirators stole at least $11.6 million, although they are believed to have stolen more than $140 million as that sum passed through the New York bank account linked to Maluf (Rohter and Hartocollis 2007, A9).

42. According to Cohn and Elias, votes on the PAS corresponded strictly to partisan lines: all center-left and left city councillors from the PSDB, PT, PV, and PC do B voted against the proposal; all members of the right-of-center parties, including PPR, PTB, PL, and PFL, voted in favor; of the twelve members from the PMDB, 1 abstained and 1 broke with the party to oppose the measure (1999, 45–47).

43. For a full description of QUALIS, see Capistrano (1999).

44. As mayor of Santos in the state of São Paulo, Capistrano initiated several public health policies to address the city's unique challenges as one of the country's most important port cities. Santos developed programs for girls and young women to reduce the incidence of prostitution and programs to curb the spread of HIV/AIDS.

45. Conselho Nacional de Secretários Municipais de Saúde (CONASEMS) is a national association of municipal health secretaries; the association publishes research and organizes national and regional meetings.

46. This point was made by Luiz Odorico de Andrade in reference to CONASEMS (interview 2004). The municipal secretary of health under Marta Suplicy (São Paulo) acknowledged a large rift between northeastern and southeastern professionals, stating that many public health experts were dismissive of innovations from the poor northeast as unrelated to the needs of their region (interview Martins Alves 2004).

47. Adib Jatene, a prominent cardiologist, has worked in various administrative public health positions, first serving as state secretary of health under Governor Paulo Maluf during the military regime. Later he accepted the position of minister of health under Presidents Fernando Collor do Mello (PRN) and Fernando Henrique Cardoso (PSDB). Dr. David Capistrano, Jr., was firmly entrenched in the leftist *movimento sanitário* and had served as the mayor of Santos (PT), a port city in the state of São Paulo. David Capistrano not only worked across partisan lines by partnering with Adib Jatane, but he also built a solid relationship with José Serra of the PSDB; see, for example, Serra's warm obituary for Capistrano (2000, 195–98).

48. As Adib Jatene explained, David Capistrano's father was a Communist and activist who had been persecuted by the government. Although the military government later issued an amnesty to political opponents, then-secretary Adib Jatene was under pressure to fire him. Since there was no evidence that Capistrano had misused his post for political reasons, Jatene refused to do so. Although their paths did not cross for many years, Jatene would take an interest in Capistrano's later accomplishments in Bauru and Santos. Dr. Jatene held David Capistrano, Jr., in the highest regard for his work in public health. He was especially impressed by the fact that Capistrano left both Bauru and Santos with empty pockets; in other words, unlike other politicians, he had not enriched himself by stealing public resources (interview Jatene 2003).

49. For instance, members of his health policy team from Santos expressed deep skepticism about the PSF program; they thought it was a "poor program for the poor." But he managed to turn around Silveira and Mattos, who joined him in administering QUALIS (interview Silveira 2003; Mattos 2003).

50. Capistrano died in October 2000, thus I was unable to interview him for this research.

51. Fiscal transfers for PSF were calculated on a sliding scale (from R$28,000 to R$54,000 per team per year) and depended on the overall percentage of the population covered under the program and the number of health teams in place. The formula favored cities that adopted the program with expansive coverage of the population (Ministério da Saúde, Portaria no. 1329, Dec. 12, 1999, as cited in World Bank 2002, 46).

52. Cristovam Buarque was affiliated with the PT, which was in opposition to then-president Fernando Henrique Cardoso of the PSDB. During the Joaquim Roriz (PMDB) administrations (1998–2002; 2002–6) Brasília officials encountered resistance from the federal government, which only intensified once President Luis Inácio Lula da Silva (PT) took office in 2002.

53. According to officials in Salvador, each PSF team has an estimated operational cost of R$30,000 (about US$10,000), of which the Ministry of Health provides R$2,800 (US$933) (i.e., less than 10 percent). The ministry also provides R$40,000 (US$13,333) for the development of each new PSF facility. Thus, by their calculations the financial incentives were too small for a large city like Salvador (interview Queiroz 2004; interview Nossa 2004). Professionals who worked on PSF in Salvador certainly believed they had limited resources to operate the program. These figures cited by Queiroz and Nossa are lower than those established by the Ministry of Health in guidelines

established in November 12, 1999 (Ministry of Health 1999a). Unfortunately, officials in Salvador's Health Department were not forthcoming in providing budget revenue and expenditure data across programmatic areas.

Chapter 6. Conclusion

1. This is one reason why I observed that supervisors pay close attention to community health agents and prohibit political activities while "on the job." Agents are barred from wearing campaign pins, for example.

2. For example, Martins Alves noted that in São Paulo the PT was fiercely opposed to PSF on ideological grounds (interview 2004).

3. In the study of American politics, incrementalism is a main feature of policy making, rather than wholesale reinvention or reversal (Lindblom 1959; Pierson 1994).

4. The ABRASCO membership database was managed in a similar manner.

5. Data for the 1992 mayoral elections is unavailable for most municipalities. Even data on the city of São Paulo is unavailable from the state's election tribunal.

6. At the time of Salvador's brief political turnover, Senator Antônio Carlos Magalhães had supported President Collor. When Collor was impeached on corruption charges, ACM, who had long been implicated in shady deals himself, lost some political capital.

7. Scholars in various fields have examined how simple or "flexible" ideas make them more likely to diffuse. See, for instance, Mossberger (2000) on the diffusion of empire zones in the American context, and Heath and Heath (2007) on why some ideas stick and others do not.

8. Most doctors with municipal contracts who worked in the four research sites were employed with part-time shifts. Thus, in practice many doctors in Brazil hold two jobs to fill a full-time schedule. PSF, however, requires not only that doctors work within a designated territory but that they do so full-time. Contract negotiations with municipal health care workers were often a source of conflict between labor unions and municipal administrators (interview M. Souza 2004; interview Costa 2003; interview D'Agostini 2003; interview Camara 2004).

9. One of the job requirements for the ACS is residency in the district in which the person works. If a community health agent moves, she is subject to job loss. Thus, administrators often need flexibility in both hiring

and firing. One mechanism municipal authorities have used to ensure flexibility is to subcontract work through nonprofit associations. For instance, São Paulo established partnerships with fourteen institutions to implement PSF throughout the municipality (Sousa 2003, 93).

10. Several scholars have examined the impact of complex, simple, and flexible ideas on policy making; see especially Mossberger 2000.

11. See Cueto (2004) and Magnussen, Ehiri, and Jolly (2004) for more on the framing and origins of selective versus comprehensive primary care debates in the world health community.

12. Cristovam Buarque himself credits the simplicity of the idea as one of its general appeals (interview 2004).

13. I am grateful to Peter K. Spink, who made this observation.

14. For instance, the ministry's preference for PSF meant that in practice, cities such as Niterói with the Programa Médico da Família did not qualify for federal PSF funds. Later, the ministry would support "similar" programs, albeit with reduced levels of funding.

15. Mossberger defines policy labels as general concepts, with or without some elements of policy design, and symbolism (2000, 116–17).

16. Macinko et al. (2007) confirm these findings for the years 1999–2004, a period of rapid PSF expansion, when infant mortality rates declined about 13 percent. McGuire notes that despite serious challenges in implementation, PSF has contributed to a significant decline in infant mortality (2010, 170–71)

17. Bolsa Família is legally established in Law 10.836 of January 9, 2004, and Decree No. 5.209 of September 17, 2004.

18. Brazil has made notable strides in lowering poverty rates, due in large measure to macroeconomic growth, low unemployment rates, and several social policy measures (including Bolsa Família). For recent analyses on the effects of Bolsa Família, see Castro and Modesto (2010a, 2010b).

19. For more on the overall structure of social spending in Brazil, including discussion of the regressive features of Social Security and education spending, see Hunter and Sugiyama (2009).

20. Innovations are more likely to spread when innovative ideas are compatible with preexisting values and beliefs (Rogers 2003, 240–43). Mensch et al. (1999) argue that gendered norms can be difficult to change. For instance, despite laws banning female circumcision, clitoridectomy remained a common practice in Ghana; a diffusion campaign to outlaw the practice made slow progress because the policy conflicted with cultural norms (as cited in Rogers 2003, 242–43).

21. As chapter 4 explains, Senator Eduardo Suplicy had initially proposed a minimum income for all individuals, regardless of marital status and number of dependents. This individualistic approach to social policy was rejected by Brazilian policy makers who embrace the idea that social policy ought to be centered on vulnerable families with children.

22. Here I refer to traditional development concerns surrounding family planning and fertility as well as international public health goals (GOBI) that include promotion of maternal breast feeding.

23. In practice, health teams in the four research sites explain that they view "family" in terms of "household." The registry of families includes all persons in the same domicile, regardless of relational ties.

24. Lipsky coined the term "street-level bureaucrats" to describe public service workers who interact with citizens in the course of their jobs (1980, 3).

25. On SEDESOL, see Bruhn (1996) and Fox (1994).

26. To my knowledge, there was minimal initial contact between Mexican and Brazilian policy makers at the *design* stage of these programs.

27. Mexican officials have undoubtedly contributed tremendously in this capacity as well, by lending expertise at international meetings, writing publications, and hosting international visitors. I focus here on the contributions of Brazilian officials in the transnational diffusion process.

28. See Hagopian (1996) for discussion of traditional politics in Brazil.

REFERENCES

Interviews

Aguiar, Marcelo. 2003. Chief of Staff at Ministry of Education. November 24. Brasília.

Almeida, Aide. 2003. Administrator in Health Program, UNESCO-Brasília. December 16. Brasília.

Almeida, Ivonette Santiago de. 2003. Administrator, Finance Department in Secretary of Health (Federal District). December 3. Brasília.

Alves, Rita de Cassia. 2003. Administrator, Finance Department in Municipal Department of Health. September 17. São Paulo.

Andrade, Luiz Odorico Monteiro de. 2004. President of CONASEMS and Municipal Secretary of Health of Sobral (CE). March 20. Natal.

Araújo, Raimundo Caires. 2004. Municipal Secretary of Work and Social Development. July. Salvador.

Arruda, Maria Arindelita Neves de. 2003. Coordinator of PSF in Brasília under Governor Cristovam Buarque. December 8. Brasília.

Augusti, Maria Teresa. 2003. President, Instituto Florestan Fernandes. October 27. São Paulo.

Bandeira, Célia. 2004. Former Special Secretary for Monitoring for Mayor Lídice da Mata. July 9. Salvador.

Barbosa, Alfonso Celso Renan. 2003. Former Coordinator of Bolsa Escola in Municipal Department of Education. March 22. Belo Horizonte.

Bisol, Jairo. 2004. Public Prosecutor, Public Prosecutor's Office for the Federal District. May 4. Brasília.

Boa Sorte, Alfredo. 2004. President of Sindicato dos Médicos. May 31. Salvador.

Borio, Jõao Carlos. 2003. Administrator, Municipal Department of Workforce and Social Development. September 15. São Paulo.

Bruno, Naire. 2000. Staff member, Municipal Department of Public Assistance. November 13. São Paulo.

Buarque, Cristovam. 2004. Senator and former governor of the Federal District. April 26. Brasília.

———. 2009. Senator and former governor of the Federal District. Discussion at conference On the Origins, Implementation, and Diffusion of Conditional Cash Transfer Programs, sponsored by the University of Texas at Austin. April 18.

Camara, Gilherme Ribeiro. 2004. Representative, Sindicato dos Médicos–MG. April 6. Belo Horizonte.

Campos, Claúdia Valentina de Arruda. 2003. Researcher with Fundação Getúlio Vargas–São Paulo consulting group. September 17. São Paulo.

Castro, Laura Alfonso. 2004. Bolsa Escola Administrator, Municipal Department of Education. March 4. Belo Horizonte.

Castro, Marcelo Lúcio Ottoni de. 2004. Senate health researcher. May 3. Brasília.

Castro, Maria Céres Pimenta Spínola. 2004. Former Secretary of Education. February 11. Belo Horizonte.

Coelho, Cristina. 2004. Administrator of Programa Saúde da Família, Municipal Department of Health. February 16. Belo Horizonte.

Conceição, Maria José da (Maninha). 2003. Former Health Secretary of the Federal District. December 1. Brasília.

Correia, Rogério. 2004. Former City Councilor for Belo Horizonte. March 29. Belo Horizonte.

Costa, Célia Regina. 2003. Union representative, SINDESAÚDE. October 30. São Paulo.

Cunha, Célio da. 2004. National program officer, UNESCO-Brasília. January 22. Brasília.

D'Agostini, Angelo. 2003. Union representative, SINDESAÚDE. October 30. São Paulo.

D'Angelo, Francisco. 2004. Secretary of Health, Municipal Department of Health for Niterói. March 17. Natal.

Dimitrov, Pedro. 2003. Senior Adviser to Secretary of Health Eduardo Jorge Martins Alves. November 6. São Paulo.

Elias, Paulo. 2003. Professor and researcher, CEDEC. September 19. São Paulo.

Eon, Fábio. 2003. Administrator, Communications Department, UNESCO-Brasília. December 16. Brasília.

Escorel de Moraes, Sarah Maria. 2004. Professor at Fundação Oswaldo Cruz and consultant to Ministry of Health. March 18. Natal.

Fernandes, Silvio. 2004. Secretary of Health, Municipal Department of Health of Londrina. March 19. Natal.

Fontes, Alexandre. 2003. Archivist with Fundação Perseu Abramo. September 18. São Paulo.

Franco, Túlio Batista. 2004. Adjunct Secretary of Health of Belo Horizonte. February 12. Belo Horizonte.

Freitas, Estanislau de. 2003. Administrator, Municipal Department of Workforce and Social Development. October 2. São Paulo.

Galeano, Paula. 2004. Former Chief of Staff to Coordinator of Bolsa Escola Federal, Ministry of Education. April 16. São Paulo.

Geddes, José. 2003. Former State Secretary of Health. November 4. São Paulo.

Goldbaum, Moisés. 2003. Professor and President of ABRASCO. October 27. São Paulo.

Gomes, Cid. 2004. Mayor of Sobral (CE). July 8. Sobral.

Gouvea, Isamara. 2003. Administrator of Programa Saúde da Família for Municipal Department of Health. October 1. São Paulo.

Guedes, Ana Cláudia. 2003. Executive Secretary of CEBES. October 20. Rio de Janeiro.

Ibañez, Antonio. 2003. Former Secretary of Education of the Federal District. December 15. Brasília.

Jatene, Adib. 2003. Former Minister of Health. October 16. São Paulo.

Junkeira, Virgínia. 2003. Researcher, State Institute of Health. October 15. São Paulo.

Kayano, Jorge. 2003. Staff member, PÓLIS Institute. October 18. São Paulo.

La Forgia, Gerald M. 2004. Program Officer, Health Division, World Bank–Brazil. May 4. Brasília.

Lavinas, Lena. 2004. Professor of Economics, Federal University of Rio de Janeiro. January 14. Rio de Janeiro.

Leitão, Elizabeth. 2004. Former Director of Bolsa Escola Municipal in Belo Horizonte. January 19. Brasília.

Lima, Lílian Carneiro. 2003. Coordinator of Renda Minha for the Department of Education of the Federal District. December 10. Brasília.

Lopes, Conceição Zotta. 2003. Administrator of Bolsa Escola for the Department of Education of the Federal District. November 20. Brasília.

Lorenzo, Rosicler Aparecida Viegas Di. 2003. State Coordinator of Programa Saúde da Família. November 18. São Paulo.

Machado, Heloísa. 2003. Former Director of PSF, Ministry of Health. November 21. Brasília.

Madeira, Wilma. 2003. Staff member, Instituto Florestan Fernandes. October 27. São Paulo.

Magalhães, Ines. 2004. Former official at Workers' Party national headquarters. January 28. Brasília.

Manfredini, Marco. 2003. Chief of Staff in the office of City Councilor Carlos Neder. September 24. São Paulo.

Mariani, Mônica. 2003. Staff member, ABRASCO. October 20. Rio de Janeiro.

Martins Alves Sobrinho, Jorge Eduardo. 2004. Former Secretary of Health of São Paulo. March 19. Natal.

Mata, Lídice da. 2004. Former Mayor of Salvador. July 16. Salvador.

Mendes, Vera. 2004. Professor, School of Public Administration at the Federal University of Bahia. May 23. Salvador.

Meneses, Milton. 2004. Director of Programa Saúde da Família in the Federal District. January. Brasília.

Miura, Hiromi. 2003. Administrator, Secretary of Health of the Federal District. December 9. Brasília.

Modesto, Lucia. 2011. Former National Secretary of Income and Citizenship (SENARC), 2005–10, and Director of the Unified Registry, Ministry of Social Development. July 1. Brasília.

Nossa, Sonia. 2004. Staff member of Programa Saúde da Família, Municipal Department of Health. June 28. Salvador.

Oliveira, Leandro Valquer JL de. 2003. President, SINDSEP-SP. November 10. São Paulo.

Oswaldo, José. 2004. Coordinator of the Municipal Health Council. March 12. Belo Horizonte.

Pacheco, Marisa. 2004. Former Coordinator of Bolsa Escola, Department of Education of the Federal District. January 27. Brasília.

Paixão, Marcia. 2003. Coordinator of Municipal Renda Mínima program. October 9. São Paulo.

Passoni, Armelindo. 2003. Administrator, Department of Workforce and Social Development. October 2. São Paulo.

Paulics, Veronika. 2003. Staff member, PÓLIS Institute. October 8. São Paulo.

Peixinho, Albaneide Maria Lima. 2004. Former administrator for the Federal District's Department of Health. January 21. Brasília.

Pena, Moacir Ricoy. 2004. Administrator of Bolsa Escola for the Municipal Department of Education. March 9. Belo Horizonte.

Pesaro, Antonio Floriano. 2004. Former Coordinator of Bolsa Escola Federal for the Ministry of Education. April 16. São Paulo.

Pochman, Márcio. 2003. Secretary of Workforce and Social Development for São Paulo. November 4. São Paulo.

Queiróz Jorge da Silva, Iêda Zilmara de. 2004. Staff member of Programa Saúde da Família for the Municipal Department of Health. June 28. Salvador.

Ribeiro, Teresa. 2003. Staff member of the Liderança do PT for the City Council. September 12. São Paulo.

Rocha, Sonia. 2003. Former researcher at the Instituto de Pesquisa Aplicada (IPEA). October 21. Rio de Janeiro.

Rodrigues, Almira Correia de Caldas. 2003. Professor of Sociology at the University of Brasília and affiliate of Centro Feminista de Estudos e Assessoria (CFEMEA). December 4. Brasília.

Romero, Luis Carlos Pelizari. 2004. Senate health researcher in the Brazilian Senate. May 3. Brasília.

Santos, Fausto Perreira. 2004. Former Adjunct Secretary of Health for Belo Horizonte. January 26. Brasília.

Santos, Rosa Maria Barros dos. 2003. Coordinator, QUALIS–São Paulo. October 14. São Paulo.

Santos Filho, Serafim Barbosa. 2003. Administrator of PROESF in the Ministry of Health. November 25. Brasília.

Schneider, Alessandra. 2003. Administrator in health program at UNESCO-Brasília. December 16, Brasília.

Silva, Célio. 2003. President of Missão Criança. November 25. Brasília.

Silva, Edimar Gomes da. 2003. Chief of Staff for municipal city council president. October 3. São Paulo.

Silva, Joanna. 2003. Coordinator, Programa Sáude da Família for the Municipal Department of Health. October 15. São Paulo.

Silva, Maria de Salete. 2004. Former Secretary of Administration and Secretary of Education in the Lídice da Mata administration. June 1. Salvador.

Silveira, Lídia Tobias. 2003. Administrator, Municipal Department of Health. October 6. São Paulo.

Soares, Ana Maria da Silva. 2004. Staff member of Rede Feminista and member of the Municipal Health Council. March 10. Belo Horizonte.

Sousa, Maria Fátima de. 2003. Chief of Staff at Ministry of Health. December 1. Brasília.

Sousa, Valdomiro. 2003. Administrator, Federal Bolsa Escola program, Ministry of Education and Culture. November 24. Brasília.

———. 2011. Former Chief of International Information, Ministry of Social Development. July 4. Brasília.
Souza, Maria Aladilce de. 2004. President of Sindisaúde-Salvador. June 16. Salvador.
Souza, Paulo Renato. 2004. Former Minister of Education. April 16. São Paulo.
Suassuna, Afra. 2003. Director of Basic Health Care in the Ministry of Health. December 17. Brasília.
Suplicy, Eduardo. 2003. Senator, Brazilian Senate. October 31. São Paulo.
Turci, Maria. 2004. Adviser to the Department of Basic Health, Municipal Department of Health. February 16. Belo Horizonte.
Vasconcelos, Sonia. 2004. Administrator, Bolsa Escola program, Municipal Department of Education. March 4. Belo Horizonte.
Vaz, José Carlos. 2003. Staff member, PÓLIS Institute. October 8. São Paulo.
Weber, Silke. 2011. Former State Secretary of Education of Pernambuco, 1987–90 and 1995–98. July 8. Recife.
Woo, William. 2003. City Councilor and leader of the PSDB. November 12. São Paulo.

Focus Groups

Citizen Representatives to the Belo Horizonte Health Council. 2004. February 16. Belo Horizonte.
Citizen Representatives to the Salvador Health Council and Affiliates with Pastoral da Saúde. 2004. June 29. Salvador.

Additional Sources

Abers, Rebecca. 2000. *Inventing Local Democracy.* Boulder, CO: Lynne Rienner.
Abrantes, Raquel Pêgo, and Célia Almeida. 2002. Ámbito y papel de los especialitas en las reformas en los sistemas de salud: Los casos de Brasil y México. Working Paper no. 299 (September). Notre Dame, IN: Kellogg Institute.
Abrucio, Fernando Luiz. 2002. *Os barões da federação: Os governadores e a redemocratização brasileira.* 2nd ed. São Paulo: Editora Hucitec.

Affonso, Rui de Britto Álvares, and Pedro Luiz Barros Silva, eds. 1996. *Descentralização e políticas sociais.* São Paulo: FUNDAP.

Aguiar, Marcelo, and Carlos Henrique Araújo. 2002. *Bolsa-Escola: Education to Confront Poverty.* Brasília: UNESCO.

Allison, Paul D. 1984. *Event History Analysis: Regression for Longitudinal Event Data.* Vol. 07-046. Beverly Hills, CA: Sage Publications.

Almeida, Carlos, Tatiana Baptista, Claudia Travassos, and Silvia Porto. 2000. Health Sector Reform in Brazil. Inter-American Development Bank. Retrieved April 2, 2007, from http://www.iadb.org/sds/specialprograms/lachealthaccounts/documents/brasil_health_sector_reform.pdf.

Alvarez, Sonia E. 1990. *Engendering Democracy in Brazil: Women's Movements in Transition Politics.* Princeton: Princeton University Press.

———. 1994. The (Trans)formation of Feminism(s) and Gender Politics in Democratizing Brazil. In *The Women's Movement in Latin America,* edited by Jane S. Jaquette. Boulder, CO: Westview Press.

———. 1999. Advocating Feminism: The Latin American Feminist NGO "Boom." *International Feminist Journal of Politics* 1(2): 181–209.

Alvarez, Sonia E., Evelina Dagnino, and Arturo Escobar. 1998. Introduction: The Cultural and the Political in Latin American Social Movements. In *Cultures of Politics/Politics of Cultures: Re-Visioning Latin American Social Movements,* edited by Sonia E. Alvarez, Evelina Dagnino, and Arturo Escobar, 1–29. Boulder, CO: Westview Press.

Alves, Maria Helena Moreira. 1985. *State and Opposition in Military Brazil.* Austin: University of Texas Press.

Ames, Barry. 2001. *The Deadlock of Democracy in Brazil.* Ann Arbor: University of Michigan Press.

Ames, Barry, and Timothy Power. 2007. Parties and Governability in Brazil. In *Party Politics in New Democracies,* edited by Paul Webb and Stephen White, 179–212. New York: Oxford University Press.

Apter, David Ernest. 1964. *Ideology and Discontent.* London: Free Press of Glencoe.

Araújo, Carlos Henrique, and Nair Heloísa Bicalho de Souza, eds. 1998. Programas de Renda Mínima no Brasil: Impactos e potencialidades. Vol. 30. São Paulo: PÓLIS.

Araújo, Carlos Henrique, and Eliezer Lopes. 1996. Falso Dilema. *Jornal de Brasília,* May 31, 2.

Armijo, Leslie, and Christine Kearney. 2008. Does Democratization Alter the Policy Process? Trade Policymaking in Brazil. *Democratization* 15(5): 991–1017.

Arretche, Marta. 2000. *Estado federativo e políticas sociais: Determinantes da decentralização.* Rio de Janeiro: Editora Reven.

———. 2004a. Federalismo e políticas sociais no Brasil: Problemas de coordenação e autonomia. *São Paulo em Perspectiva* 18(2): 17–26.

———. 2004b. Toward a Unified and More Equitable System: Health Reform in Brazil. In *Crucial Needs, Weak Incentives: Social Sector Reform, Democratization, and Globalization in Latin America,* edited by Robert R. Kaufman and Joan M. Nelson, 155–88. Baltimore: Johns Hopkins University Press.

Arretche, Marta, and Eduardo Marques. 2002. Municipalização da saúde no Brasil: Diferenças regionais, poder do voto e estratégias de governo. *Ciência & Saúde Coletiva* 7(3): 455–79.

Assunes, Márcia. 1997. Corte na Bolsa-Escola irrita mães. *Jornal de Brasília,* April 17, 1997, 20.

Auyero, Javier. 2000. The Logic of Clientelism in Argentina: An Ethnographic Account. *Latin American Research Review* 35(3): 55–81.

Baiocchi, Gianpaolo. 2003a. Emergent Public Spheres: Talking Politics in Participatory Governance. *American Sociological Review* 68(1): 52–74.

———, ed. 2003b. *Radicals in Power: The Workers' Party (PT) and Experiments in Urban Democracy.* New York: Zed Books/Palgrave.

Balla, Steven J. 2001. Interstate Professional Associations and the Diffusion of Policy Innovations. *American Politics Research* 29(3): 221–45.

Barrientos, Armando, and Jocelyn DeJong. 2006. Reducing Child Poverty with Cash Transfers: A Sure Thing? *Development Policy Review* 24(5): 537–52.

Barros, Andréa e Policarpo, Jr. 1996. Ajuda e até carinho fora do horror. *Véja,* October 30, 52–55.

Baud, Michiel. 1998. The Quest for Modernity: Latin American Technocratic Ideas in Historical Perspective. In *The Politics of Expertise in Latin America,* edited by M. A. Centeno and P. Silva. London: Palgrave.

Bava, Silvio Caccia. N.d. Bolsa-Escola (school bursary program): A Public Policy on Minimum Income and Education. São Paulo: Polis/Instituto de Estudos, Formação e Assessoria em Políticas Sociais.

Bava, Silvio Caccia, Vera da Silva Telles, Selva Ribas Bejarano, Carlos Henrique Araújo, and Nair Heloísa Bicalho de Sousa. N.d. Programa de Renda Mínima no Brasil: Impactos e potencialidades. International Development Research Centre (Canada). Retrieved August 16, 2005, from http://www.idrc.ca/uploads/user-S/11051078131caccia.doc.

———. 1998. *Programas de Renda Mínima no Brasil.* PÓLIS: Estudos, Formação e Assessoria em Políticas Sociais, 30, 1–130.

———. 1999. Bolsa-Escola: Uma política pública de Renda Mínima e educacional. Paper presented at the Seminario Internacional: Reformas a la Política Social en América Latina: Resultados y Perspectivas. Washington, DC, May 11–12.

Beck, Nathaniel, Jonathan N. Katz, and Richard Tucker. 1998. Taking Time Seriously: Time-Series-Cross-Section Analysis with a Binary Dependent Variable. *American Journal of Political Science* 42(4): 1260–88.

Becker, Gary S. 1999. Bribe Third World Parents to Keep Their Kids in School. *Business Week,* November 22, Economic Viewpoint no. 3656, 15.

Bennett, Andrew. 2010. Process Tracing and Causal Inference. In *Rethinking Social Inquiry: Diverse Tools, Shared Standards,* 2nd ed., edited by Henry E. Brady and David Collier, 207–19. Lanham, MD: Rowman and Littlefield.

Bennett, Colin J. 1991. What Is Policy Convergence and What Causes It? *British Journal of Political Science* 21(2): 215–33.

Berman, Sheri. 2001. Ideas, Norms, and Culture in Political Analysis. *Comparative Politics* 33(2): 231–50.

Berry, Frances Stokes. 1994. Sizing Up State Policy Innovation Research. *Policy Studies Journal* 22(3): 443.

Berry, Frances Stokes, and William D. Berry. 1990. State Lottery Adoptions as Policy Innovations: An Event History Analysis. *American Political Science Review* 84(2): 395–415.

———. 1992. Tax Innovation in the States: Capitalizing on Political Opportunity. *American Journal of Political Science* 36(3): 715–42.

———. 1999. Innovation and Diffusion Models in Policy Research. In *Theories of the Policy Process,* edited by Paul A. Sabatier. Boulder, CO: Westview Press.

Birdsall, Nancy, Barbara Bruns, and Richard H. Sabot. 1996. Education in Brazil: Playing a Bad Hand Badly. In Birdsall and Sabot 1996, 7–47.

Birdsall, Nancy, and Richard H. Sabot, eds. 1996. *Opportunity Foregone: Education in Brazil.* Washington, DC: Inter-American Development Bank.

Boix, Carles. 2000. Partisan Governments, the International Economy, and Macroeconomic Policies in Advanced Nations, 1960–93. *World Politics* 53 (October): 38–73.

Bolsa da sobrevivência. 1997. *Jornal de Brasília,* November 9, 6.

Bolsa-Escola um exemplo de Brasília. 1996. *Ciência Hoje* 21 (November/December): 56–62.

Box-Steffensmeier, Janet M., and Bradford S. Jones. 1997. Time Is of the Essence: Event History Models in Political Science. *American Journal of Political Science* 41(4): 1414–61.

———. 2004a. *Event History Modeling: A Guide for Social Scientists.* New York: Cambridge University Press.

———. 2004b. *Timing and Political Change: Event History Modeling in Political Science.* Ann Arbor: University of Michigan Press.

Brady, Henry E. 2004. Doing Good and Doing Better: How Far Does the Quantitative Template Get Us? In *Rethinking Social Inquiry: Diverse Tools, Shared Standards,* edited by Henry E. Brady and David Collier, 53–67. Lanham, MD: Rowman and Littlefield.

Brazil Constitution. 1988.

Brazil: Schooling the Multitudes. 1997. *The Economist,* U.S. ed., October, 18, 38.

Brinks, Daniel, and Michael Coppedge. 2006. Diffusion Is No Illusion: Neighbor Emulation in the Third Wave of Democracy. *Comparative Political Studies* 39(5): 463–89.

Brooks, Sarah M. 2002. Social Protection and Economic Integration. *Comparative Political Studies* 35(5): 491–523.

Bruhn, Kathleen. 1996. Social Spending and Political Support: The "Lessons" of the National Solidarity Programme in Mexico. *Comparative Politics* 28(2): 151–77.

Buarque, Cristovam, Vanessa Castro, and Marcelo Aguiar. 2002. Um pouco da história do Bolsa Escola. *Serviço Social e Sociedade* 66: 126–44.

Burt, Ronald S. 1987. Social Contagion and Innovation: Cohesion versus Structural Equivalence. *American Journal of Sociology* 92(6): 1287–1335.

Caldas, Eduardo de Lima, and Estêvão Passos Eller. 2005. Programa Paidéia de Saúde da Família: Campinas (SP). In *20 Experiências de Gestão Pública e Cidadania—Ciclo de premiação 2003,* edited by F. M. D. Oliveira, H. B. Barboza, and M. A. C. Teixeira, 287–97. São Paulo: Programa Gestão Pública e Cidadania, Fundação Getúlio Vargas–São Paulo.

Câmara dos Deputados. Comissião de Educação, Cultura e Desporto, Brazil. 2002. Renda Mínima Vinculada à Educação: Seminario Nacional. Brasília: Centro de Documentação e Informação (CEDI)/Coordenação de Publicações (CODEP).

Camargo, José Márcio. 1993. Os miseraveis. *Folha de São Paulo,* March 23.

Capistrano Filho, David. 1999. O Programa de Saúde da Família em São Paulo. *Estudos Avançados* 13(35): 89–100.

Carmines, Edward G., and James A. Stimson. 1993. On the Evolution of Political Issues. In *Agenda Formation,* edited by William H. Riker, 151–68. Ann Arbor: University of Michigan Press.

Castro, Claudio de Moura, and Philip Musgrove. 1998. On the Nonexistence of "The Social Sector" or Why Education and Health Are More Different Than Alike. Washington, DC: Inter-American Development Bank/Education Unit Sustainable Development Department.

Castro, Jorge Abrahão de, and Lúcia Modesto, eds. 2010a. *Bolsa Família 2003–2010: Avanços e desafios.* Vol. 1. Brasília: Instituto de Pesquisa Econômica Aplicada (IPEA).

———, eds. 2010b. *Bolsa Família 2003–2010: Avanços e desafios.* Vol. 2. Brasília: Instituto de Pesquisa Econômica Aplicada (IPEA).

CENPEC. 2001. *Fontes de educação: Guia para jornalistas.* Brasília, DF: Fórum Mídia & Educação.

Cesar, Juraci A., Marcelo A. Cavaleti, Ricardo S. Holthausen, and Luis Gustavo S. de Lima. 2002. Mudanças em indicadores de saúde infantil em um município com agentes comunitários: O caso de Itapirapuã Paulista, Vale do Ribeira, São Paulo, Brasil. *Caderno de Saúde Pública* 18(6): 1647–54.

Chiaravalloti Neto, Francisco, Angelita A. C. Barbosa, Marisa B. Cesarino, Eliane A. Favaro, Adriano Mondini, Amena A. Ferraz, Margareth R. Dibo, and Maria Elenice Vicentini. 2006. Controle do dengue em uma area urbana do Brasil: Avaliação do impacto do Programa Saúde da Família com relação ao programa tradicional de controle. *Caderno de Saúde Pública* 22(5): 987–97.

Cohen, Ernesto, Rolando Franco, and Pablo Villatoro. 2006. México: El Programa de Desarrollo Humano Oportunidades. In *Transferencias con corresponsabilidade: Una mirada latino-americana,* edited by Ernesto Cohen and Rolando Franco, 87–136. México: SEDESOL.

Cohn, Amélia. 1989. Caminhos da reforma sanitária. *Lua Nova* 19: 123–40.

Cohn, Amélia, and Paulo E. Elias, eds. 1999. *O público e o privado na saúde: O PAS em São Paulo.* São Paulo: Editora Cortez.

Collier, David, and Richard E. Messick. 1975. Prerequisites versus Diffusion: Testing Alternative Explanations of Social Security Adoption. *American Political Science Review* 69(4): 1299–1315.

Collier, Ruth Berins, and David Collier. 1979. Inducements versus Constraints: Disaggregating "Corporatism." *American Political Science Review* 73(4): 967–86.

Coppedge, Michael. 1996. A Classification of Latin American Political Parties. University of Notre Dame Kellogg Institute Working Paper 144 (November). Available at http://www.nd.edu/~kellogg/publications/workingpapers/WPS/244.pdf. Accessed on February 20, 2009.

———. 1999. Thickening Thin Concepts and Theories: Combining Large N and Small in Comparative Politics. *Comparative Politics* 31(4): 465–76.

Corrales, Javier. 1999. The Politics of Education Reform: Bolstering the Supply and Demand; Overcoming Institutional Blocks. Washington, DC: World Bank.

Corréa, Marcos Sá. 1996. A grande revolução silenciosa. *Véja,* July 10, 48–53.

Costa, Cláudia Soares Costa, and Gabriel Rangel Visconti. 2001. Terceiro setor e desenvolvimento social. Brazil: BNDES. Available at: http://www.bndes.gov.br/conhecimento/relato/tsetor.pdf

Crianças darão nota à Bolsa-Escola. 1997. *Correio Braziliense,* September 24, 12.

Cueto, Marcos. 1990. The Rockefeller Foundation's Medical Policy and Scientific Research in Latin America: The Case of Physiology. *Social Studies of Science* 20(2): 229–54.

———. 2004. The Origins of Primary Health Care and Selective Primary Care. *American Journal of Public Health* 94(11): 1864–74.

De Ferranti, David, Guillermo E. Perry, Francisco H. G. Ferreira, and Michael Walton. 2004. Inequality in Latin America: Breaking with History? Washington, DC: World Bank.

Derthick, Martha. 1970. *The Influence of Federal Grants: Public Assistance in Massachusetts.* Cambridge, MA: Harvard University Press.

Desposato, Scott. 2007. How Does Vote Buying Shape the Legislative Arena? In *Elections for Sale: The Causes and Consequences of Vote Buying,* edited by Frederic Charles Schaffer, 101–22. Boulder, CO: Lynn Rienner.

Diamond, Larry. 1999. *Developing Democracy: Toward Consolidation.* Baltimore: Johns Hopkins University Press.

DiMaggio, Paul J., and Walter W. Powell. 1983. The Iron Cage Revisited: Institutional Isomorphism and Collective Rationality in Organizational Fields. *American Sociological Review* 48(2): 147–60.

Dimenstein, Gilberto. 1997. Bolsa Mágica. *Folha de São Paulo,* August 6, A19.

Dion, Michelle. 2010. *Workers and Welfare.* Pittsburgh, PA: University of Pittsburgh Press.

Downs, Anthony. 1957. *An Economic Theory of Democracy.* New York: Harper.

Draibe, Sonia. N.d. Programa de Agentes Comunitários de Saúde. Retrieved March 4, 2007. Available at http://www.mre.gov.br/cdbrasil/itamaraty/web/port/polsoc/asocial/progfed/agcomsau/index.htm.

———. 2004. Federal Leverage in a Decentralized System: Education Reform in Brazil. In *Crucial Needs, Weak Incentives: Social Sector Reform, Democratization, and Globalization in Latin America,* edited by Robert R. Kaufman and Joan M. Nelson, 375–406. Baltimore: Johns Hopkins University Press.

Draibe, Sonia M. 1985. *Rumos e metamorfoses: Um estudo sobre a constituição do estado e as alternativas da industrializacao no Brasil, 1930–1960.* Rio de Janeiro, RJ: Paz e Terra.

———. 1994. As políticas sociais do regime militar brasileiro. In *25 Anos de regime militar,* edited by Glaúcio Soares, A. Dillon, and Maria Celina D. Araújo. Rio de Janeiro: Fundação Getúlio Vargas.

Draibe, Sonia Miriam, Marta Teresa Arretche, Ana Maria Medeiros da Fonseca, Aparecida Neri de Souza, Geraldo di Giovani, Helena Kerr do Amaral, and Juarez Rubens Brandão Lopes. 1995. Politicas sociales y programas de combate a la pobreza en el Brasil. In *Estrategias para combatir la pobreza en America Latina: Programas, instituciones y recursos,* edited by Dagmar Raczynski, 97–161. Chile: Inter-American Development Bank.

Dresang, Lee T., Laurie Brebrick, Danielle Murray, Ann Shallue, and Lisa Sullivan-Vedder. 2005. Family Medicine in Cuba: Community-Oriented Primary Care and Complementary and Alternative Medicine. *Journal of the American Board of Family Practice* 18(4): 297–303.

Drèze, Jean, and Amartya Sen. 1989. *Hunger and Public Action.* Oxford: Clarendon.

Dugger, Celia W. 2004. To Help Poor Be Pupils, Not Wage Earners, Brazil Pays Parents. *New York Times,* January 3, A1, A6.

Elkins, Zachary, and Beth Simmons. 2005. On Waves, Clusters, and Diffusion: A Conceptual Framework. *Annals of the American Academy of Political and Social Science* 598(1): 33–51.

Encarnación, Omar G. 2003. *The Myth of Civil Society: Social Capital and Democratic Consolidation in Spain and Brazil.* New York: Palgrave Macmillan.

Epstein, Daniel J. 2009. Clientelism versus Ideology: Problems of Party Development in Brazil. *Party Politics* 15(3): 335–55.

Escobar, Arturo, and Sonia E. Alvarez. 1992. *The Making of Social Movements in Latin America: Identity, Strategy, and Democracy.* Boulder, CO: Westview Press.

Escorel, Sarah. 1999. *Reviravolta na saúde: Origem e articulacao do movimento sanitário.* Rio de Janeiro: Editora Fiocruz.

Evans, Mark, ed. 2004. *Policy Transfer in Global Perspective.* Burlington, VT: Ashgate.

Ewig, Christina. 2010. *Second-Wave Neoliberalism: Gender, Race, and Health Sector Reforms in Peru.* University Park: Pennsylvania State University Press.

Farah, Marta Ferreira Santos, and Hélio Batista Barboza, eds. 2000. *Novas experiências de gestão pública e cidadania.* Rio de Janeiro: Editora FGV.

Fausto, Boris. 1999. *A Concise History of Brazil.* New York: Cambridge University Press.

Fernandes, Antônio Sérgio Araújo. 2004. *Gestão municipal e participação social no Brasil: A trajetória de Recífe e Salvador (1986–2000).* São Paulo: AnnaBlume.

Fernandes, Diana. 2001. Dois em um. *O Globo,* January 5, 2.

Finnemore, Martha. 1993. International Organizations as Teachers of Norms: The United Nations Educational, Scientific, and Cultural Organization and Science Policy. *International Organization* 47(4): 565–97.

———. 1996. *National Interests in International Society.* Ithaca, NY: Cornell University Press.

Finnemore, Martha, and Kathryn Sikkink. 1998. International Norm Dynamics and Political Change. *International Organization* 52(4): 887–917.

Fiszbein, Ariel, Norbert Schady, Francisco H. G. Ferreira, Margaret Grosh, Nial Kelleher, Pedro Olinto, and Emmanuel Skoufias. 2009. Conditional Cash Transfers: Reducing Present and Future Poverty. World Bank Policy Research Report. Washington, DC: World Bank.

Fleischer, David. *Brazil Focus.* Electronic newsletter, July 5–11. Brasília, Brazil.

Fonseca, Ana Maria Medeiros da. 2001. *Família e política da Renda Mínima.* São Paulo: Cortez Editora.

Fortes, Paulo Antonio de Carvalho, and Simone Ribeiro Spinetti. 2004. O agente comunitário de saúde e a privacidade das informações dos usuários. *Caderno de Saúde Pública* 20(5): 1328–33.

Fox, Jonathan. 1994. The Difficult Transition from Clientelism to Citizenship: Lessons from Mexico. *World Politics* 46(2): 151–84.

Friedkin, Noah E. 1993. Structural Bases of Interpersonal Influence in Groups: A Longitudinal Case Study. *American Sociological Review* 58(6): 861–72.

FUNASA (Fundação Nacional de Saúde), Brazil. 1994. *Programa de Saúde da Família: Saúde dentro da casa.* Brasília: MS. FUNASA.

Garrett, Geoffrey, and Peter Lange. 1989. Government Partisanship and Economic Performance: When and How Does "Who Governs" Matter? *Journal of Politics* 51(3): 676–93.

Gay, Robert. 2006. The Even More Difficult Transition from Clientelism to Citizenship: Lessons from Brazil. In *Out of the Shadows,* edited by Patricia Fernández-Kelly and Jon Shefner, 195–218. University Park: Pennsylvania State University Press.

Geddes, Barbara. 1990. How the Cases You Choose Affect the Answers You Get. *Political Analysis* 2: 131–52.

———. 2003. *Paradigms and Sand Castles: Theory Building and Research Design in Comparative Politics.* Ann Arbor: University of Michigan Press.

George, Alexander L., and Andrew Bennett. 2005. *Case Studies and Theory Development in the Social Sciences.* Cambridge, MA: MIT Press.

George, Alexander L., and Timothy J. McKeown. 1985. Case Studies and Theories of Organizational Decision Making. In *Advances in Information Processing in Organizations,* vol. 2, edited by Robert F. Coulam and Richard A. Smith. Greenwich, CT: JAI Press.

Geraldes, Déborah. 1999. ONG leva Bolsa-Escola a Paracatu. *Correio Braziliense,* September 5, 8.

Gerring, John. 1997. Ideology: A Definitional Analysis. *Political Research Quarterly* 50(4): 957–94.

Goldbaum, Moisés, Reinaldo José Gianinia, Hillegonda Maria Dutilh Novaesa, and Chester Luiz Galvão César. 2005. Health Services Utilization in Areas Covered by the Family Health Program (Qualis) in São Paulo City, Brazil. *Revista de Saúde Pública* 39(1): 1–9.

Goldsteen, Raymond L., Julio Cesar Pereira, and Karen Goldsteen. 1990. The Engine or the Caboose: Health Policy in Developing Countries. *Revista de Saúde Pública* 24(6): 523–27.

Goulart, Flavio A. de Andrade. 1995. Municipalização: Veredas (Caminhos do Movimento Municipalista de Saúde no Brasil). Unpublished manuscript, Brasília.

Gouveia, Roberto, and José João Palma. 1999. SUS: Na contamão do neoliberalism e da exclusão social. *Estudos Avançados* 13(35): 139–46.

Graham, Carol. 1995. The Politics of Safety Nets. In *Economic Reform and Democracy,* edited by Larry Diamond and Mark F. Plattner. Baltimore: Johns Hopkins University Press.

Granovetter, Mark. 1973. The Strength of Weak Ties. *American Journal of Sociology* 78(6): 1360–80.

———. 1983. The Strength of Weak Ties: A Network Theory Revisited. *Sociological Theory* 1: 201–33.

Gray, Virginia. 1973. Innovation in the States: A Diffusion Study. *American Political Science Review* 67(4): 1174–85.

Grindle, Merilee Serrill. 1997. The Good Government Imperative: Human Resources, Organizations, and Institutions. In *Getting Good Government: Capacity Building in the Public Sectors of Developing Countries,* edited by Marilee S. Grindle, chap. 1. Cambridge, MA: Harvard University Press.

———. 2000. *Audacious Reforms: Institutional Invention and Democracy in Latin America.* Baltimore: Johns Hopkins University Press.

———. 2004. *Despite the Odds: The Contentious Politics of Education Reform.* Princeton: Princeton University Press.

———. 2007. *Going Local: Decentralization, Democratization, and the Promise of Good Governance.* Princeton: Princeton University Press.

Grindle, Merilee Serrill, and John W. Thomas. 1991. *Public Choices and Policy Change: The Political Economy of Reform in Developing Countries.* Baltimore: Johns Hopkins University Press.

Gross, Neal C. 1942. The Diffusion of a Culture Trait in Two Iowa Townships. MS thesis, Iowa State College, Ames, IA.

Grossback, Lawrence J., Sean Nicholson-Crotty, and David A. M. Peterson. 2004. Ideology and Learning in Policy Diffusion. *American Politics Research* 32(5): 521–45.

Haas, Peter M. 1989. Do Regimes Matter: Epistemic Communities and Mediterranean Pollution Coordination—Introduction. *International Organization* 46(1): 1–35.

Hagopian, Frances. 1996. *Traditional Politics and Regime Change in Brazil.* New York: Cambridge University Press.

Haider-Markel, Donald. 2001. Policy Diffusion as a Geographical Expansion of the Scope of Political Conflict: Same-Sex Marriage Bans in the 1990s. *State Politics and Policy Quarterly* 1(1): 5–26.

Hall, Anthony. 2006. From Fome Zero to Bolsa Família: Social Policies and Poverty Alleviation under Lula. *Journal of Latin American Studies* 38(4): 689–709.

Hassim, Shireen. 2005. Turning Gender Rights into Entitlements: Women and Welfare Provision in Postapartheid South Africa. *Social Research* 72(3): 621–46.

Heath, Chip, and Dan Heath. 2007. *Made to Stick: Why Some Ideas Survive and Others Die.* New York: Random House.

Hechter, Michael, and Karl-Dieter Opp, eds. 2001. *Social Norms.* New York: Russell Sage Foundation.

Holzmann, Robert, Mitchell Orenstein, and Michal Rutkowski, eds. 2003. *Pension Reform in Europe: Process and Progress.* Washington, DC: World Bank.

Horne, Christine. 2001. Sociological Perspectives on the Emergence of Social Norms. In Hechter and Opp 2001, 3–34.

Huber, Evelyn. 1996. Options for Social Policy in Latin America. In *Welfare States in Transition,* edited by G. Esping-Anderson, 141–91. London: Sage.

Hübner, Luiz Carlos Moreira, and Túlio Batista Franco. 2007. O Programa Médico de Família de Niterói como estrategia de implementação de um modelo de atenção que contemple os princípios e diretrizes do SUS. *PHYSIS: Revista de Saúde Coletiva* 17(1): 173–91.

Hunter, Wendy. 2003. Brazil's New Direction. *Journal of Democracy* 14(2): 151–62.

Hunter, Wendy, and Timothy J. Power. 2005. Lula's Brazil at Midterm. *Journal of Democracy* 16(3): 127–39.

———. 2007. Rewarding Lula: Executive Power, Social Policy, and the Brazilian Elections of 2006. *Latin American Politics & Society* 49(1): 1–30.

Hunter, Wendy, and Natasha Borges Sugiyama. 2009. Democracy and Social Policy in Brazil: Advancing Basic Needs, Preserving Privileged Interests. *Latin American Politics & Society* 51(2): 29–57.

Huntington, Samuel P. 1957. Conservatism as an Ideology. *American Political Science Review* 51(2): 454–73.

Husseini, Samya. 1996. Bolsa Escola recebe prêmio do UNICEF. *Correio Braziliense,* November 12, 14.

Ibañez Ruiz, Antonio. 1996. Querem Acabar com a Bolsa-Escola. *Jornal de Brasília,* October 22, 6.

———. 1997. A coerência da Bolsa Escola. *Correio Braziliense,* May 26, 2.

Instituto Nacional de Estudos e Pesquisas Educacionais (INEP). N.d. *Mapa do analfabetismo no Brasil.* Ministério de Educação. Brasília, Brazil. Available at www.publicacoes.inep.gov.br/arquivos/%7B3D805070-D9D0-42DC-97AC-5524E567FC02%7D_MAPA%20DO%20ANALFABETISMO%20NO%20BRASIL.pdf. Accessed on November 25, 2009.

Instituto de Pesquisa Econômica Aplicada, Ipea data. 2007. Pobreza, pessoas indigentes, desígualdade (índice de gini). Instituto de Pesquisa

Econômica Aplicada. Brasília, Brazil. Available at www.ipeadata.gov.br. Accessed on November 14.

Jacobo Waiselfisz, Julio, Miriam Abramovay, and Carla Andrade. 1998. *Bolsa Escola melhoria educacional e redução da pobreza.* Brasília: UNESCO.

Jaquette, Jane S. 1994. *The Women's Movement in Latin America: Participation and Democracy.* 2nd ed. Boulder, CO: Westview Press.

Jaquette, Jane S., and Sharon L. Wolchik. 1998. *Women and Democracy: Latin America and Central and Eastern Europe.* Baltimore: Johns Hopkins University Press.

Jatene, Adib. 2000. Um rebelde com causa. *Folha de São Paulo,* November 17.

Jordan, Jason. 2006. Mothers, Wives, and Workers: Explaining Gendered Dimensions of the Welfare State. *Comparative Political Studies* 39(9): 1109–32.

Jordana, Jacint, and David Levi-Faur. 2005. The Diffusion of Regulatory Capitalism in Latin America: Sectoral and National Channels in the Making of a New Order. *Annals of the American Academy of Political and Social Science* 598: 102–24.

Karch, Andrew. 2007. *Democratic Laboratories: Policy Diffusion among the American States.* Ann Arbor: University of Michigan Press.

Karl, Terry. 2000. Economic Inequality and Democratic Instability. *Journal of Democracy* 11(1): 149–56.

Kaufman, Jason, and Orlando Patterson. 2005. Cross-National Cultural Diffusion: The Global Spread of Cricket. *American Sociological Review* 70(1): 82–110.

Kaufman, Robert R. 1999. Approaches to the Study of State Reform in Latin American and Postsocialist Countries. *Comparative Politics* 31(3): 357–75.

Kaufman, Robert R., and Joan M. Nelson, eds. 2004. *Crucial Needs, Weak Incentives: Social Sector Reform, Democratization, and Globalization in Latin America.* Washington, DC: Woodrow Wilson Center Press.

Keck, Margaret E. 1992. *The Workers' Party and Democratization in Brazil.* New Haven: Yale University Press.

Keck, Margaret E., and Kathryn Sikkink. 1998. *Activists Beyond Borders: Advocacy Networks in International Politics.* Ithaca, NY: Cornell University Press.

Kilduff, Martin, and Wenpin Tsai. 2003. *Social Networks and Organizations.* Thousand Oaks, CA: Sage Publications.

King, Gary, Robert Keohane, and Sidney Verba. 1994. *Designing Social Inquiry.* Princeton: Princeton University Press.

Kingdon, John W. 1995. *Agendas, Alternatives, and Public Policies.* 2nd ed. New York: Longman.

Klingman, David. 1980. Temporal and Spatial Diffusion in the Comparative Analysis of Social Change. *American Political Science Review* 74(1): 123–37.

Knight, Kathleen. 2006. Transformations of the Concept of Ideology in the Twentieth Century. *American Political Science Review* 100(4): 619–26.

Krook, Mona Lena. 2006. Reforming Representation: The Diffusion of Candidate Gender Quotas Worldwide. *Politics and Gender* 2: 303–27.

LaFranchi, Howard. 1998. Paying Parents $65 a Month to Keep Kids in School. *Christian Science Monitor,* April 15.

Lago, Rudolfo. 2001. Lento e Bem-Vindo Investimento. *Correio Braziliense,* January 4, 16.

Lana, Xenia, and Mark Evans. 2004. Policy Transfer between Developing Countries: The Transfer of the Bolsa-Escola Programme to Ecuador. In *Policy Transfer in Global Perspective,* edited by Mark Evans, 190–210. Burlington, VT: Ashgate.

Lavinas, Lena, and Maria Ligia de Oliveira Barbosa. 2000. Combater a pobreza estimulando a freqüência escolar: O estudo de case do Programa Bolsa-Escola do Recife. *DADOS—Revista de Ciências Sociais* 43(3): 447–77.

Lavinas, Lena, Maria Ligia de Oliveira Barbosa, and Octávio Tourinho. 2001. Assessing Local Minimum Income Programs in Brazil. Geneva: International Labour Organisation/World Bank.

Levi-Faur, David. 2005. The Global Diffusion of Regulatory Capitalism. *Annals of the American Academy of Political and Social Science* 598: 12–32.

Levitsky, Steven. 2003. *Transforming Labor-Based Parties in Latin America: Argentine Peronism in Comparative Perspective.* New York: Cambridge University Press.

Lieberman, Evan S. 2003. *Race and Regionalism in the Politics of Taxation in Brazil and South Africa.* New York: Cambridge University Press.

———. 2005. Nested Analysis as a Mixed-Method Strategy for Comparative Research. *American Political Science Review* 99(3): 435–52.

Lijphart, Arend. 1971. Comparative Politics and the Comparative Method. *American Political Science Review* 65(3): 682–93.

———. 1975. The Comparable-Case Strategy in Comparative Research. *Comparative Political Studies* 8(2): 158–77.

Lima, Roberto Teixeira, and Nilton Maciel Mangueira. 2001. Avaliação de implantação de ações básicas de saúde. *Revista Brasileira de Ciências de Saúde* 5(2): 149–58.

Lindblom, Charles E. 1959. The "Science" of Muddling Through. *Public Administration Review* 19(2): 79–88.

Lindert, Kathy. 2006. Brazil: Bolsa Família—Scaling up Cash Transfers to the Poor. In *MfDR: Principles in Action: Sourcebook on Emerging Good Practice,* 67–74. Paris/Washington, DC: OECD/World Bank. Available at http://www.mfdr.org/sourcebook/3-1stEdition.html. Accessed on October 12, 2007.

Lipsky, Michael. 1980. *Street-Level Bureaucracy: Dilemmas of the Individual in Public Services.* New York: Russell Sage Foundation.

Lobato, Ana Lucia, and André Urani, eds. 1998. *Garantia de renda mínima: Ensaios e propostas.* Brasília: Instituto de Pesquisa Econômica Aplicada.

Lowi, Theodore. 1963. Toward Functionalism in Political Science: The Case of Innovation in Party Systems. *American Political Science Review* 57(3): 570–83.

———. 1995. Distribution, Regulation, Redistribution. In *Public Policy: The Essential Readings,* edited by Stella Theodoulou and Mathew Cahn. Englewood Cliffs, NJ: Prentice Hall.

Lucas, Kevin, and David Samuels. 2010. The Ideological Coherence of the Brazilian Party System, 1990–2009. *Journal of Politics in Latin America* 2(3): 39–69.

Macinko, James, Inês Dourado, Rosana Aquino, Palmira de Fátima Bonolo, Maria Fernanda Lima Costa, Maria Guadalupe Medina, Eduardo Mota, Veneza Berenice de Oliveira, and Maria Aparecida Turci. 2010. Major Expansion of Primary Care in Brazil Linked to the Decline in Unnecessary Hospitalization. *Health Affairs* 29(12): 2149–60.

Macinko, James, Maria de Fátima Marinho de Souza, Frederico C. Guanais, and Celso Cardoso da Silva Simões. 2007. Going to Scale with Community-Based Primary Care: An Analysis of the Family Health Program and Infant Mortality in Brazil, 1999–2004. *Social Science & Medicine* 65: 2070–80.

Macinko, James, Frederico C. Guanais, and Maria de Fátima Marinho de Souza. 2006. Evaluation of the Impact of the Family Health Program on Infant Mortality in Brazil, 1990–2002. *Journal of Epidemiology and Community Health* 60: 13–19.

Madrid, Raúl L. 2003. *Retiring the State: The Politics of Pension Privatization in Latin America and Beyond.* Stanford, CA: Stanford University Press.

Magnussen, Lesley, John Ehiri, and Pauline Jolly. 2004. Comprehensive versus Selective Primary Health Care: Lesson for Global Health Policy. *Health Affairs* 23(3): 167–76.

Mahoney, James, and Gary Goertz. 2006. A Tale of Two Cultures: Contrasting Quantitative and Qualitative Research. *Political Analysis* 14: 227–49.

Mainwaring, Scott. 1999. *Rethinking Party Systems in the Third Wave of Democratization: The Case of Brazil.* Stanford, CA: Stanford University Press.

Mainwaring, Scott, Rachel Meneguello, and Timothy J. Power. 2000. Conservative Parties, Democracy, and Economic Reform in Contemporary Brazil. In *Conservative Parties, the Right, and Democracy in Latin America,* edited by Kevin Middlebrook, 164–222. Baltimore: Johns Hopkins University Press.

Malloy, James M. 1979. The Politics of Social Security in Brazil. Pittsburgh, PA: University of Pittsburgh Press.

Martins, Roberto Borges, and José Carlos Libânio, eds. 2005. *Atlas do desenvolvimento humano no Brasil.* Retrieved May 17, 2005. Available at http://www.pnud.org.br/atlas/.

Mattos, Maria do Socorro. 2003. Public presentation, community meeting. November 3. São Paulo, Brazil.

Mazur, Amy G. 2002. *Theorizing Feminist Policy.* New York: Oxford University Press.

McGuire, James W. 2010. *Wealth, Health, and Democracy in East Asia and Latin America.* New York: Cambridge University Press.

McKeown, Timothy J. 2004. Case Studies and the Limits of the Quantitative Worldview. In *Rethinking Social Inquiry: Diverse Tools, Shared Standards,* edited by Henry E. Brady and David Collier, 139–67. Lanham, MD: Rowman and Littlefield.

Medeiros, Marcelo. 2001. A trajetória do welfare state no Brasil: Paper redistributivo das políticas sociais dos anos 1930 aos anos 1990. Brasília: Instituto de Pequisa Econômica Aplicada (IPEA) Texto Para Discussão, 852, 1–24.

Melamed, Clarice, and Nilson do Rosário Costa. 2003. Inovações no financiamento federal à atenção básica. *Ciência & Saúde Coletiva* 8(2): 393–401.

Mello, Alessandra. 2000. Bolsa-Escola reduz pobreza no país. *Jornal de Brasília,* December 3, 13.

Mello, Carlos Gentile de. 1977. *Saúde e assistência médica no Brasil.* São Paulo: CEBES-Hucitec.

Melo, Marcus Andre. 2008. Unexpected Successes, Unanticipated Failures: Social Policy from Cardoso to Lula. In *Democratic Brazil Revisited,* edited by Peter K. Kingstone and Timothy J. Power, 161–84. Pittsburgh, PA: University of Pittsburgh Press.

Mendonça, Ana Valéria Machado, Fernanda Morais, Keyla Antunes Kikushi Câmara, Maria de Fátima Sousa, Maria do Socorro Monteiro Freire, and Maria Lúcia Matias Ferreira. 2004. Primeira mostra de saúde da família—Camaragibe dez anos: Uma síntese das rodadas de diálogo. *Divulgação Saúde em Debate* 31: 28–37.

Menocal, Alina Rocha. 2001. Do Old Habits Die Hard? A Statistical Exploration of the Politicisation of Progresa, Mexico's Latest Federal Poverty-Alleviation Programme, under the Zedillo Administration. *Journal of Latin American Studies* 33(3): 513–38.

Mesa-Lago, Carmelo. 1978. *Social Security in Latin America: Pressure Groups, Stratification and Inequality.* Pittsburgh, PA: University of Pittsburgh Press.

———. 1997. Social Welfare Reform in the Context of Economic-Political Liberalization: Latin American Cases. *World Development* 25(4): 497–517.

Meseguer, Covadonga. 2004. What Role for Learning? The Diffusion of Privatisation in OECD and Latin American Countries. *Journal of Public Policy* 24(3): 299–325.

Meseguer, Covadonga, and Fabrizio Gilardi. 2009. What Is New in the Study of Policy Diffusion? *Review of International Political Economy* 16(3): 527–43.

Ministry of Education and Culture, Brazil. 2002. Relatório de Atividades 2001. Available at http://www.mec.gov.br/bolsaesc/.

———. 2004. The Development of Education: Quality Education for All Young People: Challenges, Trends, and Priorities. Paper presented at the International Conference on Education, 47th Session, Geneva, Switzerland, September 8–11.

———. N.d. Secretaria do Programa Nacional do Bolsa Escola. Available at http://www.mec.gov.br/home/bolsaesc/default.shtm.

Ministry of Education and Sports, Brazil. 1996. Development of Education in Brazil. Paper presented at the International Conference on Education, Geneva, Switzerland, September 30–October 5.

Ministry of Health, Brazil. 1997. *Saúde da Família: Uma estratégia para a reorientação do modelo assistencial.* Brasília: MS.

———. 1999a. Portaria no. 1329, Gabinete do Ministro. December 12.

———. 1999b. *I seminário de experiências internacionais em Saúde da Família: Relatório final.* Brasília: MS.

———. 2002a. Desafios e conquistas do PSF. *Revista Brasileira de Saúde da Família* 2(5) (May): 7–24.

———. 2002b. *Relatório de gestão, 1998–2002.* (MS. DAB Departamento de Atenção Básica.) Brasília: MS. DAB.

———. 2002c. *Experiências inovadoras no SUS.* (MS. SAS Secretaria de Assistência à Saúde.) Brasília: MS. SAS.

———. 2002d. *Avaliação da implementação do programa Saúde da Família em dez grandes centros urbanos: Sintese dos principais resultados.* Brasília: Ministério da Saúde.

———. 2003. *A produção sobre saúde da família: Trabalhos apresentados no VII Congresso Brasilieiro de Saúde Coletiva ABRASCO 2003.* Brasília: Ministério da Saúde.

———. 2009. Historical data on Programa Saúde da Família. Departamento de Atenção Básica e Saúde da Família. Retrieved on December 4, 2009, from http://dtr2004. Saúde.gov.br/dab/abnumeros.php#historico.

———. 2011. Departamento de Atenção Básica website. Accessed on August 4, 2011, from http://dab. Saúde.gov.br/abnumeros.php#mapas.

Ministry of Justice, Brazil. 2007. Organizações da Sociedade Civil de Interesse Público: OSCIP Lista de Entidades. Available at http://www.mj .gov.br/snj/oscip/. Accessed on February 18, 2007.

Ministry of Social Development, Brazil. 2009. Programa Bolsa Família. Available at http://www.mds.gov.br/bolsafamilia/. Accessed on January 15, 2009.

Ministry of Treasury, Brazil. 2004. Perfil e evolução das finanças municipais (1998–2003) (August). Brasília: Ministério da Fazenda. Available at http://www.tesouro.fazenda.gov.br/estados_municipios. Accessed on September 23, 2011.

Mintrom, Michael. 1997. Policy Entrepreneurs and the Diffusion of Innovation. *American Journal of Political Science* 41(3): 738–70.

Mintrom, Michael, and Sandra Vergari. 1998. Policy Networks and Innovation Diffusion: The Case of State Education Reforms. *Journal of Politics* 60(1): 126–48.

Mishima, Silvana Martins, Eliete Maria Silva, Maria Luiza Anselmi, and Sílvia Lúcia Ferreira. 1992. Agentes comunitários de saúde: Bom para o Ceará . . . bom para o Brasil? *Saúde em Debate* 37: 70–75.

Missão Criança. 2001. What Is Bolsa Escola? Available at unesdoc.unesco .org/images/0013/001364/136427eo.pdf.

Molyneux, Maxine. 2006. Mothers at the Service of the New Poverty Agenda: Progresa/Oportunidades, Mexico's Conditional Cash Transfer Program. *Social Policy and Administration* 40(4): 425–49.

Montero, Alfred P. 2001. Decentralizing Democracy: Spain and Brazil in Comparative Perspective. *Comparative Politics* 33(2): 146–69.

Montero, Alfred P., and David Samuels. 2004. The Political Determinants of Decentralization in Latin America: Causes and Consequences. In *Decentralization and Democracy in Latin America,* edited by Alfred P. Montero and David Samuels, 3–32. Notre Dame, IN: University of Notre Dame Press.

Mooney, Christopher Z. 2001. Modeling Regional Effects on State Policy Diffusion. *Political Research Quarterly* 54(1): 103–24.

Mooney, Christopher Z., and Mei-Hsien Lee. 1995. Legislating Morality in the American States: The Case of Pre-Roe Abortion Regulation Reform. *American Journal of Political Science* 39(3): 599–627.

Moraes, Reginaldo C. 2002. Reformas neoliberais e políticas públicas: Hegemonia ideológia e redefinição das relações estado-sociedade. *Educação e Sociedade* 23(80): 13–24.

Mossberger, Karen. 1999. State-Federal Diffusion and Policy Learning: From Enterprise Zones to Empowerment Zones. *Publius: The Journal of Federalism* 29(3): 31–50.

———. 2000. *The Politics of Ideas and the Spread of Enterprise Zones.* Washington, DC: Georgetown University Press.

Mullins, Willard A. 1972. On the Concept of Ideology in Political Science. *American Political Science Review* 66(2): 498–510.

Munck, Gerardo L. 2004. Tools for Qualitative Research. In *Rethinking Social Inquiry: Diverse Tools, Shared Standards,* edited by Henry E. Brady and David Collier, 105–21. Lanham, MD: Rowman and Littlefield.

Myers, David J., and Henry A. Dietz, eds. 2002. *Capital City Politics in Latin America: Democratization and Empowerment.* Boulder, CO: Lynne Rienner.

98% das pessoas que requisitaram o Bolsa-Escola são mulheres, 28% estão desempregadas e 39% não trabalham. 1997. *Correio Braziliense.* Brasília, 5.

North, Douglass C. 1981. *Structure and Change in Economic History.* New York: Norton.

———. 1990. *Institutions, Institutional Change, and Economic Performance.* New York: Cambridge University Press.

Nunn, Amy. 2008. *The Politics and History of AIDS Treatment in Brazil.* New York: Springer.

Nylen, William R. 2003. *Participatory Democracy vs. Elitist Democracy: Lessons from Brazil.* New York: Palgrave Macmillan.

OECD. 2004. OECD Economic Survey of Brazil: Better Targeting Government Spending. *OECD Economic Survey of Brazil.* Available at http://www.oecd.org/dataoecd/12/10/34427527.pdf.

Oliveira, Anna Cynthia, and Sérgio Haddad. 2001. As organizações da sociedade civil e as ongs de educação. *Cadernos de Pesquisa* 112 (March): 61–83.

Oliveira, Marina. 2001. À margem do Bolsa Escola: Pedir dá mais lucro que Renda Mínima. *Correio Braziliense,* January 2, 6.

Olson, Mancur. 1965. *The Logic of Collective Action: Public Goods and the Theory of Groups.* Cambridge, MA: Harvard University Press.

Orenstein, Mitchell. 2003. Mapping the Diffusion of Pension Innovation. In *Pension Reform in Europe: Process and Progress,* edited by Robert Holzmann, Mitchell Orenstein, and Michal Rutkowski, 171–94. Washington, DC: World Bank.

Passy, Florence. 2003. Social Networks Matter. But How? In *Social Movements and Networks: Relational Approaches to Collective Action,* edited by Mario Diani and Doug McAdam. New York: Oxford University Press.

Paulics, Veronika. 2000. *125 Dicas: Ideais para a ação municipal.* São Paulo: Pólis/Rio de Janeiro: Banco Nacional de Desenvolvimento Econômico e Social.

———. 2003. Disseminação do programa de garantia de Renda Mínima no Brasil (1991–1997). Master's thesis, Fundação Getúlio Vargas–São Paulo, São Paulo.

———. 2004. Disseminação de inovações em gestão local. Paper presented at the 2004 meeting of the Latin American Studies Association, Las Vegas, Nevada, October 7–9.

Peterson, George E. 1997. Decentralization in Latin America: Learning through Experience. Washington, DC: World Bank.

Pierson, Paul. 1994. *Dismantling the Welfare State.* New York: Cambridge University Press.

Plank, David N. 1990. The Politics of Basic Education Reform in Brazil. *Comparative Education Review* 34(4) (November): 538–59.

Plank, David N., José Amaral Sobrinho, and Antonio Carlos da Ressureição Xavier. 1996. Why Brazil Lags behind in Educational Development. In Birdsall and Sabot 1996, 117–45.

Policarpo Jr. and Sandra Brasil. 1996. "Casa e escolar." *Véja* 1516: 74–76.

Potter, Joseph. 2009. PROGRESA/Oportunidades. Presentation at conference, Origins, Implementation, and Spread of Conditional Cash

Transfer Programs in Latin America, University of Texas at Austin, April 17.

Power, Timothy J. 2000. *The Political Right in Postauthoritarian Brazil: Elites, Institutions, and Democratization.* University Park: Pennsylvania State University Press.

Power, Timothy, and Cesar Zucco. 2009. Estimating Ideology of Brazilian Legislative Parties, 1990–2005. *Latin American Research Review* 44(1): 218–46.

Ramachandran, V. K. 2000. Human Development Achievements in an Indian State. In Social Development and Public Policy, edited by Dharam Ghai. New York: St. Martin's.

Riker, William H., and Peter C. Ordeshook. 1973. *An Introduction to Positive Political Theory.* Englewood Cliffs, NJ: Prentice Hall.

Rocha, Sonia, and Guilherme Sedlack. 1999. The Bolsa-Escola Program. Paper presented at conference, Social Protection: Strategies for Improving Policies in LAC, Washington, DC, June 7.

Rodrigues, Leôncio Martins. 2002. Partidos, ideologia e composição social. *Revista Brasileira de Ciências Sociais* 17(48): 31–47.

Rogers, Everett M. 2003. *Diffusion of Innovations.* 5th ed. New York: Free Press.

Rohter, Larry, and Anemona Hartocollis. 2007. Brazilian Politician Indicted in New York in Kickback Scheme. *New York Times,* March 9, A9.

Roma, Celso. 2002. A institucionalização do PSDB entre 1988 e 1999. *Revista Brasileira de Ciências Sociais* 17(49): 71–92.

Roncalli, Angelo Giuseppe, and Kenio Costa de Lima. 2006. Impacto do Programa Saúde da Família sobre indicadores de saúde da criança em municípios de grande porte da região Nordeste do Brasil. *Ciência & Saúde Coletiva* 11(3): 713–24.

Rose, Douglas D. 1973. National and Local Forces in State Politics: The Implications of Multi-Level Policy Analysis. *American Political Science Review* 67(4): 1162–73.

Rose, Richard. 1989. *Ordinary People in Public Policy: A Behavioural Analysis.* Newbury Park, CA: Sage Publications.

———. 1993. *Lesson-Drawing in Public Policy: A Guide to Learning across Time and Space.* Chatham, NJ: Chatham House.

———. 2004. *Learning from Comparative Public Policy: A Guide to Lesson-Drawing.* New York: Routledge.

Rossi, Amamaria. 1997. Cristovam faz fé na Bolsa Escola. *Correio Braziliense,* September 30, 2.

Rueschemeyer, Dietrich, and Peter B. Evans. 1985. The State and Economic Transformation: Toward an Analysis of the Conditions Underlying Effective Intervention. In *Bringing the State Back In*, edited by Peter B. Evans, Dietrich Rueschemeyer, and Theda Skocpol, 44–77. New York: Cambridge University Press.

Ryan, Bryce, and Neal C. Gross. 1943. The Diffusion of Hybrid Seed Corn in Two Iowa Communities. *Rural Sociology* 8: 15–24.

———. 1950. *Acceptance and Diffusion of Hybrid Corn Seed in Two Iowa Communities*. Research Bulletin 372, Agricultural Experiment Station, Ames, IA.

Sabatier, Paul A. 1999. *Theories of the Policy Process*. Boulder, CO: Westview Press.

Sabatier, Paul A., and Hank C. Jenkins-Smith. 1993. *Policy Change and Learning: An Advocacy Coalition Approach*. Boulder, CO: Westview Press.

Samuels, David. 2000. Reinventing Local Government: Municipalities and Intergovernmental Relations in Democracy Brazil. In *Democratic Brazil: Actors, Institutions, and Processes*, edited by Peter R. Kingstone and Timothy J. Power, 77– 98. Pittsburgh, PA: University of Pittsburgh Press.

———. 2003. *Ambition, Federalism, and Legislative Politics in Brazil.* New York: Cambridge University Press.

———. 2004. The Political Logic of Decentralization in Brazil. In Montero and Samuels 2004, 67–93.

Samuels, David, and Scott Mainwaring. 2004. Strong Federalism, Constraints on the Central Government, and Economic Reform in Brazil. In *Federalism and Democracy in Latin America*, edited by Edward L. Gibson. Baltimore: Johns Hopkins University Press.

SANARE: Revista de Políticas Públicas. 2003. Vol. 1(4). Available at http://www.esf.org.br/downloads/sanare/Sanare_v4_n1.pdf.

Sartori, Giovanni. 1969. Politics, Ideology, and Belief Systems. *American Political Science Review* 63(2): 398–411.

Schady, Norbert R. 2000. The Political Economy of Expenditures by the Peruvian Social Fund (FONCODES), 1991–95. *American Political Science Review* 94(2): 289–304.

Scholz, Imme. 2005. Environmental Policy Cooperation among Organised Civil Society, National Public Actors and International Actors in the Brazilian Amazon. *European Journal of Development Research* 17(4): 681–705.

Sen, Amartya. 1999. *Development as Freedom*. New York: Alfred A. Knopf.

Serra, José. 2000. *Ampliando o possível: A política de saúde do Brasil.* São Paulo: Hucitec.

Shipan, Charles R., and Craig Volden. 2006. Bottom-up Federalism: The Diffusion of Antismoking Policies from U.S. Cities to States. *American Journal of Political Science* 50(4): 825–43.

———. 2008. The Mechanisms of Diffusion. *American Journal of Political Science* 52(4): 840–57.

Silva, Joana Azevedo da, and Ana Sílvia Whitaker Dalmaso. 2002. *Agente comunitário de saúde.* Rio de Janeiro: Editora Fiocruz.

Silva, Maria Josefina da, and Rui Martinho Rodrigues. 2000. O agente comunitário de saúde no processo de municipalização da saúde. *Revista Eletrônica de Enfermagem* 2(1).

Silva, Sônia Cristina. 1996. Complemento a renda familiar reduz evasão escolar no Distrito Federal. *O Estado de São Paulo*, February 5, A11.

Simmons, Beth A., Frank Dobbin, and Geoffrey Garrett. 2006. Introduction: The Diffusion of Liberalism. *International Organization* 60(4): 781–810.

———, eds. 2008. *The Global Diffusion of Markets and Democracy.* New York: Cambridge University Press.

Simmons, Beth A., and Zachary Elkins. 2004. The Globalization of Liberalization: Policy Diffusion in the International Political Economy. *American Political Science Review* 98(1): 171–89.

Skocpol, Theda. 1979. *States and Social Revolutions: A Comparative Analysis of France, Russia, and China.* New York: Cambridge University Press.

Skofias, Emmanuel, and Bonnie McClafferty. 2000. Is PROGRESA Working? Summary of the Results of an Evaluation by IFPRI. International Food Policy Research Institute (IFPRI). Available at www.ifpri.org/publication/PROGRESA-working-0.

Snyder, Richard, and Richard Owen. 2001. Devaluing the Vote in Latin America. *Journal of Democracy* 12(1): 146–59.

Solla, Jorge José Pereira, Maria Guadalupe Medina, and Maria Beatriz Pragana Dantas. 1996. O PACS na Bahia: Avaliação do trabalho dos agentes comunitários de saúde. *Saúde em Debate* 51: 4–15.

Sousa, Maria de Fátima de, ed. 2002. *Os sinais vermelhos do PSF.* São Paulo: Editora Hucitec.

———. 2003. O PSF na cidade de São Paulo trabalhando em parceria: O compromisso possível. In Sousa and Mendes 2003, 91–94.

Sousa, Maria Fátima de, and Áquilas Mendes. 2003. *Tempos radicais da saúde em São Paulo: A construção do SUS na maior cidade Brasiliera.* São Paulo: Editora Hucitec.

Spink, Peter K. 2006. Learning from Innovation: Educational Policies Seen through the Public Management and Citizenship Program. *Cadernos Gestão Pública e Cidadania* 11: 109–28.

Spink, Peter K., Silvio Caccia Bava, and Veronika Paulics, eds. 2002. *Novos contornos da gestão local: Conceitos em construção*. São Paulo: Pólis/Programa Gestão Pública e Cidadania–FGV-EAESP.

Steck, Juliana. 1997. Unesco adota project da Bolsa-Escola: Programa do GDF vai ser implantado em outros países com o financiamento do órgão do ONU. *Jornal de Brasília*, July 5, 21.

Stepan, Alfred. 1978. *The State and Society: Peru in Comparative Perspective*. Princeton: Princeton University Press.

Stepan, Nancy. 1976. *Beginnings of Brazilian Science: Oswaldo Cruz, Medical Research and Policy, 1890–1920.* New York: Science History Publications.

Stone, Deborah A. 1989. Causal Stories and the Formation of Policy Agendas. *Political Science Quarterly* 104(2): 281–300.

Stone, Diane. 1999. Learning Lessons and Transferring Policy across Time, Space, and Disciplines. *Politics* 19(1): 51–59.

Strang, David, and John W. Meyer. 1993. Institutional Conditions for Diffusion. *Theory and Society* 22(4): 487–511.

Strang, David, and Sarah A. Soule. 1998. Diffusion in Organizations and Social Movements: From Hybrid Corn to Poison Pills. *Annual Review of Sociology* 24: 265–90.

Sugiyama, Natasha Borges. 2008a. Ideology and Social Networks: The Politics of Social Policy Diffusion in Brazil. *Latin American Research Review* 43(3): 82–108.

———. 2008b. Theories of Diffusion: Social Sector Reform in Brazil. *Comparative Political Studies* 41(2) (February): 193–218.

———. 2011a. Bottom-up Policy Diffusion: National Emulation of a Conditional Cash Transfer Program in Brazil. *Publius: The Journal of Federalism.* First published July 20, 2011. DOI: 10.1093/publius/pjr019.

———. 2011b. The Diffusion of Conditional Cash Transfer Programs in the Americas. *Global Social Policy*, 1–29. DOI: 10.1177/1468018111421295.

Suplicy, Eduardo Matarazzo. 2002. *Renda de cidadania: A saída é Pela Porta.* São Paulo: Cortez Editora/Editora Fundação Perseu Abramo.

Tarrow, Sidney. 2004. Bridging the Quantitative-Qualitative Divide. In *Rethinking Social Inquiry: Diverse Tools, Shared Standards*, edited by Henry E. Brady and David Collier, 171–80. Lanham, MD: Rowman and Littlefield.

———. 2010. Bridging the Quantitative-Qualititative Divide. In *Rethinking Social Inquiry: Diverse Tools, Shared Standards*, 2nd ed., edited by Henry E. Brady and David Collier, 101–10. Lanham, MD: Rowman and Littlefield.

Taylor, Michael. 2006. *Rationality and the Ideology of Disconnection*. New York: Cambridge University Press.

Teixeira, Suely C. S., Valéria de O Monteiro, and Verônica A. Miranda. 1999. Programa Médico de Família no município de Niterói. *Estudos Avançados* 13(35): 147–55.

Tendler, Judith. 1997a. *Good Government in the Tropics*. Baltimore: Johns Hopkins University Press.

———. 1997b. Ceará vs. Kerela. In *Rethinking Development in East Asia and Latin America*, edited by James McGuire, 109–22. Los Angeles: Council on International Policy.

Terra, Valéria, and Ana Maria Malik. 1998. Programa Médico de Família de Niterói. In *20 Experiências de Gestão Pública e Cidadania*, edited by Luis Fujiwara, Nelson Alessio, and Marta Farah. São Paulo: Programa Gestão Pública e Cidadania, FGV-EAESP.

Terra de Souza, Ana Cristina, Ennio Cufino, Karen E. Peterson, Jane Gardner, Maria Ines Vasconcelos do Amaral, and Alberto Ascherio. 1999. Variations in Infant Mortality Rates among Municipalities in the State of Ceará, Northeast Brazil. *International Journal of Epidemiology* 28(2): 267–75.

Teruel, Graciela, and Benjamin Davis. 2000. Final Report: An Evaluation of the Impact of Progresa Cash Payments on Private Inter-Household Transfers. Washington, DC: International Food Policy Research Institute.

Thelen, Kathleen, and Sven Steinmo. 1992. Historical Institutionalism in Comparative Politics. In *Structuring Politics: Historical Institutionalism in Comparative Analysis*, edited by Sven Steinmo, Kathleen Thelen, and Frank Longstenth, 1–32. New York: Cambridge University Press.

Theodoulou, Stella, and Matthew Cahn. 1995. *Public Policy: The Essential Readings*. Englewood Cliffs, NJ: Prentice Hall.

Transparency International. 2004. *Global Corruption Report 2004*. Available at http://www.transparency.org/publications/gcr/gcr_2004#download.

True, Jacqui, and Michael Mintrom. 2001. Transnational Networks and Policy Diffusion. *International Studies Quarterly* 45(1): 27–57.

Tulchin, Joseph S., and Allison M. Garland. 2000. *Social Development in Latin America: The Politics of Reform*. Boulder, CO: Lynne Rienner.

UNESCO. 2007. Brazil. World Data on Education. UNESCO–International Bureau of Education. Retrieved on January 9, 2007, from http://www.ibe.unesco.org/.

União espera beneficiar 5 milhões de crianças com Bolsa-Escola. 2000. *Estado de São Paulo*, C1.

U.S. Supreme Court. 1932. New State Ice Co. v. Liebmann, 285 U.S. 262 (1932).

Vasconcellos, Maria da Penha Costa. 1999. Reflexões sobre a saúde da família. In *A saúde no nível local*, edited by Eugênio Villaça Mendes, 155–72. São Paulo: Hucitec.

Vawda, Ayesha. N.d. Brazil: Stipends to Increase School Enrollment and Decrease Child Labor: A Case of Demand-Side Financing. Available at http://www.ifc.org/edinvest/brazil.htm.

Véja. 1996. Um Projeto Para o Brasil. June 26, 40–41.

Viana, Ana Luiza D'Ávila, and Mario Roberto Dal Poz. 1998. A reforma do sistema de saúde no Brasil e o programa de saúde da família. *PHYSIS: Revista Saúde Coletiva* 8(2): 11–42.

Villaméa, Luiza. 2001. Made in Brasil. *Istoé* 1634: 38–39.

Villatoro, Pablo. 2004. *Programas de reducción de la pobreza en América Latina: Un análisis de cinco experiencias*. No. 87. Santiago, Chile.

Walker, Jack L. 1969. The Diffusion of Innovations among the American States. *American Political Science Review* 63(3): 880–99.

Walt, Stephen. 2000. Fads, Fevers, and Firestorms. *Foreign Policy* 121: 34–42.

Wampler, Brian. 2004. Expanding Accountability through Participatory Institutions: Mayors, Citizens, and Budgeting in Three Brazilian Municipalities. *Latin American Politics & Society* 46(2): 73–99.

Wampler, Brian, and Leonardo Avritzer. 2004. Participatory Publics. *Comparative Politics* 36(3): 291–312.

Wejnert, Barbara. 2002. Integrating Models of Diffusion of Innovations: A Conceptual Framework. *Annual Review of Sociology* 28: 297–326.

———. 2005. Diffusion, Development, and Democracy, 1800–1999. *American Sociological Review* 70(1): 53–81.

Welch, Susan, and Kay Thompson. 1980. The Impact of Federal Incentives on State Policy Innovation. *American Journal of Political Science* 24(4): 715–29.

Werneck, Felipe. 2001. Bolsa Escola terã R$1.7 bilhão. *O Estado de São Paulo*, A9.

Weyland, Kurt. 1996. *Democracy without Equity: Failures of Reform in Brazil.* Pittsburgh, PA: University of Pittsburgh Press.

———, ed. 2004. *Learning from Foreign Models in Latin American Policy Reform.* Washington, DC: Woodrow Wilson Center Press.

———. 2005. Theories of Policy Diffusion: Lessons from Latin American Pension Reform. *World Politics* 57(2): 262–95.

———. 2007. *Bounded Rationality and Policy Diffusion: Social Sector Reform in Latin America.* Princeton: Princeton University Press.

———. 2010a. The Performance of Leftist Governments in Latin America: Conceptual and Theoretical Issues. In *Leftist Governments in Latin America: Successes and Shortcomings*, edited by Kurt Weyland, Raúl Madrid, and Wendy Hunter, 1–27. New York: Cambridge University Press.

———. 2010b. The Diffusion of Regime Contention in European Democratization, 1830–1940. *Comparative Political Studies* 43(8–9): 1148–76.

Whitehead, Laurence. 2000. The Politics of Expertise. *Brazilian Journal of Political Economy* 20(2): 23–35.

Wodon, Quentin, Rodrigo Castro-Fernandez, Kihoon Lee, Gladys Lopez-Acevedo, Corinne Siaens, Carlos Sobrado, and Jean-Philippe Tre. 2001. Poverty in Latin America: Trends (1986–1998) and Determinants. *Cuad. Econ.* 38(114): 127–53.

World Bank. 2001. Brazil: An Assessment of the Bolsa Escola Programs. Retrieved June 6, 2005, from http://www.wds.worldbank.org/servlet/WDSContentServer/WDSP/IB/2001/04/24/000094946_01041107221120/Rendered/PDF/multi0page.pdf.

———. 2002. Brazil: Maternal and Child Health. Report no. 23811-BR. Retrieved on December 10, 2009, from http://siteresources.worldbank.org/BRAZILINPOREXTN/Resources/3817166-1185895645304/4044168-1186326902607/32pub_br56.pdf.

———. 2004. *Brazil: Equitable, Competitive, Sustainable: Contributions for Debate.* Washington, DC: World Bank.

———. 2005a. World Development Indicators. Retrieved on July 27, 2009, from http://devdata.worldbank.org/wdi2005/Cover.htm.

———. 2005b. Brazil's Bolsa Família Program Celebrates Progress in Lifting Families out of Poverty. World Bank News and Broadcasts, December 19, 2005. Available at http://go.worldbank.org/5NAMSEOR60.

Zedillo, Ernesto. 2009. Keynote Address: A Look at Progresa's Genesis. Presentation at conference, The Origins, Implementation, and Spread of Conditional Cash Transfer Programs in Latin America, University of Texas at Austin, April 17.

INDEX

abertura, 46, 78, 204n32
Abrinq, 47
Agentes Comunitários de Saúde (ACS), 129, 213n24, 214n30, 218n9
agricultural workers, 210n2
Aguiar, Marcelo, 92–93
Albuquerque, José Carlos de, 213n20
Alma Ata Declaration, 136–37, 138, 139, 146
Alternative Approaches to Meeting Basic Health Needs in Developing Countries (WHO/UNICEF), 136
Alvarez, Sonia E., 47
Ananias, Patrus, 106, 112
Andrade, Luiz Odorico de, 212n17, 216n46
  and PSF, 125, 139–40, 163
Annan, Kofi, 107–8, 182
Araújo, Raimundo Caires, 104
Argentina, 36
Associação Brasileira de Pós-Graduação em Saúde Coletiva (ABRASCO), 47, 144, 160
  and PSF, 145, 150, 163, 167
Auyero, Javier, 35–36
Bacha, Edmar, 199n6
Belo Horizonte, 95, 97, 209n30
  Bolsa Escola in, 96, 99, 103, 106, 109–10, 171, 210n39
  PSF in, 128, 131–32, 143, 148
Bennett, Andrew, 19
Berry, Frances Stokes, 29, 35
Berry, William D., 29, 35
Birdsall, Nancy, 80
Bisol, Jairo, 134, 214n29
Boix, Charles, 203n29
Bolivia, 39
Bolsa Escola
  as award-winning program, 14, 42, 91, 107, 200n14, 208n18
  in Belo Horizonte, 96, 99, 103, 106, 109–10, 171, 210n39
  in Brasília, 7, 8, 88–92, 105, 110, 210n34
  broad appeal, 78, 97, 108
  clientelism and, 44, 78
  diffusion statistics, 8, 51, 52, 53–54
  efficacy, 175–76
  event history analysis of diffusion, 63–74
  federal program, 85, 93–94, 175, 177, 219n17, 268n23

Bolsa Escola (*cont.*)
framing, 170, 178, 220n21
funding, 93, 203n25, 209n30
good governance features, 45, 152, 177
ideology as incentive for adoption, 12, 58–59, 78, 101–3, 105–6, 112, 186
international support for, 107–8, 182–83
left and, 46, 157
measuring adoption probability, 71–72, 73–74
media coverage, 91–92, 97, 155
Ministry of Education and, 52, 175, 203n25, 208n23
origins, 88–89
policy design, 7–8
policy flexibility, 170–71
political incentives for adoption, 58, 96–101, 187
poverty alleviation and, 37, 86, 160
Renda Mínima and, 85, 89–90
in Salvador, 94–95, 96, 103
in São Paulo, 103, 208n23
simplicity of, 169, 170, 172, 219n12
social networks as incentive for adoption, 60–62, 78, 107–11, 112, 162
teachers and, 99–100, 107
technocrats and, 156, 171
UNICEF and, 91, 107, 208n18
women and mothers as focus, 92–93, 178, 208n22
See also Renda Mínima
Brandeis, Louis D., 199n4
Brasília, 16, 51, 95, 97, 103, 109, 166
Bolsa Escola in, 7, 8, 88–92, 105, 110, 210n34
PSF in, 128, 131, 134, 143
Brazilian Democratic Movement (MDB), 5
Brazilian history, 3, 41
abertura, 46, 78, 204n32
military dictatorships, 116, 210n2
Bruns, Barbara, 80
Buarque, Cristovam, 86, 153, 210n36, 217n52
and Bolsa Escola, 7, 88, 92, 93, 98, 100, 103–4, 110, 136, 169, 170, 183, 219n12
and PSF, 131, 135, 143, 148
technocratic background of, 48–49
bureaucracy, 6, 200n8
Business Week, 92

Caixa de Aposentadoria e Pensão (CAP), 115–16, 210n1
Camargo, José Márcio, 87
Campinas, 51, 89–90, 109, 112, 207n12
minimum income program in, 7, 8, 87–88, 89–92, 101
Capistrano Filho, David, 216n44, 216n47, 217n48, 217n50
and Jatene, 139, 145, 146–47, 216n47, 217n48
and PSF, 139, 142, 145, 150, 158, 163
Cardoso, Fernando Henrique, 83, 87, 93, 98, 139, 158, 177
Castillo, Oscar, 212n17

Castro, Célio de, 48–49, 153, 214n31
  and Bolsa Escola, 98, 103
  and PSF, 131–32, 135, 143
Ceará, 122, 212n11, 212n13
Center for Contemporary Brazilian Studies, 88
Centro Brasileiro de Estudos de Saúde (CEBES), 47, 60, 160
  and PSF, 62, 70, 72–73, 144, 150, 163, 167
Centros Educacionais Unificados (CEU), 136
Chile, 39
Christian Science Monitor, 92
civil servants, 40, 48, 109, 170, 200n8, 212n15, 213n23
civil society engagement, 4, 47, 82–83
clientelism, 5, 43, 75, 185
  education and, 11, 35–36, 44, 77, 82
  health care and, 11, 36–37, 118
Cohn, Amélia, 211nn4–5
collective health, 211n4
Collier, David, 28
Collor de Mello, Fernando, 87, 139, 218n6
comparative politics, 1, 2, 29, 31
complexity, 169–70
compulsory voting, 11, 96
Conceição, Maria José da (Maninha), 131, 135
conditional cash transfer programs (CCTs), 51, 52, 78, 87, 99, 183–84
  Bolsa Escola and Renda Mínima as, 7, 78, 93, 175
  federal government and, 12, 93–94, 98, 175
  international support for, 107–8, 173
  political incentives and, 98, 101, 155
  transnational diffusion of, 172, 180–84
  See also Bolsa Escola; Renda Mínima
Conferência Nacional de Saúde, VIII (1986), 146
Conselho Nacional de Secretários de Educação (CONSED), 107
Conselho Nacional de Secretários Municipais de Saúde (CONASEMS), 140, 160, 216nn45–46
  and PSF, 144–45, 150, 163, 167
Constitution of Brazil, 3–4, 205n8
  on education, 4, 80–81, 199n2
  on health care, 4, 117–18, 119–20, 199n2
corporatism, 2, 100, 107, 116
Correia, Rogério, 109–10, 162
Correio Braziliense, 92
corruption, 44, 141, 154, 203n28, 215n41
  in health care system, 134, 185, 214n29
Costa Lima, Humberto Sérgio, 213n20
Cruz, Oswaldo, 115
Cuba, 9, 121–22, 200n11
Cueto, Marcos, 214n32

Dagnino, Evelina, 47
Dal Poz, Mario Roberto, 124, 212n17, 213n23

da Silva Guedes, José, 142
decentralization, 4, 6, 50
  education, 83
  health care, 114, 118, 119, 120, 126, 211n7
democracy, 21
  Brazil's transition to, 46, 78, 117, 185–86, 204n32
dentistry, 174–75
diffusion studies, 20, 25, 30, 171
  Brazil as opportunity for, 21, 184–85
  evolution of, 28–34
  motivation as question for, 10–11, 31–32, 33, 186–87, 200n12, 201n9
  shortcomings of, 13–14, 33
  statistical techniques in, 33, 34
  See also policy diffusion
DiMaggio, Paul J., 203n24
Dobbin, Frank, 32, 33
domestic violence, 178–79
Downs, Anthony, 202n17, 202n21
Draibe, Sonia N., 44, 82

The Economist, 92
Ecuador, 183
Educação para Todos, 81–82
education, 7, 12, 77–112, 169–70
  Brazilian Constitution on, 4, 80–81, 199n2
  under Cardoso, 83–85
  civil society advocacy and, 82–83
  clientelism and, 11, 35–36, 44, 77, 82
  contemporary deficits in, 78, 79, 80
  decentralization, 83
  federal funding, 83–84, 207nn3–4
  General Law on, 83
  local experimentation and innovation, 85–94
  patronage and, 8, 44, 77, 81–82
  poor and, 11, 79–80, 88
  poverty alleviation and, 37, 86, 160
  professional associations and, 107, 161
  upper classes and, 79–80
  See also Bolsa Escola; Ministry of Education and Culture
elections
  for congressional office, 5–6
  municipal, 42, 56–57, 185, 205nn11–12
  patronage and, 43–44, 112, 154
  vote buying, 2, 43, 44, 102, 203n28
electoral incentives. *See* political and electoral incentives
Elkins, Zachary, 202n16, 204n2
Eloy Chaves law, 115–16
El Salvador, 39
Escobar, Arturo, 47
Estado de São Paulo, 92
Evans, Mark, 183
event history analysis, 14, 63, 165, 201n5
  in diffusion studies, 29–30, 33, 34
  of PSF and Bolsa Escola adoption, 63–74

federal financing
for Bolsa Escola, 93, 203n25, 209n30
for municipalities, 40, 67, 203n25
for PSF, 70, 203n25, 219n14
federalism, 31, 41, 199n4, 201n8, 205n8
Federal University in Campinas (UNICAMP), 132, 145
Finnemore, Martha, 39
flexibility, 170–71, 218n7
Folha de São Paulo, 87
Fonseca, Ana, 110–11
Fox, Jonathan, 36
Fox, Vicente, 181
Franco, Itamar, 87
Friedkin, Noah E., 159
Fujimori, Alberto, 36
Fundação Fio Cruz, 138
Fundação Getúlio Vargas, 47, 91, 108, 109, 121, 210n34
Fundação Perseu Abramo, 56
Fundo de Manutenção e Desenvolvimento do Ensino Fundamental e de Valorização do Magistério (FUNDEF), 83–84, 85, 93

Galton's problem, 28
Garrett, Geoffrey, 32, 33, 203n29
Geddes, Barbara, 19
gender, 177–80, 219n20
See also women
General Law on Education, 83
George, Alexander L., 19
Gilardi, Fabrizio, 33–34
Girade, Halim Antônio, 212n17
GOBI, 137, 220n22
Goertz, Gary, 165
good governance, 1, 3, 13, 21, 45, 108, 186
Bolsa Escola and PSF as models of, 152, 177, 200n14
civic associations and, 47, 86, 208n19
in developing countries, 2, 22
Grindle, Merilee, 2, 209n28

Hagopian, Frances, 5
health agents, 9, 122
and clientelism, 44–45, 154, 218n1
hiring of, 123, 170, 218n9
and PSF, 124, 125, 129, 131
health care, 113–50
Brazilian Constitution on, 4, 117–18, 119–20, 199n2
clientelism and, 11, 36–37, 118
community, 8, 9, 120, 123, 124, 125, 149
cooperative clinics, 123, 141, 212nn15–16
corruption, 134, 185, 214n29
decentralization, 114, 118, 119, 120, 126, 211n7
expansion of coverage to population, 174–75
federal funding, 70, 123, 203n25, 219n14
history in Brazil, 113, 115–16
local experimentation and innovation, 120–26
patronage and, 8, 44–45, 118, 129, 133, 134, 154
for poor, 11, 113
preventive, 8–9, 117, 126

health care (*cont.*)
reform process for, 117, 119
regional differences in, 117, 145, 174, 216n46
taxes for, 118–19
Unified Health System, 118, 126
wealthy elite and, 113, 116
women's, 178–79
See also Programa de Agentes Comunitários de Saúde (PACS); Programa Saúde da Família (PSF); sanitarian movement

Ibañez, Antonio, 109
ideology, 12, 20–21, 36–37, 41, 161, 164, 166
Bolsa Escola diffusion and, 12, 58–59, 78, 101–6, 112, 186
definitions of, 36, 202n21
diffusion studies and, 33
event history analysis of diffusion, 65, 68, 70, 74–75
leftist, 46, 106, 111–12, 138, 141–43, 150, 157–58, 162–63, 203n30
measuring impact of, 57–59, 166–68
motivations as, 36–37
PSF diffusion and, 12, 58–59, 135–43, 150, 162–64
Renda Mínima diffusion and, 101–6, 186
Imbassahy, Antônio, 102–3, 104, 133, 136, 168
and Bolsa Escola, 99
and PSF, 132, 134, 135, 143, 154
incrementalism, 218n3
Índice de Desenvolvimento Humano Municipal (IDH-M), 68, 70
infant mortality, 9, 114, 122, 212n11, 212n13
PSF reduction of, 139, 173, 219n16
informal networks, 38, 47–48
Bolsa Escola diffusion and, 109–10
PSF diffusion and, 145–47, 150, 160–61, 163
innovation
diffusion and, 12, 30, 219n20
municipal governments and, 4, 6–7, 85–94, 120–26, 199n4
Instituto de Pesquisa Econômica Aplicada (IPEA), 52, 125, 212n19
Instituto Florestan Fernandes, 135
Instituto Nacional de Assistência Médica da Previdência Social (INAMPS), 113, 116
Instituto Pólis, 109
Inter-American Development Bank, 182
International Conference on Primary Health Care, 136, 214n32
International Food Policy Research Institute (IFPRI), 181
International Labour Organization, 182
Istoé, 91

Jatene, Adib, 118, 213n20, 216n47
and Capistrano, 139, 145, 146–47, 216n47, 217n48
and PSF, 125, 139, 141–42, 145, 163, 213n21, 213n26, 215n34

Jornal de Brasíla, 92
Junkeira, Virginia, 215n35

Karl, Terry, 21
Keck, Margaret E., 203n23
Keohane, Robert, 19, 75
King, Gary, 19, 75

La Forgia, Jerry, 215n35
Lana, Xenia, 183
Lange, Peter, 203n29
large-n analysis, 14, 16, 18–19, 23, 33, 165, 166
Latin America, 20–21, 35–36, 185
  conditional cash transfer programs in, 180–82, 198
  dominance of capital cities in, 41–42, 203n26
left, 45, 167, 185
  and Bolsa Escola, 46, 157
  ideology of, 46, 106, 111–12, 138, 141–43, 150, 157–58, 162–63, 203n30
  and PSF, 46, 130, 138, 141, 142–43, 150, 157–58, 162–63, 215n40, 216n42, 218n2
Levitsky, Steven, 35–36
Lieberman, Evan S., 200n15
Lijphart, Arend, 19
Lima, Lílian Carneiro, 105
Lipsky, Michael, 220n24
Londrina, 149
Lowi, Theodore, 35, 201n9
Lucas, Kevin, 204n31
Lula da Silva, Luiz Inácio, 41, 98, 175, 177, 207n10, 217n52

Machado, Heloísa, 125, 139
Macinko, James, 215nn38–39, 219n16
Magalhães, Antônio Carlos, 5, 168, 199n7, 218n6
Magalhães Teixeira, Roberto, 88
Mahoney, James, 165
Malan, Pedro, 118–19
Maluf, Paulo, 104, 123, 130, 140–41
  and corruption, 141, 215n41
  and PSF, 136, 140–41, 148
Maninha. *See* Conceição, Maria José da
Maranhão, 5
Martins Alves, Eduardo Jorge, 147, 150, 163
Mata, Lídice da, 136, 162, 168
  and education, 98, 100, 101
  and Renda Mínima, 103–4, 109, 161
maternal mortality, 9, 139
mayoralship, 5, 6, 49, 200n9
McGuire, James W., 212n11
media, 91–92, 97, 155
medical schools, 211n4
Médici, Emílio, 210n2
Melo, Marcus Andre, 12, 43, 98, 177
Mendes, Eugênio Villaça, 212n17
Menocal, Alina Rocha, 36
Meseguer, Covadonga, 33–34
Messick, Richard E., 28
Mexico, 2, 36, 180–82, 220nn26–27
military dictatorships, 116, 210n2
minimum income, 86, 87, 89, 100–101, 207n9, 208n17

Ministry of Education and Culture (MEC), 81, 83
and Bolsa Escola, 52, 175, 203n25, 208n23
clientelism and patronage in, 44, 82
Ministry of Finance, 119
Ministry of Health, 119, 120, 206n19, 213n20
funding by, 67, 123, 217n53
and health agents, 8–9, 122–23
and PSF, 10, 52, 124, 125–26, 134, 138, 147, 171, 215n34, 217n53, 219n14
responsibilities of, 113, 116
Ministry of Justice, 107, 210n35
Ministry of Social Development (MDS), 183
Missão Criança, 183, 210n36
Molyneux, Maxine, 178
Morgenthau, Robert, 216n41
Mossberger, Karen, 219n15
Mullins, Willard A., 37
municipal elections, 42, 56–57, 185, 205nn11–12
municipal governments, 4, 165–66, 184, 207n11
autonomy of, 3, 16, 50, 52
and education, 11, 85–94, 200n13
federal financing of, 40, 67, 203n25
and health care, 119, 120, 126, 211n7
innovative programs by, 4, 6–7, 85–94, 120–26, 199n4
municipalization, 83, 119, 132, 206n1
National Action Party (PAN, Mexico), 181
National Confederation of Rural Workers (CONTAG), 210n2
Negri, Barjas, 213n20
neoliberalism, 21, 45, 46
Niterói, 9, 120–22, 149, 200n11
Norma Operacional Básica (NOB), 211nn7–8
North, Douglass C., 36, 202n19

Pacheco, Marisa, 92, 109
Pan-American Health Organization (PAHO), 124, 137–38, 212n17
Paranoá, 89
Partido Comunista do Brasil (PC do B), 46, 216n42
Partido da Frente Liberal (PFL), 46, 82, 104, 216n42
Partido da Social Democracia Brasileira (PSDB), 83, 100–102, 109, 216n42
as centrist party, 103, 209n32
PT and, 43, 106, 177
Partido Democrático Social (PDS), 104, 123
Partido do Movimento Democrático Brasileiro (PMDB), 82, 104, 128
Partido dos Trabalhadores (PT), 7, 103, 106, 204n31, 216n42
and PSDB, 43, 106, 177
and PSF, 141, 215n40, 218n2
social policies of, 46, 101–2
wings of, 100
Partido Liberal (PL), 46, 82, 216n42

Partido Progressista Brasileiro (PPB), 104
Partido Socialista Brasileiro (PSB), 101–2, 103, 106
Partido Trabalhista Brasileiro (PTB), 216n42
Partido Verde (PV), 216n42, 225n13
Pastoral da Criança, 47
patronage, 75, 185
  education and, 8, 44, 77, 81–82
  elections and, 43–44, 112, 154
  health care and, 8, 44–45, 118, 129, 133, 134, 154
pensions, 116
personalism, 5, 42, 46, 98
Peru, 36
Pimentel, Fernando, 214n31
Pitta, Celso, 104, 130, 136, 140–41
Plank, David N., 82
Plano de Atendimento à Saúde (PAS, São Paulo), 123–24, 130, 212nn14–16
policy diffusion, 12, 21, 24–49
  definitions, 25–26, 202n16, 204n2
  and flexibility, 170–71, 218n7
  lagged neighborhood effect, 70
  measuring probability, 71–75
  motivational approach to studying, 10–11, 15, 20, 31–35, 49, 186–87, 200n12, 201n9
  nature of, 24–28
  and policy reversal, 96, 104, 105, 166
  regional influence on, 66–67
  statistics on Bolsa Escola, 8, 51, 52, 53–54
  statistics on PSF, 10, 51, 52, 54–55, 126, 173–74, 193–96
  theoretical questions, 34–40, 184–88
  transnational, 180–84
  vertical, 209n30
  See also diffusion studies; ideology; political and electoral incentives; social networks
political and electoral incentives, 41, 44–46, 75
  as deficient explanation for diffusion, 12, 112, 152–57, 164, 187
  education reform and, 96–101, 185
  event history analysis of diffusion, 65, 68, 74
  health care reform and, 127–35, 149, 185
  measuring, 56–57, 168
political appointees, 6, 99
political parties, 46, 205n13, 216n42
  and macroeconomic policy, 45, 203n29
  party switching, 206n14
Porto Alegre, 112, 210n41
Poupança-Escola, 89
poverty, 2, 7, 21
  Bolsa Escola and, 176, 219n18
  in Brazil, 11, 79, 97, 113, 121–22
  education and, 11, 79–80, 86, 88
  electoral appeals and, 43, 96–97
  health care and, 11, 113
Powell, Walter W., 203n24

Power, Timothy J., 45, 203n30
process-tracing approach, 19, 23
professional associations, 38, 47, 65–66, 159–60
  and Bolsa Escola, 160
  and PSF, 62, 70, 72–73, 144–45, 150, 161, 163, 167
  and sanitarian movement, 47, 115, 143–44, 160
  technocrats and, 49, 161
Programa de Agentes Comunitários de Saúde (PACS), 8–9, 122–23, 137, 138
Programa de Agentes de Saúde (PAS, Ceará), 122
Programa de Educación, Salud, y Alimentación (PROGRESA), 180–82
Programa de Interiorização de Ações de Saúde e Saneamento (PIASS), 215n36
Programa de Renda Mínima Vinculada à Educação, 93
Programa Gestão Pública e Cidadania, 60, 86, 108–9, 167
Programa Médico de Família (PMF), 9, 120–22, 200n11
Programa Saúde da Família (PSF)
  as award-winning program, 14, 42, 200n14
  in Belo Horizonte, 128, 131–32, 143, 148
  in Brasília, 128, 131, 134, 143
  broad goals, 140, 172
  complexity, 170
  cost, 140, 215n39, 217n53
  creation, 8, 124
  design, 9–10
  diffusion statistics for, 10, 51, 52, 54–55, 126, 173–74, 193–96
  doctors and, 153, 170, 214n28, 218n9
  efficacy, 173–75, 215n38, 219n16
  electoral competition and, 58
  eligibility for, 125, 212n19
  event history analysis of diffusion, 63–74
  financing, 70, 148–49, 203n25, 217n51, 217n53, 219n14
  framing, 170
  gendered dimensions, 129, 178–79, 213n25
  good governance practices, 152, 186
  and health agents, 124, 125, 129, 131
  ideology as factor in diffusion, 12, 58–59, 135–43, 162–64
  and infant mortality, 139, 173, 219n16
  left view of, 46, 130, 138, 141, 142–43, 150, 157–58, 162–63, 215n40, 216n42, 218n2
  measuring adoption probability, 72–73
  Ministry of Health and, 10, 52, 124, 125–26, 134, 138, 147, 171, 215n34, 217n53, 219n14
  PACS as predecessor, 8–9, 122–23, 138
  patronage and, 129, 154
  policy flexibility, 170–71
  political incentives approach to diffusion, 127–35, 155–56, 187

"poor program for the poor" charges against, 147, 162, 217n49
preventive care and, 8–9, 114, 126
professional associations and, 62, 70, 72–73, 144–45, 150, 161, 163, 167
professional staff, 133, 154, 213n23, 214n28
PT and, 141, 215n40, 218n2
regional influences on adoption of, 160–61
right-wing parties and, 130, 140, 149, 216n42
in Salvador , 128, 132–35, 143, 146, 214n30
sanitarian movement and, 136, 139
in São Paulo, 120, 128, 130–31, 135, 148, 171, 213n26
social networks as factor in diffusion, 62–63, 143–48, 162–64
technocrats and, 146, 156, 171
UNICEF and, 124, 212n17
women and, 129, 178, 213n25
World Bank and, 138, 140, 158, 215n35

Qualidade Integral à Saúde (QUALIS), 142
qualitative methods and analysis, 19, 33, 167–68
mixed-methods research and, 19, 20, 200n15
and quantitative approach, 17, 164–65
QWERTY keyboard, 25, 201n2

rational choice, 35, 157, 202n22
rationality, 32, 34–35, 201n11, 202n17
regional differences, 4, 5
in health care, 117, 145, 174, 216n46
as influence on diffusion, 66–67
national government and, 41
Renda Minha, 105, 106
Renda Mínima, 85, 86–87, 102, 207n11
awards for, 91, 208n18
Bolsa Escola and, 89–90, 166
in Campinas, 7, 88, 208nn14–15
clientelism and, 44
federal funding, 93, 209n30
as federal program, 85, 200n10, 207n10
idea behind, 7–8
ideology as motivation for adoption, 101–6, 186
media coverage, 91–92, 97
political incentives for adoption, 96, 97
in Salvador, 104
social networks as motivation for adoption, 109–11
See also Bolsa Escola
Ribeirão Preto, 87–88
rightist parties and politicians, 104, 168, 185
and PSF, 134–35, 140
Rio de Janeiro, 5, 115
Rocha, Aldely, 132, 134
Rockefeller Foundation, 137, 215n33
Rogers, Everett M., 13–14, 26, 30, 31–32, 201n10

Roriz, Joaquim, 103, 104, 106, 136, 209n32
  and Bolsa Escola, 99, 105
  and PSF, 133–34, 148, 154
Rousseff, Dilma, 41

Sabot, Richard H., 80
Salvador, 95, 97, 102–3, 209n30
  Bolsa Escola in, 94–95, 96, 103
  municipal assistance programs in, 104, 209n33
  PSF in, 128, 132–35, 143, 146, 214n30
  Renda Mínima in, 104, 110
Samuels, David, 5, 204n31
SANARE: Revista Sobralense de Politicas Públicas, 140, 215n37
sanitarian movement, 60, 141, 211n6
  and professional associations, 47, 115, 143–44, 160
  and PSF, 136, 139
  results of, 117–18, 119–20
Santillo, Henrique Antônio, 213n20
São Paulo, 55, 95, 97, 209n30
  Bolsa Escola in, 103, 208n23
  health care initiatives in, 120, 123–24, 140–42, 149
  PSF in, 120, 128, 130–31, 135, 148, 171, 213n26
Sarney, José, 81, 82
Saúde em Casa, 133, 166, 214n27
Saúde em Debate, 60, 144–45
Schady, Norbert R., 36
Seixas, José Carlos, 213n20
Serra, José, 41, 98, 129
  as health minister, 138, 158, 213n20
Shipan, Charles R., 32–33
Sikkink, Kathryn, 203n23
Simmons, Beth A., 32, 33, 202n16, 204n2
Sistema Único de Saúde (SUS), 118
small-n analysis, 16, 19, 166
Sobral, 171, 174–75
Social Democratic Party (PSDB). *See* Partido da Social Democracia Brasileira
social inequality, 4–5, 116, 199n5
social movements, 46–47, 117, 119, 144, 160
social networks, 13, 37–38, 46–48, 59–60, 112, 159–62, 164, 186
  education reform and, 107–11, 112
  event history analysis of diffusion, 65–67, 74–75
  health care reform and, 143–48, 150, 163
  measuring, 59–63, 167
  nonpartisan nature of, 40
social security, 44, 115–16, 210n2
Sousa, Amaury de, 12, 43
Sousa, Maria Fátima de, 125, 139
Souza, Paulo Renato, 83, 85
statistical analysis, 16–17, 28, 33–34, 76, 164–65, 200n15
street-level bureaucrats, 179, 220n24
Successo no Aprender, 105
Suplicy, Eduardo, 86, 210n40
  and minimum income programs, 87, 93, 100, 110, 207nn7–8, 220n21
Suplicy, Marta, 98, 103, 136, 153, 208n23
  and PSF, 130, 131, 135, 142
systems theory, 38–39

Taylor, Michael, 15, 202n22
teachers, 99–100, 107, 169, 209n28
technocrats, 40, 48, 163–64
  and Bolsa Escola, 156, 171
  and professional associations, 49, 161
  and PSF, 146, 156, 171
Teixeira, Magalhães, 162
Tendler, Judith, 2, 213n23
Terra de Souza, Ana Cristina, 212n13
Transparency International, 203n28

UNESCO, 91, 107, 108, 182, 210n34
União dos Dirigentes Municipais de Educação (UNDIME), 107
UNICEF, 137–38, 182
  and Bolsa Escola, 91, 107, 208n18
  and PSF, 124, 212n17
United Nations Development Program, 68

Vargas, Getúlio, 113, 116
Vejá, 91
Verba, Sidney, 19, 75
Viana, Ana Luiza D'Ávila, 124, 212n17, 213n23
Volden, Craig, 32–33
vote buying, 2, 43, 44, 102, 203n28
Voto a Voto, 56

Walker, Jack L., 28, 35, 42, 65, 201n11
wealthy elite, 1–2, 4, 5, 79, 116
Weber, Silke, 44
Weyland, Kurt, 32, 37, 39, 44
Wolfensohn, James, 182–83
women, 172, 177
  Bolsa Escola and, 92–93, 178, 208n22
  PSF and, 129, 178, 213n25
women's movement, 179–80
Workers Party. *See* Partido dos Trabalhadores (PT)
World Bank, 91, 182, 210n34, 212n14
  and PSF, 138, 140, 158, 215n35

Zedillo, Ernesto, 181

NATASHA BORGES SUGIYAMA

is assistant professor of political science

at the University of Wisconsin-Milwaukee.